4 3.1 37 204 66 9/16 66 5/16 66 7/16 – 3/16
e15.5 ... 364 17 11/16 17 1/2 17 1/2 – 3/16
e22.8 ... 242 14 3/4 14 5/8 14 11/16 – 1/8
4 .6 11 1680 38 1/2 37 1/16 37 3/16 – [illegible]
e 8.3 ... 10 15 7/16 15 5/16 15 5/16 + 1/16
8 1.0 dd 924 8 3/16 7 7/8 8 + 1/16
... 19 610 10 3/16 9 15/16 10 + 1/16
... ... 2 1 3/16 1 3/16 1 3/16 ...

42 3/8 23 7/16 ♠ GPU inc GPU 2.18f 7.8 9 2232 28 3/8 27 11/16 28 1/8 ...
26 3/8 14 5/16 Gabelli A GBL ... ... 25 24 5/16 24 1/4 24 1/4 + 1/16
11 5/16 8 15/16 GabelliConv GCV .80a 8.0 ... 26 10 1/16 9 13/16 10 + 1/16
[illegible] GabelliConv pf [illegible]
[illegible] Gabelli Tr [illegible]
24 [illegible] 20 1/2 Gabelli Tr pf [illegible]
19 3/4 13 1/4 GabelliMlti GGT e ... ... 301 14 3/8 14 1/8 14 5/16 + 1/8
25 1/2 22 GabelliMlti pf 1.98 8.6 ... 8 23 5/16 23 1/8 23 1/8 – 3/16

14 11/16 4 9/16 Hlthsouth HRC ... cc 12873 7 5/8 [illegible]
29 1/4 18 11/16 ♠ HearstArgyl HTV ... 49 197 20 1/16 [illegible]
[illegible] HecIaMin [illegible] p ... dd 881 1 [illegible]
34 [illegible] [illegible] pf 3.50 18.9 ... 57 19 5/16 [illegible]
24 [illegible] [illegible] QUIPS 2.01 8.5 ... 18 23 7/8 [illegible]
23 1/2 18 7/16 Heco QUIPS HE+T 1.83 8.6 ... 13 21 5/16 [illegible]
25 1/16 12 1/4 Heico HEI .05b .3 15 436 15 5/8 [illegible]
s 21 1/8 9 7/8 Heico A HEIA .06b .5 ... 697 13 3/8 [illegible]

STOCK MARKET WIZARDS

Interviews with America's
Top Stock Traders

Jack D. Schwager

While the methods of investment described in this book are believed to be effective there is no guarantee that the methods will be profitable in specific applications, owing to the risk that is involved in investing of almost any kind. Moreover, readers are specifically advised that the author may invest in certain of the traders about which he is writing (or has written) and/or may be affiliated with hedge fund(s) that so invest with such persons or entities. Neither the publisher nor the author assumes liability for any losses that may be sustained by the use of the method described in this book, and/or this potential conflict of interest, and any such liability is hereby expressly disclaimed.

HarperCollins books may be purchased for educational, business, or sales promotional use. For information please write: Special Markets Department, HarperCollins Publishers Inc., 10 East 53rd Street, New York, NY 10022.

First HarperBusiness paperback edition published 2003
Designed by Fearn Cutler

Library of Congress Cataloging-in-Publication Data

Schwager, Jack D., 1948–
Stock market wizards : interviews with America's top stock traders / Jack D. Schwager.—
1st HarperBusiness paperback ed.
p. cm.
Originally published: 1st ed. New York : HarperBusiness, c2001.
Includes bibliographical references.
ISBN 0-06-662059-7 (alk. paper)
1. Stockbrokers—United States—Interviews. 2. Investment advisors—United States—Interviews. 3. Floor traders (Finance)—United States—Interviews. 4. Futures market—United States. 5. Financial futures—United States. I. Title.

HG4621 .S286 2003
332.64'0973—dc21 2002192229

04 05 06 07 WF 10 9 8 7 6 5

In memory of my mother, Margaret Schwager, loved by all who knew her for her kindness, empathy, and sincerity.

and

In memory of my brother, Kerwin Farkas, deeply loved by family and many friends whose support never waned—a reflection of a life well lived.

CONTENTS

AUTHOR'S NOTE TO THE PAPERBACK EDITION

The interviews for this book were conducted from mid-1999 through early 2000—in other words, just before the major top in the stock market (March 2000). Since then, the S&P 500 has been nearly halved, while the Nasdaq has lost nearly three-quarters of its value (as of the end of September 2002).

Thus readers of these interviews are likely to think: "Yes, but how have they done lately?" Fair question.

In the revised edition, detailed answers to this question have been provided at the end of each chapter, along with short follow-up interviews, focusing on the experience of the traders during this protracted bear market.

ACKNOWLEDGMENTS

Although I found most of the traders in this book through personal contacts in the industry, several money manager databases and texts provided helpful references. In particular, I would cite the following:

Barclay MAP for Windows. This software program, which is updated monthly, allows searches of an impressively large database of hedge fund managers. The program is highly intuitive and permits the investor to extract and rank those trading programs that meet multiple user-defined criteria. (Barclay Trading Group: [641] 472-3456; *www.barclaygrp.com*.)

Van Hedge Fund Advisors International Inc. (VAN). A hedge fund advisory service that compiles its own hedge fund indexes and maintains one of the largest hedge fund databases. The company provided me with the results of a computer search of hedge fund managers meeting my extremely restrictive set of criteria. ([615] 661-4748; *www.hedgefund.com*.)

The CTA Report. A quarterly comprehensive compendium of CTA performance results, containing a well-designed two-page layout of tables and charts for each CTA. There is also an easy-to-use Web site for monthly updates. As the name implies, this service covers managers who specialize in futures trading; only a small portion of these managers focus on equity derivatives. (International Traders Research, Inc.: [858] 459-0818; *www.managedfutures.com*.)

The U.S. Offshore Funds Directory. An annual publication that contains one-page summaries and annual returns for over 700 offshore hedge funds. There is also a web link for updates. ([212] 371-5935; *www.hedgefundnews.com*)

When I began my search for traders worthy of inclusion in this volume, my first call was to Doug Makepeace. He has built a career on finding and investing his own and client funds with exceptional traders. Doug was most generous in sharing information with me, even though doing so threatened his ability to invest additional funds with these traders in the future if they became too well known.

Tom DeMark, a renowned technical analyst whose indicators are featured on many of the country's leading financial data services, was particularly vigorous in his efforts to help me find traders for this book. Tom is in a good position to provide such assistance, holding the unofficial world record as the technical analyst who has worked for the most (four) Market Wizards or their organizations.

Marty Schwartz and Linda Raschke were two former Market Wizards ("former" referring to the books in which their interviews appeared, not their trading talent) who helped me find new Market Wizards for this book.

Other industry contacts who were particularly helpful in aiding my search for great trading talent include: Sol Waksman and George Van; Bob Morris, Andy Good, Tony Cimirusti, Loran Fleckenstein, and Jason Perl.

I find it extremely difficult to evaluate the writing quality of any book I am working on. I lose all sense of perspective. For this reason, it is invaluable to have someone to provide objective feedback as the book is being written. Enter my wife, Jo Ann, who read the final draft of each chapter as soon as it was completed. Her promptness in performing this task was not a reflection of her eagerness to read the material—in fact, few topics interest her less than the financial markets—but rather a resignation to the inevitable in the face of my unrelenting nagging. ("Have you read it yet?") Jo Ann provided honest comments—sometimes brutally so—and very helpful suggestions, nearly all of which were accepted. Whatever the defects of this book in its final form, I can only assure the reader they would have been that much worse without Jo Ann's input.

PROLOGUE

An Inauspicious Beginning

Men are from Mars because they missed the flight to Venus. When to leave for the airport has always been a subject that my wife and I have viewed from different perspectives—my view: late enough to make it exciting; my wife's view: early enough to allow for a traffic jam, a flat tire, airport shopping, and a full course meal before the flight.

For years I left for airports without allowing for any spare time and never missed a flight. About eighteen months ago, I moved to Martha's Vineyard, where the travel time to the airport can be accurately estimated because of the limited traffic off-season and because the airport is so small—sort of like the one in the old TV series *Wings*, only smaller. (At least it was when I began this book; a new airport has since opened.)

One morning, only a few months after we had moved to Martha's Vineyard, my wife, Jo Ann, and I were scheduled to fly to Boston. I was so cocky about the predictability of getting to the airport on time that I left our house—approximately a twenty-minute drive away—only thirty-five minutes before the scheduled departure time. The drive took a few minutes longer than expected, due to being stuck behind a slow driver on the no-passing, single-lane road; I realized I had cut it just a little bit too tight.

"We'll still make it," I assured my wife, "but we won't have much extra time." She seemed skeptical—irrationally so, I thought. We pulled into the airport entrance only ten minutes before flight time. Even though the parking lot was only a stone's throw from the terminal, I dropped Jo Ann at the entrance, saying, "Let them know we're here."

When I returned about one minute later, I found Jo Ann standing outside waiting for me with a troubled expression. Confused to see her there, I asked, "What's wrong?"

"The plane left," she said in a voice that was a cross between disappointment and "I told you so."

"What do you mean, the plane left?" I asked, glancing at my watch, even though I knew the exact time. "It's only eight minutes to ten."

I went into the terminal, angry that the small prop plane had left without us before the scheduled time. "I don't get it," I said to the woman at the airline counter, all prepared to be the aggrieved customer.

She couldn't have been nicer. "Our planes leave as soon as everyone is here. Since we hadn't heard from you to tell us you were running late, we assumed you weren't coming. If you had called, we would have held the plane." And, you know, they would have, too; that's how Martha's Vineyard works. How could I be angry at anyone other than myself after that explanation?

Fast-forward about six months—the beginning of the interview process for this book. I am scheduled to catch the first flight on an intricate itinerary that will take me to four states in four days for six interviews. This schedule has no leeway for missed flights.

Wiser from experience, I make sure to leave early for the airport, allowing for plenty of extra time. On the drive there, Jo Ann, who is dropping me off, notices that I have lint on my blue blazer. She offers the helpful hint that I should ask the people at the airport counter for tape to brush it off. We arrive about thirty minutes early. I pull up to the curb and say good-bye to Jo Ann. After checking in and sitting for a while, I realize I have enough time to take care of my lint-laden jacket. I walk up to the counter and obtain the necessary tape.

There are about a dozen people in the small waiting room. A few moments later there is an announcement for my flight: "Now boarding section one, seats one to eight." I pull out the red, plastic, envelope-size boarding pass and notice that it is emblazoned with the number 11. "How quaint," I muse, "that they would board such a small flight in two sections." I sit down and return to my lint-removal project.

I'm sitting there absentmindedly, picking lint off my jacket. Suddenly

I snap back into reality. I realize that it must be at least five or ten minutes since they called for the boarding of the first group of passengers. I look around the waiting area and, to my horror, I discover that it is virtually deserted. I jump up, run through the doors to the airstrip, and see a small plane with propellers whirring. "Wait!" I yell, waving my arms frantically as I rush toward the plane. I see my whole precisely orchestrated trip—all four days, four states, and six interviews of it—unraveling on the spot.

The airline attendant intercepts me. I flash my large red boarding pass. "You're not going anywhere," he says firmly. At first I think he means that it's too late and I missed the plane. But then he adds, "Your section will be leaving in five minutes." That's when I learned that at the Martha's Vineyard airport "sections" refer to different planes!

I slink back to my seat. The moment of panic having passed, my sense of awareness returns, and I am able to appreciate completely the full scope of my stupidity. The last time I felt that embarrassed I had just asked an infrequently seen relative when she was "expecting," only to learn subsequently that she had given birth two months earlier but had obviously retained a good portion of the gained weight. Oops.

"Okay, okay," you're saying, "a slightly amusing anecdote—maybe—but what does this have to do with trading or investing?" Simply this: If you're too busy picking the lint off your jacket, you're liable to miss the plane. In other words, don't get so caught up in the details that you miss the big picture. Here are some examples of market myopia:

- a trader who does exhaustive research trying to identify the most promising new technology companies but overlooks the fact that a 70 percent price rise in the sector during the past six months implies an unusually high-risk investment environment
- a trader who scrutinizes a company's financial statements and reports but fails to realize that the company's soaring profits have been due to a single product whose future sales are threatened by the imminent entry of new competitors
- a trader who is engrossed with finding better timing-entry methods but virtually ignores such critical questions as: When and how will positions be exited? How will risk be controlled?

All of these examples contain the same basic message: Maintain a whole-picture perspective. Focus on the entire market and the sector, not just the individual stock. Be attentive to qualitative factors, not just the available quantitative information. Develop a trading plan that encompasses all the aspects of trading, not just the entry strategy.

STOCK MARKET WIZARDS

STUART WALTON

Back from the Abyss

In June 1999, at the peak of his career, after eight years establishing one of the most extraordinary stock trading track records of the 1990s, and with $150 million under management, Stuart Walton returned all money to his investors and walked away from trading completely. The emotional repercussions of a marital breakup were interfering with his ability to focus on trading, and he did not feel it was right to manage money until he could once again devote "100 percent energy and enthusiasm" to the task. In the preceding eight years, he had achieved an astounding 115 percent average annual compounded return in trading profits (92 percent for his clients after deducting management fees), with annual returns ranging from a high of 274 percent to a low of 63 percent (excluding the 1999 partial year).

Stuart Walton's career as a trader is marked by a string of contradictions and paradoxes. He wanted to be an artist or a writer; he became a trader. Though he valued academics and disdained the financial world, the markets became his profession. He once hated trading so much that he awoke feeling that he couldn't do it for another day and quit his job that morning; several years later, the markets were his endeavor and passion. His initial forays into stock trading were marked by such ineptitude that he nearly went bankrupt, yet he subsequently became so skilled that he more than doubled his money annually.

I visited Walton, a Canadian expatriate, at his office in downtown San Francisco. I discovered that, although managing a nine-digit sum, he had no trading assistants, no back office staff, no marketing people, no programmers, not even a full-time secretary. His firm, Reindeer Capital, consisted of Stuart Walton alone. His isolation was deliberate. After having gone wrong so often by listening to tips and opinions, he had come to realize the importance of not being influenced by others while trading.

Walton was relaxed and outgoing. We talked for five hours straight without interruption. The time passed quickly.

★

Is there some significance to the name of the firm or are you just partial to reindeer?

The firm is named after my great-grandfather, William Gladstone Walton, who was given the nickname "Reindeer" for a famous trek he conceived and led. Much of what I know about him I learned from my grandfather, who passed away last year at the age of one hundred, narrowly missing the feat of having lived in three separate centuries. In 1892, at the age of twenty-three, Reindeer Walton left England to work as a missionary in northern Canada. He typically traveled over two thousand miles a year by canoe and dogsled, visiting his far-flung constituency—the Indians and Eskimos that lived around the Arctic Circle.

One year, vast forest fires swept through northern Quebec, destroying almost all the region's vegetation and game, and leaving the native population at the brink of starvation. Reindeer Walton came up with the idea of herding the Siberian reindeer, which are also called caribou, from Alaska to northern Quebec. Through sheer perseverance, he convinced the Canadian government to finance the trek, which he organized and led. It took him five years, from 1921 to 1925, to herd three thousand reindeer across northern Canada. Reindeer are not like cattle; they move only when they want to move, and they go in all different directions.

How did he keep them herded together?

Caribou will follow the feeding path. He used a lot of foresight in choosing the right route. He succeeded in getting three-quarters of the herd to migrate; the remainder died or dispersed. His trek permanently changed the migration patterns for Siberian reindeer. The portion of the herd that survived flourished in northern Quebec, and he became a local hero.

Is there some principle you wish to symbolize by the name, or is it just a matter of honoring your great-grandfather?

I tell people that my great-grandfather added more value to society than I ever will.

When did you first get involved in the markets?

As soon as I graduated from McGill University with an M.B.A. I originally wanted to be a cartoonist.

A cartoonist with an M.B.A.? Were you planning to be the world's first business cartoonist?

No, the cartoonist ambitions came earlier. When I graduated from college, I definitely wanted to be a cartoonist. I sat down with the head of the art department, and he told me, "If you feel you know how to draw and represent the human body as well as one of the masters of art history and are then prepared to make five dollars per hour drawing cartoons, then this is definitely the career path for you." His comments threw some cold water on my plans. I had also done some writing in college, and a few of my short stories had been published. I thought that journalism might be a good alternative career path that allowed some creativity.

Your interests seem to be so strongly artistic. Why did you go for an M.B.A.?

Because the journalism idea fell through as well, and I decided I needed to earn a living.

What went wrong with journalism?

I applied to several journalism schools. That summer, while visiting my parents, who were in Brazil at the time, I received a rejection call from Carleton University, which was my first choice for a journalism school. I received the call during a party. Maybe it was because I'd had too many Brazilian *caipirinhas*, which is their rum concoction, but I said to myself, "I guess this is another one of life's crossroads." So I decided to give up the idea of becoming a journalist. I guess I didn't want to do it badly enough to pursue it.

In retrospect, do you consider your rejection from journalism school a lucky event?

I consider it a huge stroke of luck. My father always told me that I had to differentiate between my hobbies and my career. I think he's right. My mother recently asked me if I had any regrets at not having pursued any of these other interests. At first I said that I didn't, because I was basking in the success I've had with this business, but every day that goes by, I regret it more and more. Eventually, I can see myself veering back.

Veering back to drawing or writing?

Maybe both, maybe neither. I always thought that the best way to combine my interests in drawing and writing was films, particularly short films. I have a lot of ideas already. Nothing that would be commercial; stuff that probably would have an end audience of three people in the world.

Have you ever made any films?

No, I would have to take a film course just to learn how to point the camera.

Are you thinking of giving up trading in lieu of these other interests?

I really admire people who do what they want to do and don't care about anything else. I had a friend in college who was determined to be a rock and roll star. He formed the band The Cowboy Junkies. When he started college, he couldn't even play a guitar, and now he is sold out at every concert. But I know myself. I like the comforts of life, and for me this business is the best way to acquire them. Although, eventually, I will probably pursue some of these other interests, it's not something I see happening in the immediate future.

What happened after you were rejected from journalism school?

I decided to go for an M.B.A because I thought it was the best way to get a job.

Did you give any thought to what you might do with your M.B.A.?

I intended to go into advertising because it was the one business career I thought might satisfy my creative side. But the opportunity never arose. When I graduated, the economy in Canada was terrible. There were only two jobs offered on campus. One was a management trainee position with Lloyds Bank. The job appealed to me because of the location: New York or London. I thought it would be great to work in either of those two cities. I applied and got the job.

They sent me to a training program in New York. I spent most of the training program in the foreign exchange trading room, which was a fluke because I was supposed to be trained as a loan officer and sent back to Canada.

So you fell into a trading environment entirely by chance.

That is one reason why I believe anyone can do this job; I don't think you have to be born to do it.

I don't know about that. I can assure you that among the hundreds of thousands of people who try trading, very few can even remotely approach your track record. What was your job at the foreign exchange desk?

I was just a flunky. I took customer orders and did other assorted tasks. I had to be at work at 3:30 A.M.—which was brutal for a single guy living in New York—to get everything ready for the traders. I clipped newspaper articles for them and made sure their order tickets were in place. It was a glorified gofer position.

Did you have any interest in financial markets at the time?

None at all. I was still wrapped up in the idealism of my previous academic life. I looked down on my M.B.A. My thoughts were, "What happens to all the learning and academics I've done? Does it all just get shoved away for the rest of my life?"

The job in the foreign exchange department didn't help matters at all. If anything, it turned me off to trading because of all the day-to-day friction. The job was my first introduction to Americans; I had been surrounded by Canadians all my life. Canadians are more laid-back; they are more concerned about etiquette than going for the jugular or getting their point across. There were traders on the desk who would just scream at me all the time. Most times, I didn't even know why. Maybe it was because they needed someone to take it out on when their positions went bad, or maybe it was because I didn't do things quickly enough for them. I would go home every night upset because someone had shouted at me.

How long did you stay at this job?

For about six months. I left because I found out through the grapevine that I was about to be transferred to Toronto. At that point, I loved living in New York, and I had also just met my wife-to-be and didn't want to leave her. Therefore, I took a job at the New York branch of another Canadian company, Wood Gundy. One attraction of the new job was that they offered to get me a green card; I had been in the United States on a temporary visa.

What was the job you got?

It was a little bit less of a flunky job. I went through Wood Gundy's training program and was placed on the equity desk. I was just an order taker, which was very boring. The customer was making the decision, and the floor broker was executing the trade; I was nothing more than an intermediary. I always laugh when brokers on the sell side of the stock business call themselves traders. Well they are not traders; they are just order takers. None of them are taking positions for the house or with their own money.

At that point, I made the first trade for my own account. My girlfriend, who later became my wife, worked for Liz Claiborne. She kept telling me how great her company was doing: "I don't even have to call my customers, they're calling me." Since I didn't have any money to invest, I called my father for a loan. "Dad," I said, "I have a great idea; you just have to lend me some money." He loaned me $10,000, and I put it all into Liz Claiborne stock. The stock quickly went up three points, and I took my profits. But the worst thing you can do as a beginning trader is to have your first trade work. Within three weeks, I had lost not only all my profits from the Liz Claiborne trade, but also all the money my father had lent me.

How did you do that?

I was so taken with the success of my first trade that I started listening to all sorts of tips and rumors. The guy delivering my coffee in the morning could tell me about a stock, and I would buy it. I was cleaned out in three weeks. It took me five years, a little bit at a time, to pay back my father.

What did your father say when you told him you had lost the money?

"Well, I thought that you would," he said, "but I appreciated that you had an idea and wanted to follow through on it." Ironically, the Liz Claiborne stock, for which I had originally borrowed the money, continued to go straight up, quintupling in a year.

What was your next trading experience?

The Wood Gundy equity desk was another version of New York verbal abuse. Once again, I found myself at a job where the guys on the desk were constantly yelling at me. It was just regular day-to-day business, but I hated it. When I looked across the room to the bond trading desk, I noticed that everyone was very quiet. They weren't shouting at each other; they were very civil. That appealed to me. I got permission to switch to the bond trading desk.

At the time, Wood Gundy was trying to become a major dealer in the U.S. bond market, and they had brought in a bunch of hired-gun traders. These guys were just blowing up left, right, and center. There were huge losses everywhere. One trader even hid his tickets to conceal his losses. Eventually almost everyone was fired, though I was still left, along with a few others.

Were you happier on the bond desk?

I had mixed feelings. I was certainly happy to get away from the verbal abuse. Also, the bond desk was very exciting because it traded huge position sizes compared with the equity desk. I liked the idea that I could make or lose five times as much as twenty people combined on the equity desk. But I didn't like being responsible for trading all sorts of illiquid issues, most of which were overseas bonds.

The Japanese would call me at 2 or 3 A.M., and I would have to make bids or offers on huge sums of illiquid bonds without even knowing where the market was. And because I was sleepy, it was possible to give them the wrong quote. If you gave them a quote that was off by 100 basis points, they would hold you to it. You could have a $1 million loss on an obvious error, and they would still insist on the trade being valid.

Did that ever happen to you?

Oh yes.

You had a $1 million error?

Well I didn't have a $1 million error, but I had a $300,000 error.

Just because you gave them the wrong quote.

I was sleepy. I thought the yield was 9.5 percent when it was really 10.5 percent.

Is it normal to be held on a trade on a quote that is obviously an error?

It certainly wouldn't be considered normal in North America, and I doubt that it would be the case anymore in Japan.

How did you do on balance in your trading?

I did well and was promoted as the youngest vice president at Wood Gundy.

On what basis were you making buy and sell decisions?

I didn't have any methodology. I almost got to the point where I thought the market was random.

But you must have been doing something right if you were making money. Was it just a matter of gut feel?

All the trading I do involves gut feel. But at that point in my life, I think I was bailed out because there was a major bull market in bonds, and my instincts were apparently good enough to keep me off the short side for the most part. In my best year, I made about $700,000 for the desk, which is really nothing, considering it has to be split among so many different people.

One time, over drinks with my boss, I said, "We're not really trading these bonds; we're really investing, just like one of our accounts. And if that is what we're doing, there are better things to invest in."

"Don't go off half-cocked," he said. "We just have to keep dodging and weaving."

It was at that point, after three years, that I really started to burn out. I went as long as I did because it was exciting having the responsibility of trading that much money.

By that point, had you developed a passion for trading?

Yes, I knew it was something I loved to do. I liked the idea that it was me against the markets. I just didn't care for the markets I was trading. One major source of frustration was that the bond issues we were trading in New York were highly illiquid. I decided to transfer to the main office of Wood Gundy in Toronto because there I could trade Canadian government bond securities, which were far more liquid. At first I was very happy to be in the main office, trading liquid bond markets, with lots of activity. After six months, however, I realized that I didn't want to work in Canada. It's a country club environment where success has more to do with politics than with your performance. I was also getting very sick of bonds and interest rates.

Why?

Because it is such a commodity. At our morning meeting a standard question always was: "What is going to happen today?" All the participants would give this spiel about why they thought the market was going up or down. They would talk about the influence of currency rate movements, fiscal and monetary policy, interest rate trends in the United States and other countries, and so on. When my turn came, I would simply say, "I think the market is going down today." When they asked me why, I would answer, "Because it went up yesterday." They didn't know whether to take me seriously or not. I had reached the point where I thought the market was so efficient that if the price went up big one day, it was just as likely to go down the next day.

One morning I woke up and realized that I didn't want to worry about interest rates again for the rest my life. I knew that I couldn't stand to trade another bond. I walked into work and quit, even though I had moved to Canada only seven months earlier. They couldn't believe it.

You quit even though you didn't have another job?

Oh yeah, I just couldn't stand it anymore. The ironic thing is that my wife called me the same day to tell me that she had quit her job, and I hadn't even hinted to her that I was going to quit mine. I knew she had been unhappy, but I didn't think she was on the verge of quitting. It was amazing that we both quit our jobs independently on the same day. We decided to delay looking for new jobs so that we could take six months to travel across the United States, going from ski resort to ski resort.

When we were at Lake Tahoe, we took a side trip to San Francisco. We loved the city and decided to move there. When we returned to Toronto after the end of our trip, we thought it would be a good idea to revisit San Francisco before actually moving, just to make sure that we still liked it as much as we had on our visit. While we were there, we looked for jobs, and we were both offered positions. We even found a house we liked and put in a bid that was accepted. We thought we were set. We flew back to Toronto, rented a truck, and moved our stuff to San Francisco. But when we got there, we found out that both jobs had fallen through.

What was the job you thought you had?

I had interviewed with a small venture capital firm. The person who interviewed me had also graduated from McGill.

You must have thought that gave you the inside track.

Yes, he was very enthusiastic. "Oh sure, we can use you. Come back out, and we will set you up." When I arrived in San Francisco, I kept calling him, but didn't receive any return phone calls. When I finally got through to him, he said, "Oh, we're not hiring M.B.A.s this year." It was a complete reversal from what he had told me before.

I had put my life savings into the down payment for the house, so we hardly had any money left. Initially we weren't worried because we thought we would get jobs in a month or two. Month after month went by, however, and neither one of us got a job offer. I couldn't believe it. I started drinking cheap beer and sleeping late.

Were you depressed?

No, I'm not that kind of person. It was just too stressful for me to get up in the morning and pound the pavement. I couldn't believe that after having a successful career in New York, I couldn't even get a hint at a job offer. I was so desperate that I even went to insurance companies to interview for sales jobs.

Sounds as if that is a job you would have hated.

Absolutely, but I was desperate. I would have taken anything. I needed money to pay my mortgage, and I didn't want to ask my family for help.

What was your wife's attitude during this ordeal?

She was pretty positive. She felt we would come up with something.

Did you run out of money?

We did. Then after we had been there for six months, my wife got the first job, a retail sales position at J. Crew, which was a large step down for her after having been a merchandise manager for Liz Claiborne. She also had reached the point where she was willing to take virtually any job. We had just run out of money that month, and she used her first paycheck to pay the mortgage.

Were you panicking before she got her job at the last minute?

I had given up hope. My attitude was that whatever happens, happens. Take the house. I don't care. I was very distraught. That's when I first learned about San Francisco. They're not impressed if you're from New York, L.A., or London. It's not a transient city like New York or L.A., where it is okay to come from other cities and get a job. San Francisco is more of a community. People want to see that you have lived in the area for a while. Now I really appreciate that aspect of the city, but at the time it was very frustrating.

Do you mean the jobs you were applying for would go to people who were local?

Absolutely, although there wasn't a huge slew of jobs anyway. I couldn't believe that I had gone from a status position to the verge of working at Starbucks. I went to the library and microfiched every financial-sounding company and sent them my résumé. Eventually, I got a call from someone who liked my résumé. "I don't have a job for you myself," he said, "but I have a friend who I think might be interested."

What about your résumé appealed to him?

He liked the variety—a combination of financial jobs and artistic interests.

Before you got that job nibble, I imagine this must have been the low point of your life.

No it wasn't. The low point is coming up. The person who had received my résumé convinced his friend who ran the sales and trading unit for Volpe, Welty & Co., a regional brokerage firm, to give me a shot at an interview. When I arrived at the interview, I had no idea what to expect. He asked me about my background, and I told him what I've just told you.

He then asked me, "How much do you want to make?"

I added $200 to my mortgage and answered, "$2,500 a month."

"How about $4,000?" he asked.

"That would be good too." I answered.

Did he know your predicament?

No, but he saw the jobs I'd held previously, and I don't think he felt right offering me as little as I was asking.

What job did he hire you for?

I was hired to be an institutional stockbroker, but I had no accounts. I had to cold-call in front of other people, which really got to me. I had gone from being Mister Bond Trader, whom everybody wanted to take out to dinner, to cold-calling no-name institutions to buy our lousy stock ideas.

When you were cold-calling, I guess a lot of people just hung up on you.

Absolutely. I used to do waves of calls. I had a list of people to call, and I just put my head down and started dialing. I don't have an aggressive nature, so I tried drawing people in by just being a nice guy. That didn't work too well. It was a relentless day-after-day process. It was difficult watching other people doing business while I was making these phone calls, knowing that it was obvious to them whenever someone hung up on me. I would have a five-second conversation, put the phone down, and look around. Then I would have to go on to the next phone call. It was such a demeaning process. I hated it, hated it. I didn't know when I would ever be able to cover my draw. I couldn't generate a trade.

You don't mean that literally?

Yes I do. I had zero trades.

How long did this go on?

I probably didn't have a single account or trade for eight months.

You cold-called for eight months without a single sale! That sounds brutal. Was this your low point?

No, this wasn't the low point *[he laughs]*. The low point happened shortly afterward. Regardless of my lack of success in selling, I knew there was a big difference between trading and selling. Eventually, after watching the markets, I decided I had to start trading again. Although I didn't have any money, I realized that I could take out a home-equity loan and do whatever I wanted with the money. I said to myself, "I can liquefy my house and invest it."

I can see it coming . . .

I started selling stocks that I thought were up too high—powerhouse stocks like Liz Claiborne and the Gap—and buying stocks that I thought were down too low. In effect, I was shorting good companies and buying bad companies.

How much of a home-equity loan did you take out?

I had placed a down payment of $75,000 on the house, and I took out a loan of $50,000 against it. Within three weeks of taking out the loan, I had lost 75 percent of the money.

How did your wife react to this turn of events?

She had no idea.

She didn't know that you took out a home-equity loan?

She knew about the loan, but she didn't know what I did with the money.

What did you tell her you were going to do with the money?

I did tell her that I was going to invest it, but I told her that I was going to invest it in a conservative dividend play that would give us a greater return than the rate we had to pay on the home-equity loan. That was my intention. But once I had the money I thought, "I'm not going to put this into some boring dividend play to make a few dollars on the spread between the dividend income and my loan rate."

When you are at a brokerage firm, there is always something exciting going on. There is always some stock doubling or tripling. You can't avoid the frenzy. I was listening to the stories being pitched all around me. The salesmen could make any story sound great.

So apparently you had failed to learn your lesson about not listening to tips and rumors. You made the same mistake all over again.

Absolutely. I couldn't bring myself to tell my wife that I had lost almost all the money. I had trouble sleeping the entire month. I made up all these excuses why I was looking so sickly. I told my wife that I had the flu. She was worried, but she had no idea what the truth was.

One day a buddy who worked beside me gave me a tip to buy Commodore Computer. "I think this story is really going to work," he said. "We're hearing that their latest game is going to be a high-flier." I was so desperate that I told myself, "I'm going to do it." I took everything that was left in my account, leveraged it at 200 percent, and bought the stock.

That was the low point in my life. The $75,000 I had put into my house was my entire savings. The thought that because of some gambling I could lose everything that I had built up in ten years of saving really scared me. It was the black abyss.

The stock went from $10 to $17, and I got out. After I liquidated, the stock reached as high as the low twenties, but it eventually went back down to zero when the company went bankrupt. That single trade was enough to almost make me whole again.

You actually were salvaged by pure luck, by a tip that could have been a disaster because the stock eventually ended up going to zero. You just happened to catch it during the right time window.

It was just luck. To this day, I look back at pivotal points in my life, and I don't know whether they were due to luck or intelligence, but I never care about the difference. It's funny how things work out. I always tell people that luck is a very important factor in this business. Maybe you have to put yourself in the position to be lucky, but I think we all get our fair share of luck—both good and bad. We just have to take it as it comes.

That Commodore trade saved me. You might think my attitude would have been: "That tip worked, so I'm going to listen to other tips." But at the time, I recognized the luck involved. I realized that I was being bailed out by the stock market gods. I did learn my lesson. From that point on, I traded so much better.

Did you say, "Thank God, I won't sin again"?

Exactly. Even though everything worked out, the stress was incredible. Therefore, when I made it back, it was a godsend. Then I just started to chip away at it. Of course, I still had a lot to learn, but at least I had that experience behind me. I think it's important to get that low and see the abyss.

How did that help you?

The shock of the experience gave me clarity. I understood that stocks don't go up and stay up because of stories, tips, or people's opinions; they go up for specific reasons. I was determined to find those reasons, shut out the world, and then act on my own knowledge. I started to do that, and over time, my record got better and better.

This was really the first time in your life that you were trading stocks with any success. What types of things were working?

The theme I noticed back then that has persisted through bull and bear markets is: Good companies, on balance, continue to go up. Grandmothers in Kansas City know that.

And how do you find these good companies?

I look for companies that have been blessed by the market. They may be blessed because of a long string of quarters they've made [quarters in which the company's reported earnings reached or exceeded expectations], or for some other reason. You can identify these stocks by how they act. For some reason, the market goes to some stocks, and it doesn't go to others, no matter how many brokers tell their clients to buy these other stocks because they are cheap.

In effect, you actually reversed what you had been doing before: Instead of buying bargains and selling stocks that had gone up a lot, you were buying the expensive stocks.

That theme has continued to this day. The hardest thing to do is to buy a high-flying stock or to sell a stock that has gone down a lot, but I always find that the hardest thing to do is the right thing to do. It's a difficult lesson to learn; I'm still learning it now.

What tells you—to use your word—that a stock is "blessed"?

It's a combination of things. The fundamentals of the stock are only about 25 percent of it.

What is the remaining 75 percent?

Another 25 percent is technical.

What are you looking at on the technical side?

I like stocks that show relative linearity in their trend. I don't want stocks that are swinging all over the place.

That's 50 percent, and you have already gone through fundamental and technical. What's left?

Another 25 percent is watching how a stock responds to different information: macroeconomic events, its own news flow. I also pay attention to how a stock reacts to going to round numbers: $20, $30, etcetera. I try to get a feel whether a company has that special shine to it.

What kind of response are you looking for?

I want to see a stock move higher on good news, such as a favorable earnings report or the announcement of a new product, and not give much ground on negative news. If the stock responds poorly to negative news then it hasn't been blessed.

That's 75 percent. What's left?

The last 25 percent is my gut feeling for the direction of the market as a whole, which is based on my sense of how the market is responding to macroeconomic news and other events. It's almost like looking at the entire market as if it were an individual stock.

How long do you typically hold a stock once you buy it?

I don't day trade, but I only hold a stock for an average of about a few weeks. Also, when I buy a stock, even if it's a core position of a few hundred thousand shares, I might be in and out of it twice in the same day and six times in the same week, trying to get a feel about whether I'm doing the right thing. If I'm not comfortable with the way the stock is trading, I get out. That's one thing I love about running a hedge fund. I don't have to worry about my customers seeing the schizophrenia in my trading. I used to work for a company where the customers received a confirmation statement for every trade that I did. They would go nuts. They would call up and say, "Are you crazy? What are you doing? I thought you were supposed to be doing real research."

What prompts you to get out of a stock?

I get out either because the stock looks as though it's rolling over, and I am in danger of losing what I have made, or because the stock has made too much money in too short a period of time.

Would you then look to buy back the stock on a correction?

Yes.

Does that work, or do you often end up missing the rest of the move?

I often end up missing the rest of the move because the stocks I am buying are good companies, and they usually continue to go up.

Have you considered changing your trading approach so that you hold stocks longer?

I have changed gradually over the years, but to this day, I still fall prey to the mistake of getting out too early.

When you get out of a stock, do you sometimes buy it back at a higher price?

Sure, all the time.

So you are at least able to bite the bullet and admit that you made a mistake by getting out, and then get back in at a higher price. You don't say, "I can't get buy it now; I sold it $10 lower."

I may have done that in earlier years, but now buying back a stock at a higher price doesn't bother me at all. To me, the successful stock is not one that I bought at 10 and held to a 100, but one where I picked up 7 points here, 5 here, another 8 here, and caught a major part of the move.

But it sounds as if it would be easier to just buy one of these blessed stocks and hold it.

Sometimes, but it really depends on market conditions. For example, right now valuations are so high that I don't have any core positions that I intend to hold on to.

That brings me to a question I was going to ask: In this type of market, where the leading stocks have already seen such extraordinary price run-ups, do you still use the same approach? If not, how do you adjust your methodology?

To be honest, I'm having a hard time adjusting. My philosophy is to float like a jellyfish and let the market push me where it wants to go. I don't draw a line in the sand and say this is my strategy and I'm going to wait for the market to come to me. I try to figure out what strategies are working in the market. One year it might be momentum, another year it might be value.

So you adopt your strategy to match your perception of the market environment.

Exactly, I try to anticipate what the market is going to pay for.

How do you know when there is a sea change?

I'll look at everything and listen to as many people as I can, from cabdrivers to stock analysts. Then I sit back and try to see what idea rises to the top. Sometimes the opportunities are so obvious that you almost can't lose when they come around; the only problem is that they don't come around that often. The key is not to lose money in the times in between.

Give me an example of an opportunity that was that obvious.

Last year [1998] it was very clear to me—I don't like saying stuff like this because it makes it sound as though I have a crystal ball—that the market had a very good chance of rolling over in a serious way during August.

What made you so sure?

I constantly evaluate market sentiment—Is the market hopeful? Is it fearful?—and wait for the price action to confirm my assessment. Throughout last winter and spring, the situation was very confounding. There were lots of reports about potential problems in Asia, but the market ignored everything. Therefore, the only way to make money was to be long, even in the face of this potential trouble.

So I decided to get really long in July. The leaders were performing great, and the market was roaring. At one point, I was up 15 percent for the month. Then all of a sudden, in a matter of days, I lost everything and actually found myself down 3 percent for the month. The market took the money away so quickly that just by looking at my own portfolio, which was filled with market leaders, not stocks with poor fundamentals, I knew something had to be wrong.

What did you do at the time? You said you had started out the month heavily long. Did you cover your entire position? Did you go net short?

I was 130 percent long. What I typically do when I believe there's a major bearish event occurring in the market is to sell everything and then just watch. That's what I did then.

Did you go short?

Yes, about two weeks later. I thought that the Asian crisis that precipitated the break would have a second leg to it. Usually you don't just hear about a problem and then have it end. We also started seeing headlines about potential problems in Russia. Although we had seen these types of news reports before, the difference this time around was that prices were responding. I felt convinced that the situation would continue. Russia was not going to get fixed the next day, neither would Thailand or Korea, and prices were reflecting these fears. During the second week of August, I went 130 percent net short, and the scenario played out. To me it was very obvious.

When did you cover your short position?

I covered my shorts during the second week of October. I have a number of rules taped to my quote machine. One of these is: Buy on extreme weakness and sell on extreme strength. The only way to identify extremes is to get a feel for the sentiment, whether it is euphoria or pessimism. Then you have to act on it quickly, because there are often abrupt peaks and bottoms. By the second week of October, I felt that I had to take advantage of the opportunity of the market's extreme weakness to cover all my shorts. I covered the entire position in one day and actually went net long 25 percent.

Was there anything significant about that day in particular that prompted you to reverse your position?

That day, stocks like Dell went down from 50 to 40, and before the end of the day they were going up 2 or 3 points at a clip.

So you were buying these stocks at much higher prices than they were trading at earlier the same morning.

Absolutely. Actually one of the things I like to see when I'm trying to buy stocks is that they become very difficult to buy. I put an order in to buy Dell at 42, and I got a fill back at 45. I love that.

Do you just put your buy orders in at the market, or do you try to get filled at a particular price?

I always buy and sell at the market. I never mess around trying to get the best fill. I'm a broker's dream.

You said you went long about 25 percent. When did you increase that long position?

Whenever I start to go back in on the long side, I like to wait and see that the market rebound continues the next day and that there is no further bearish news. If there is additional bearish news and the market doesn't go down, then I really go nuts.

Did that happen then?

It didn't happen the next day, but it happened later in the week. There was more news about the collapse of Long Term Capital. [The multibillion-dollar hedge fund was overleveraged in the bond market and suffered enormous losses, leading to fears of repercussions to the entire financial system. See David Shaw interview.] The market just shrugged it off. That gave me greater confidence to just plow in on the long side. I had a chance to buy all these market leaders while they were down sharply from their peaks, which I love to do.

Did the all-or-nothing trade that recouped most of the money you had lost from your home-equity loan mark the beginning of your successful trading career? Did you stay true to your vow to give up your trading transgressions?

For the most part. I immediately started trafficking in quality growth names. I bought the stocks that went up more than the market when the market was going up. I figured those were the horses to bet on. I forced myself to buy these stocks on down days. I found these stocks would often go up five points in a week, whereas I would have been lucky to get five points in a year in the low-quality stocks I had previously been buying.

The only time I really got into trouble was when I fell prey to a great sales pitch. The most dangerous thing on the Street is the ability to communicate. I worked with some great salesmen. They would say, "Stuart, you have to look at this." And sometimes in a weak moment, I would rationalize that I'd done well and had some extra money to speculate with. Maybe this trade would work, and if it didn't, I'd get out quickly. Before I knew it, I would be down 20 or 30 percent on the trade. It's a lesson that I continually have to learn.

Do you still find yourself vulnerable to listening to tips even now?

Absolutely. At some level, I have a gambling urge, which I decided a long time ago I needed to satisfy, but in a small way. Therefore, I set aside a small amount of money in the fund for doing these speculative trades.

On balance, do you end up winning or losing on these trades?

About breakeven.

How did you go from being a stockbroker to a fund manager? For that matter, did you ever make a sale?

Eventually I started to do okay as a stockbroker because I learned how to sell.

How do you sell?

You need to find out what the customer wants and package your sales pitch—not the product—accordingly.

What did the customer want?

Instant gratification, excitement, sizzle, the comfort of knowing that lots of other people were buying the same stock, and a million reasons why the stock would go up.

So you tried to make the stock sound as good as possible without any qualifications?

Absolutely. That's what all stockbrokers do.

Weren't you troubled by making something uncertain sound certain?

Sure, but it wasn't exactly lying, because I had no idea whether the stock would go up or not. It was, however, a huge embellishment. After a while, I just couldn't hack it anymore.

How did you get out of it?

After I started doing well in my own account, I began recommending some of my own ideas, not just the stocks that were part of the company line. I was bailed out by one of my accounts who liked my style and offered me a job to manage money for them. That was really what I wanted to do. If I hadn't landed that job, I would have had to quit because I was once again at the point of waking up in the morning and feeling I can't do this anymore.

What kind of firm was it?

It was a registered investment advisory firm that managed about $300 million in institutional accounts. They had their own strategy on how to invest.

Were you allowed to make your own trading decisions, or did you have to follow their guidelines?

I could buy any stock I wanted, but it had to meet their investment criteria.

What were those restrictions?

The price/earnings ratio had to be below 15. Earnings had to be growing by at least 20 percent per year. There were also some balance sheet and liquidity conditions that had to be met.

Was that a help or a hindrance?

It was a huge impediment because it dramatically narrowed the universe of companies that I could invest in.

What stocks were you missing because of this policy?

For example, I couldn't buy a Microsoft or a Cisco; instead I had to buy a Novell or a 3Com.

Because the price/earnings ratio was greater than fifteen?

Right.

Do you feel it is a flawed investment policy to try to buy stocks that have low price/earnings ratios?

Not necessarily. I would never adopt that type of strategy myself, but I feel that any sound strategy will work as long as you stick to it.

Were there any restrictions on the stocks you bought for your own account?

I was allowed to buy any stocks I wanted to, as long as they were not the same names I was buying for the company's clients.

What was the difference in performance between your own account and the accounts you were managing for the company?

For the company accounts, I would only be up an average of 15 to 20 percent per year, while on my own account, I was averaging well over 100 percent per year.

Did you try going to management and saying, "Look, here's what I've been doing for my own account without any restrictions. Let me trade the company accounts the same way."

Sure, but they had geared the firm to follow their particular philosophy, and that's what the customers bought into. The last thing an investor wants to see is a change in strategy.

My idea, however, was to try to adapt to any new strategies that seemed to be working. Eventually I built up enough capital in my own account so that I could go my own way. I started a fund with $1.3 million, about half of which was my own.

How did you get investors?

Strictly word of mouth. I didn't do any marketing.

I see that you're here completely on your own, which is amazing for a hedge fund managing $150 million. Don't you have any help?

I have a secretary who comes in every other day.

That's it? Don't you need any additional assistance?

I hired someone last year—a great guy who is now off on his own—but I knew immediately that it wasn't for me.

Why is that?

I found that having another opinion in the office was very destabilizing. My problem is that I am very impressionable. If I have someone working for me every day, he may as well be running the money because I'm no longer making my own decisions.

I like quiet. I talk all day on the phone, and that's enough for me. I don't need committees, group meetings, and hand-holding to rationalize why a stock is going down. I even like the fact that my assistant only comes in every other day, so that every alternate day I am completely on my own and can sit here and germinate.

I understand that completely, because I work in a home office. I find that when you work on your own, you can get completely engrossed in what you are doing.

Exactly. That's the main reason I like to be on my own. People come in here and ask me, "How could you manage this much money on your own? Don't you want to become a bigger firm?"

What do you tell them?

Well it's worked for me so far. The only thing that matters is how well I do, not the amount of zeros I'm managing.

With your track record, you could easily raise a lot more money.

That would just kill everything. The only way I can possibly maintain my track record is to make sure I don't overwhelm myself with assets. Right now, if I have a good quarter, it ramps up the amount of money I am managing. By growing through capital appreciation, I can evolve my trading style to accommodate the increase in assets managed.

I guess you would rather make 50 percent plus on a $150 million than 20 percent on $1 billion.

Exactly. A lot of people who do well and decide to dramatically increase their assets find that their first year is their best year. After that, it's downhill. Of course, they still make huge sums of money. But I want to feel good about coming in every day. I want to have happy customers and see my assets steadily growing. I don't want to be cranking out a great living on a business that is deteriorating. I have almost no overhead, so I still make a great income. There is no need to get greedy.

Do you think the experience of coming close to the edge of bankruptcy helped you become successful?

Definitely.

In what way?

The odd thing about this industry is that no matter how successful you become, if you let your ego get involved, then one bad phone call can put you out of business. My having seen the abyss might spare me from making that phone call. I know how quickly things can go bad. Any stock can go to zero, and you need to realize that.

When I talk to potential new investors I focus on my mistakes. Because if you are going to invest with someone, you want that person to have made mistakes on his own tab and not to make them on yours. Someone who has never made a mistake is dangerous, because mistakes will happen. If you've made mistakes, you realize they can recur, and it makes you more careful.

We've talked about the mistakes you've made early in your career. What mistakes have you made during your more recent successful years?

This year I got very bearish without waiting for prices to confirm my opinion.

What made you so blindly bearish?

I became very concerned about the rise in interest rates. In the past, higher interest rates had always led to lower stock prices, and I assumed the same pattern would repeat this year. The market, however, chose to look at other factors. I didn't wait for the market to confirm the fear of higher interest rates, and I lost money very quickly. I was down 7 percent in March, which is a pretty big one-month drop for me.

Any other mistakes come to mind?

In January 1998 I invested in a bunch of small-cap initial public offerings (IPOs), which all performed incredibly poorly in the first quarter they went public.

What was your mistake there?

My mistake was getting involved in illiquid securities without doing sufficient research.

What prompted you to buy these stocks?

Market sentiment. The market was getting very excited about conceptual IPOs—stocks with a dream and a story but no earnings. When stocks like these go sour, they can go down 70 percent or more very quickly. It was as if a tornado had swept through my portfolio. I was down 12 percent for the month and decided to liquidate everything. One stock that I bought at 18, I sold at 2.

If these stocks were down that much, wouldn't you have been better off holding them in case they bounced back? What happened to these stocks after you liquidated them?

They bounced, but not by much. As I liquidated these stocks, I used the money to buy the types of stocks that I should've been buying—good companies at much higher prices.

So you had deviated from your philosophy.

Yes, once again. It's like a junkie who is off drugs for three years and then runs into some crack dealer who is able to convince him to start again. I don't mean to blame other people for convincing me. It was my own fault for allowing myself to be susceptible to these stories. I think I've learned not to trade on those types of stories anymore. The good news is that I quickly switched back to buying the types of companies that I like. By the end of the quarter, I had recovered all my losses.

I guess the implication is that holding on to a losing stock can be a mistake, *even if it bounces back,* if the money could have been utilized more effectively elsewhere.

Absolutely. By cleaning out my portfolio and reinvesting in solid stocks, I made back much more money than I would have if I had kept the other stocks and waited for a dead cat bounce.

Do you talk to companies at all?

I used to visit companies all the time when I was working for the investment advisory firm.

Did it help at all?

Hardly at all. I found that either they told me what they had previously told everyone else, and it was already factored into the price, or else they lied to me. Once in a blue moon you would learn something valuable, but there was a huge opportunity cost traveling from company to company to get that one piece of useful information.

Can you give me an example of a situation where management lied to you.

The examples are almost too numerous to remember.

Pick out one that stands out as being particularly egregious.

I saw Autumn Software* make a presentation at a conference. I had never heard such a great story. They produced software that was used in computer backup systems all around the world. The management team was very believable and articulate. The stock was high, but I felt it was a big momentum horse. I bought half a million shares, and the stock started to crumble almost immediately.

I called management and asked them what was happening. "We have no idea," they said. "Business is actually better than last month." One day I was out at Nantucket, and I received a phone call informing me that Autumn had just preannounced that they would have a disappointing quarter. The stock, which had closed at 30 that day, opened at 7 the next morning. It was funny because every time I had talked to the company, "business had never been better." That proved to me that as an outside investor you never know the truth.

Is this an example of a situation in which you ignored your own rule of paying careful attention to how a stock responds to news, or if it goes down for no apparent reason?

Unfortunately for my former employer, I was still learning that lesson at the time.

Did that experience sour you completely on talking to management?

Not completely. I might call a company's management when its stock is very low and no one is talking to them, because that is when they are usually desperate enough to talk to anyone. My hope is that I might learn about some catalyst that could cause the stock to turn around.

What are the traits of a successful trader?

I think a lot of successful traders are unemotional, hardworking, and

*Pseudonym

disciplined. Ironically, I find myself lacking on each of those counts. I get very emotional; I really don't work that hard; and I'm not as disciplined as I should be. I would attribute my own success to having both conviction about my gut feelings and the ability to act on them quickly. That is so critical.

So in your own case, you've been able to offset some other drawbacks simply by having the ability to pull the trigger?

Exactly, that's a very good point.

What is the biggest misconception people have about the stock market?

Currently, the biggest misconception is the widespread belief that it is easy to make a living trading in the stock market. People feel they can give up their jobs and trade for a living; most of them are bound to be disappointed.

What are the trading rules you have posted on your computer?

- Be patient—wait for the opportunity.
- Trade on your own ideas and style.
- Never trade impulsively, especially on other people's advice.
- Don't risk too much on one event or company.
- Stay focused, especially when the markets are moving.
- Anticipate, don't react.
- Listen to the market, not outside opinions.
- Think trades through, including profit/loss exit points, before you put them on.
- If you are unsure about a position, just get out.
- Force yourself to trade against the consensus.
- Trade pattern recognition.
- Look past tomorrow; develop a six-month and one-year outlook.
- Prices move before fundamentals.
- It is a warning flag if the market is not responding to data correctly.
- Be totally flexible; be able to admit when you are wrong.
- You will be wrong often; recognize winners and losers fast.
- Start each day from last night's close, not your original cost.
- Adding to losers is easy but usually wrong.
- Force yourself to buy on extreme weakness and sell on extreme strength.

- Get rid of all distractions.
- Remain confident—the opportunities never stop.

I know you have no desire to be working with anyone, but let's say five years from now you decided to pursue a new career making films. Could you train someone to take over for you and invest in accordance with your guidelines?

I could teach someone the basic rules, but I couldn't teach another person how to replicate what I do, because so much of that is based on experience and gut feeling, which is different for each person.

After you reach a certain level of financial success, what is the motivation to keep on going?

The challenge of performance and the tremendous satisfaction I get from knowing that I contributed to people's financial security. It's fantastic. I have a lot of clients, some of whom are my own age, who I have been able to lead to total financial independence.

How do you handle a losing streak?

I trade smaller. By doing that, I know I'm not going to make a lot, but I also know I'm not going to lose a lot. It's like a pit stop. I need to refresh myself. Then when the next big opportunity comes around—and it always does—if I catch it right, it won't make any difference if I've missed some trades in the interim.

What advice do you have for novices?

Either go at it full force or don't go at it at all. Don't dabble.

Is there anything pertinent that we haven't talked about?

It is very important to me to treat people with fairness and civility. Maybe it's a reaction to all the abuse I took in the New York trading rooms. But, whatever the reason, the everyday effort to treat others with decency has come back to me in many positive ways.

Stuart Walton had no burning desire to be a trader, no special analytical or mathematical skills, and was prone to emotional trading decisions that caused him to lose all or nearly all his money on several occasions. Why, then, did he succeed, let alone succeed so spectacularly?

There are five key elements:

Persistence. He did not let multiple failures stop him.

Self-awareness. He realized his weakness, which was listening to other people's opinions, and took steps to counteract this personal flaw. To this end, he decided to work entirely alone and to set aside a small amount of capital—too small to do any damage—to vent his tip-following, gambling urges.

Methodology. Walton became successful exactly when he developed a specific market philosophy and methodology.

Flexibility. Although Walton started out by selling powerhouse stocks and buying bargains, he was flexible enough to completely reverse his initial strategy based on his empirical observations of what actually worked in the market. If he believes a stock he previously owned is going higher, he is able to buy it back at a higher price without hesitation. If he realizes he has made a mistake, he has no reservation about liquidating a stock, even if it has already fallen far below his purchase price. Finally, he adjusts his strategy to fit his perception of the prevailing market environment. In Walton's words, "One year it might be momentum, another year it might be value."

Diagnostic capability. Most great traders have some special skill or ability. Walton's talent lies in not only observing the same news and information as everyone else, but also in having a clearer insight into the broad market's probable direction—sometimes to the point where the market's future trend appears obvious to him. This market diagnostic capability is probably innate rather than learned. As an analogy, two equally intelligent people can go to the same medical school, work equally hard, and intern in the same hospital, yet one will have much greater diagnostic skill because ability also depends on intrinsic talent.

Walton's case history demonstrates that early failure does not preclude later success. It also exemplifies the critical importance of developing your own methodology and shutting out all other opinions.

Update on Stuart Walton

Walton left trading in the midst of a roaring bull market after eight years in which he achieved a remarkable triple-digit average annual return (gross). He returned to trading in the midst of a bear market (January 2001), out of step with the changed environment. In the twenty-one months since his return, he experienced an indexlike cumulative decline, losing 6 percent more than the S&P 500 and 4 percent less than the Nasdaq. In this follow-up interview, we discussed the reasons for Walton's drastic performance reversal and the changes he has made in his trading approach as a result.

You had an eight-year run with exceptional returns, then took a sabbatical, and experienced a terrible year on your return. What happened?

When I stopped trading in mid-1999, the Nasdaq had not yet reached its frenzied overdrive phase. It had been going up over 20 percent per year, but in the mere eight months after I quit, it shot up another 75 percent. So I didn't trade through that period of explosive price gains and market euphoria. Similarly, I didn't trade through the subsequent bursting of that bubble. When I returned in 2001, since I hadn't lived through the excesses the market had gone through, I didn't fully appreciate the extent of the emotional damage the market had sustained in 2000. My most recent trading experience had been the success I had witnessed in the 1990s by zigging and zagging to the rhythm of the markets. As a result, instead of playing for the big trade, which was the continuation of the downmove, I was still trying to play the market from both sides. With the benefit of hindsight, it is clear that I suffered from a lack of perspective.

Many of the indicators that have worked reliably for decades have ceased working in the current bear market, leaving many professional market participants looking foolish. The problem is that most of us have not seen a comparable stock market in our lifetimes. Very few of us have lived through the aftermath of the bursting of a market bubble. The closest analogy would the 1930s in the United States or the 1990s in Japan.

Do you mean to suggest that the current bear market could be as protracted as those extreme examples?

The analogy is not totally appropriate insofar as the current U.S. economy is far sounder than the U.S. economy of the 1930s or the

Japanese economy during the past ten to fifteen years. But one reason to think this way is that I don't believe the current stock market malaise will come to a permanent end until memories of the 1990s bull market are completely erased. There are still too many people ready to try to pick bottoms and buy tech stocks.

If you just look at some of these tech companies on the basis of their fundamentals—negative earnings, huge debt, high valuations—there would no conceivable reason to go near them. Yet many people are still jumping in any time these stocks begin to rebound. Why? Because they still have the memory of how these stocks went from $10 to $200 in the late 1990s. It is reminiscent of the typewriter companies with the advent of the computer. Investors had been so taken, for so long, with the dominance of the typewriter, that even as it became clear that the PC revolution had started, people were still willing to buy Smith Corona all the way down to zero. The same kind of general dynamic seems to have taken hold in the technology and speculative portions of the current market.

As another example, you couldn't get a more frightening, destabilizing event than what occurred on September 11. Yet the market failed to remotely approach the extreme levels it had seen many times in the past, particularly in times of crisis. I found that amazing; it made me realize that it would take a long time for this process to unwind itself. Every time one of these rallies fails and the market falls to new lows, as was the case with the recent breaking of the September 2001 lows, it disenchants more and more people. But the absence of extremes suggests this process still has to be repeated before the bear market comes to an end.

By extremes, do you mean extreme low valuations?

Yes, certainly valuation levels in September 2001, and even the lower lows in July 2002, were well above levels seen at past market bottoms, but I am also talking about measures of extreme emotion, such as downside volume versus upside volume. In this context, the levels seen in the aftermath of September 11 and the July 2002 lows were nowhere near other past extremes, which is one of the main reasons why I believe we are going to see more unwinding of the excesses of the 1990s. Nevertheless, if the market is going to have a strong three-month rally, I want to participate in that rebound regardless of my long-term viewpoint.

How do you distinguish between a market that is beginning an intermediate rally and one that is just witnessing a one-week pop?

From a technical perspective, I would look for lots of trendlines being broken and stocks moving up on volume. Also I approach the market one stock at a time, one day at a time. I don't just say now is a good time to play for a three-month upmove and load up on long positions. If a stock's fundamentals look sound, the stock and sector are acting well technically, and the general market tone is improving, I may put on a position and stay with it as long as these factors don't deteriorate significantly.

Do you always use stops?

Yes.

Why didn't that help in 2001?

I was using stops, but I had one horrendous month—February—in which my entire portfolio got stopped out twice. Leading companies had gone down 50 to 70 percent, so I bought a basket of these stocks, which then promptly proceeded to go down another 10 percent, stopping me out. I tried the same set of trades later in the month, and was stopped out again. I now use risk controls at the portfolio level in addition to stops on individual stocks. If the portfolio is down 5 percent in any month, I will pare down the exposure, and if it declines by 10 percent, I will go completely to cash.

Besides the failure to focus sufficiently on risk at the portfolio level, what has been the worst mistake you have made since your return to trading?

Not appreciating how drastically a bear market can change the balance between return and risk. For example, say you like a pharmaceutical company because you have done thorough research that leads you to believe there is an 80 percent probability that the FDA will approve their drug application. In the current bear market environment, even if you are right about the odds, the trade may be a bad bet because the stock might go up only 5 percent with a favorable ruling, but go down 50 percent with an unfavorable ruling.

What is the most important lesson you have learned from your difficult experience in 2001?

The importance of only trading with an edge—not to trade when there is no trade.

Are you trading less now?

Yes, radically less. I've re-examined my trading at my prior hedge funds and found that during those periods in which my turnover was the highest, I never made any real progress. When I look back at those times, I realize they were the same periods when my emotions were running at their highest. Too much emotion tends to lead to too much turnover and bad decisions. Although I still like to be spontaneous, I now put myself through more mental drills before I decide to put on a trade.

STEVE WATSON

Dialing for Dollars

Steve Watson has never had a problem taking risks. He fondly recalls the childhood summer ritual of catching snakes with his cousin in the Ozark Mountains. When he was eleven, he and his cousin thought it would be "fun" to move up from capturing nonpoisonous snakes to the poisonous variety. They found two large water moccasins. After pinning each snake down with a long branch and grabbing it tightly just below the head, they decided it would be a good idea to carry their quarry back to the family cabin, approximately a mile downriver, to proudly show their fathers what they had caught. After sloshing through the shallow river for about half a mile, with the snakes wrapped around their arms and their hands tiring from the tight grip needed to keep the snakes' heads immobile, they had some second thoughts. "Maybe this wasn't such a good idea," they agreed. Finally, unable to maintain their grips for much longer, they hurled the snakes into the water and darted in the opposite direction. In comparison, buying and shorting stocks must seem pretty tame.

Watson has also been willing to take risks in his career. Two years after becoming a broker, he faced the growing realization that he had chosen the wrong path toward fulfilling his goal to trade stocks, so he quit and set off for New York. He did so without the comfort of any business contacts, job leads, or supportive résumé. In fact, there was absolutely no logical reason for Steve Watson to succeed in his quest—other than his determination. Several years later, he quit a secure job with a major fund to start his own hedge fund. He launched his new business without even enough money to rent office space.

When it comes to trading, however, Watson is willing to accept risk but not to take risks. "You have to be willing to accept a certain level of risk," Watson says, "or else you will never pull the trigger." But he believes in keeping the risk under firm control. His net long position is typically less than 50 percent of assets, often significantly less. Since starting his fund four and a half years ago his worst drawdown from an equity peak to a subsequent low has been just under 4 percent—the same level as his average monthly return after deducting fees. In terms of return to risk, this performance places him at the very top tier of fund managers.

One of the major lessons that I have learned by conducting the interviews for the *Market Wizard* books is that, invariably, successful traders end up using a methodology that fits their personality. Watson has chosen an approach that is heavily dependent on communicating with and getting information from other people, a style that is a good match for his easygoing manner. Asked whether he found it difficult to get people who were often complete strangers to take the time to speak with him, Watson said, "My father is one of the nicest people you could ever hope to meet. One thing he taught me was, 'Don't treat anyone differently than you would your best friends.' I find if you approach people with that attitude, most of the time they will try to help you out."

I met with Watson in a conference room at his firm's Manhattan office. He was relaxed and friendly, and spoke with an accent that reflected his Arkansas origins.

★

When did you first get interested in the stock market?

I came from a family that never read *The Wall Street Journal*, never bought a share of stock, and never invested in mutual funds. I didn't know anything about the stock market until I was in college. When I attended the University of Arkansas, I took an investment course that sparked my interest.

What about the course intrigued you?

Doing research on a stock. As a main project for the course, we were required to pick a stock and write a report on it. My group picked a local utility company that was experiencing some trouble. We did our analysis and came to the conclusion that it was a terrible company. We were all prepared to trash the stock in our presentation.

The day before the presentation, someone in our group came up with the bright idea of going to the local brokerage office and seeing what they said about the stock. The brokerage firm had this beautiful glossy report on the company, which was filled with all sorts of positive commentary and concluded with a recommendation to buy the stock. Here we were, a group of undergraduate students taking an elementary investment course, and we thought that since these guys get paid to do this for a living, we must be wrong. We completely transformed our report so that it reached a positive conclusion, even though it was the exact opposite of what we believed.

The next day, we gave our presentation, and the professor just tore it apart. "This is a terrible company!" he exclaimed, citing a list of reasons to support his conclusion—all of which had been in our original report. Of course, we couldn't say anything *[he laughs]*.

What ultimately happened to the stock?

It went down. That's when I learned my first and most important lesson about the stock market: Stick to your own beliefs.

Did that course clinch your decision to pursue a career in the stock market?

Yes. After I graduated, I moved to Dallas, which was the only big city I had ever visited, to look for a job as a stockbroker. I thought being a stockbroker meant that you got to manage other people's money and play the stock market all day long. I quickly found out that it was more of a sales job, and quite frankly, I'm a terrible salesperson. I picked up my largest client because his own broker wouldn't answer the phone on the day of the October 1987 stock market crash—he couldn't face talking to his customers—and I was the only one his client could reach.

After I was there for about two years, I remember calling up my dad and saying, "I don't like being a stockbroker. All I do is cold-call people all day, trying to sell them stuff they probably don't need in the first place." Verbalizing my feelings helped me decide to quit. I knew I really wanted to be a money manager. I moved to New York City to find a job more closely aligned with my goal.

Had you been successful picking stocks as a broker?

No, I had been very unsuccessful.

What then gave you the confidence that you could manage money successfully?

I didn't expect to get a job managing money on day one. I just wanted to break into the business. Once I decide I am going to do something, I become determined to succeed, regardless of the obstacles. If I didn't have that attitude, I never would have made it.

When I arrived in New York, I didn't have any contacts, and my résumé—a 2.7 GPA from Arkansas University—and two years' experience as a stockbroker were certainly not going to impress anyone. I couldn't compete against people who had gone to Harvard and interned at Goldman Sachs. Therefore, I had to do it the hard way. I went to work for an insurance company, doing credit analysis, essentially to pay the bills, but also to gain some analytical experience. I also applied to business school at NYU but couldn't get in. I enrolled at Fordham University for a semester, received good grades, and then transferred.

After I graduated, I interviewed with about forty different hedge fund managers, which was very helpful, because it gave me a feeling for what other people were doing. I landed a job at Bankers Trust working in the small cap department [group that invested in stocks with small capitalization]. Even though I was new to the game, the reason I was hired was that I knew small cap stocks better than anyone else. I can't tell you how many nights I stayed up until 3 A.M., flipping through stocks on the Bloomberg. At that point, I probably knew something about every exchange-listed stock under the $300 million market cap level.

Why had you decided to focus on small cap stocks?

Small caps have always been a love for me because I can't get an edge on stocks like Microsoft or Intel. I can't call up the CFOs of those companies. In college, even though I didn't have a job, I would call up CFOs, tell them that I was doing a project on their company, and ask them questions. I had stacks of company reports filling up my apartment.

What were your responsibilities at Bankers Trust?

I worked as Bill Newman's right-hand person for one of the firm's two small cap funds. He gave me tremendous leeway. If I liked an idea, he let me go with it. It was almost as if I were a portfolio manager because he rarely turned down one of my stock picks. Unfortunately, he left the firm three months after I joined. I didn't get along with his replacement—our investment philosophies clashed.

In what way?

My new boss—who, incidentally, was one of the worst stock pickers I have ever seen—was a momentum player who believed in buying high P/E stocks [stocks trading at large multiples of their earnings] that were moving up rapidly, whereas I believed in buying value stocks and doing a lot of detailed research on a company. I left about a half year later, and after another extensive Wall Street job search found a job with Friess Associates, which ran the Brandywine Fund.

What job were you hired for?

Officially, I was hired as a consultant because I worked in a satellite office. At the time, the firm's main branch was located in Wilmington, Delaware, and I worked in Manhattan. The way Friess operated was that everyone was both a research analyst and portfolio manager. They used what they called "a-pig-at-the-trough" approach. If you found a stock that you liked and wanted to buy, you had to convince one of the other people to liquidate one of their holdings to make room in the portfolio, just like one pig has to push another pig out of the way if he wants to get a spot at the trough.

How long were you there?

About two years.

Why did you leave?

The assets of the fund were growing rapidly. I love small cap stocks. But the assets of the fund were getting too large to bother with small cap stocks, and the fund's focus shifted almost exclusively to mid cap and large cap stocks, which made it harder to get a hold of the CFOs and ask questions. Also, as the assets grew, the number of analysts increased. When there are fifteen analysts, your performance doesn't have too much impact on the fund. I wanted to be in a situation where I had control over the performance. I decided to leave to start my own fund.

Where did you get the money to start your fund?

At the time, I only had about $20,000 to my name. I went to a few CFOs to whom I had given stock tips for their own personal accounts—recommendations that had worked out very well for them. I only raised $700,000 in assets; I'm the worst salesman in the world. But that was enough to start the fund.

How did you cover your operating expenses?

I was extremely lucky. Ed McGuinn, the man from whom I was renting office space at the time, wanted to help me get started. He knew I couldn't afford to rent space on my own, so he let me have the use of a small office for free. It was the smallest office I had ever seen—about 12 feet by 5—but I was extremely grateful. He even paid the monthly fee for my Bloomberg.

I noticed that in your first year as a fund manager, your net exposure was considerably higher, probably double what it has been since then. Why is that?

I had a different risk/reward perspective the first year because I was managing less than $1 million. I allowed my net exposure to get up to 70 to 80 percent and individual positions to get as high as 5 or 6 percent of assets. As a result, we had triple-digit returns that year.

How do you select the stocks you buy?

We have two funds: the microfund, which invests in companies with a market capitalization of under $350 million, and a small cap fund that invests in companies with a capitalization of $350 million to $1.5 billion. In both funds, we begin by looking for companies that are relatively cheap—trading between eight to twelve times earnings. Within this group, we try to identify those companies for which investors' perceptions are about to change. Typically, these may be companies that are having some trouble now, but their business is about to turn around. We try to find out that information before everyone else does.

How do you do that?

We make a lot of phone calls. The difference between our firm and most other hedge funds is that talking to companies is our primary focus. I have two people who spend three-quarters of their time booking calls with company management and five research people who spend virtually their entire day calling companies and talking to CFOs.

In this business, you can't wait for a new product to come out and be successful. By that time, you will have to pay three times as much for the stock. We are trying to add value by doing our own research. If you are buying stocks that are washed out—stocks that are trading at only eight to twelve times earnings—any significant change can dramatically impact the stock price.

Won't CFOs tend to paint a rosy picture of their company?

Of course. You can't go strictly by what they say. CFOs are only human, and they will tend to exaggerate how well their company is doing. But we also speak to distributors, customers, and competitors. If we are going to own something, we're going to talk not only to the company, but also to the people selling and using their products.

What did you teach your research people about doing phone interviews?

You want the other person to be on your side. Don't ever tell a CFO he is wrong or try to tell him how to run his business. If you do, he probably won't take your phone call the next time. You also have to ask questions the right way. You don't want to ask a CFO a direct question such as, "What are earnings going to be this quarter?" because, obviously, he can't tell you. But if instead you ask him about how his company will be affected by a product his competitor is putting out, you may well get some useful information. We are detectives. We are trying to find out information that is not widely dispersed and then put all the pieces together to get an edge.

What else do you look for when you buy a stock?

A low price and the prospect for imminent change are the two key components. Beyond that, it also helps if there is insider buying by management, which confirms prospects for an improvement in the company outlook.

Is insider buying something that you look at regularly?

Yeah, but I'd rather not put that in print.

Why not?

Because I don't want to give away secrets.

But insider buying is not exactly a secret. In fact, it came up in a number of other interviews I did for this book.

Over the course of the two times in my career that I looked for a job on Wall Street, I must have interviewed with as many as eighty firms. I was amazed by how many hedge fund managers used charts and sell-side information [brokerage research] but didn't use insider buying. In fact, I had a lot of managers tell me that using insider buying was stupid *[he laughs]*.

Stock investing is not an exact science. The greater the number of useful things you can look at, the greater you increase your odds. The odds are better that we will make correct investment decisions if we talk to a company than if we don't talk to them. Similarly, if we focus on companies with insider buying, it doesn't mean that these stocks will go up, but it certainly improves our odds.

Do you also mean to imply that you don't use charts or Wall Street research?

I never looked at a chart for 99 percent of the stocks I bought for our funds.

Is the reason you don't use charts because you tried using them but couldn't find any value or because you never explored this avenue of research?

Too many people use charts. If too many people are using an approach, I feel that I can't get a competitive edge.

What about brokerage research? Is that also something you never use?

I will look at analysts' earnings estimates because part of my job is to find out whether a company is doing better or worse than people perceive. But I have never called a sell-side analyst to ask for an opinion. Don't get me wrong; there are some great analysts out there. But it really comes down to my philosophy: It's much more valuable to do your own research so that you can make your own decisions about when to get in and out.

If I buy a company because of an analyst's recommendation, and the stock suddenly drops 20 percent, I'm going to be dependent on that analyst for information. If I call the analyst and he says, "Everything is fine," and then try to call the CFO of the company, he may well not return my call because he doesn't know who I am. In the meantime, he's talking to ten other people with whom he has built a relationship. If I was the guy who built the relationship with the company, maybe I would be the first person the CFO called back.

Another aspect is that sell-side research tends to be biased; it is driven by investment banking relationships. If a brokerage firm earns several million dollars doing an underwriting for a stock, it is very difficult for an analyst of that firm to issue anything other than a buy rating, even if he believes the company has significant problems. Some of my research analysts have good friends who are sell-side analysts and have seen them pressured to recommend stocks they didn't like.

Let's say a stock is trading in the 8 to 12 P/E range and you like the fundamentals. How do you decide when to buy it? Obviously, you're not using any technical analysis for timing, since you don't even look at charts.

You need a catalyst that will make the stock go higher.

Give me an example of a catalyst that prompted you to buy a stock.

A current example is Amerigon. Two weeks ago, they put out a press release announcing a five-year agreement with Ford Motors to manufacture ventilated car seats. The press release didn't contain much information about the size of the contract. But by talking not only to the company but also to someone at Ford, we know the contract is huge. We also know that they're working on similar agreements with the other car manufactures.

What is another example of a catalyst?

A change that will lead to a dynamic improvement in margins. Another one of our long positions is Windmere, which is a manufacturer of personal care products, such as hair dryers. Last year, they bought a division of Black & Decker and overpaid for it. The high operating costs of the acquired division acted as a drag on their earnings. We bought the stock recently when we learned that the company planned to close down some of these unprofitable facilities—an action that will bring their costs down and lead to better-than-expected earnings in coming quarters.

Any other examples of a catalyst?

Sometimes the catalyst can be a new product. One of our biggest winners last year was LTXX, a semiconductor company. They had come out with a new product, and by talking to their customers, we knew the sales were going to be very good. Wall Street didn't know about it because the sales of this new product hadn't shown up in earnings reports. When the earnings starting showing up above expectations, the stock took off.

If you buy a stock and it moves higher, when do you decide to liquidate the position?

Too early [*he laughs*]. We are always rotating our stocks. If we buy a stock at ten times earnings and it goes up, usually by the time it gets to twenty times earnings, we are out of it. We will rotate the money down to another stock with similar qualities so that we can keep the risk/reward of the portfolio as low as possible. LTXX is a good example. We started buying the stock around $5 and got out when it went up to $15, even though our earnings projections for the stock were still positive. Today the stock is trading at $45. That's fairly typical. But that same trait of liquidating stocks too early has also helped us during market declines because we're not long the stocks with the high price/earnings ratios that get hit hardest in a market correction.

If you buy a stock and it just sits there, at what point do you decide to get out?

If it looks like dead money and what I originally thought would happen is not happening, then it's probably better to just move on.

In other words, you liquidate once it becomes clear that the reasons you went in are no longer valid?

Or because I have a better idea. We're working with a finite amount of money. Consequently, it's important to stay invested in your best ideas.

How many positions do you have at one time?

Over a hundred. We won't let any single position get very large. Our largest holding will be about 3 percent of assets, and even that is rare. For shorts, our maximum position will be half that large.

What is your balance between long and short positions?

Our total exposure will normally range between about 20 and 50 percent net long, although it could be even lower if I get very bearish on the market. Right now we're about 80 percent long and 40 percent short, which is fairly typical. We've always kept a pretty good-size short position and will continue to do so. Part of the reason for that is that I am a perennial bear.

A perennial bear in the greatest bull market in history—that doesn't like a beneficial trait. Why do you have a bearish bias?

Thank goodness we've been able to make money anyway. I have felt this way for a while, but certainly now [March 2000], I think we are seeing a mania in certain sectors, such as the Internet and technology. Valuations are up there in the ozone layer. It is no different from the market manias we've seen in the past: the Russian market a few years ago, the Japanese market during the 1980s, the real estate market in the 1970s, even the Dutch tulip craze in the seventeenth century. Right now, when everyone's golf buddy is making money buying these stocks, there's a lot of peer pressure to follow the group. You have a locomotive while prices are going up, but the problem is, what happens when the locomotive stops and reverses direction, as it invariably will.

Are we near a top or will the top form three years from now? I can't answer that question. All I can do is control the factors over which I have an influence. I can control the number of CFOs and customers we talk to each day, but I can't determine what the market is going to do.

Isn't it difficult to talk to the CFOs of companies you are shorting? I imagine they wouldn't be too eager to talk to managers who are selling their stock.

We don't really talk to CFOs on the short side anymore.

Because of the access problem?

No, because we got talked out of some of our best short positions. In earlier years, there were a number of times when I changed my mind about selling a stock because a CFO assured me that everything was fine, and then the stock tanked. If we are considering a stock on the short side, we spend a lot of time talking to customers, suppliers, and competitors.

How do you select your short positions?

We certainly look for the higher-priced stocks—companies trading at thirty to forty times earnings, or stocks that have no earnings. Within that group, we seek to identify those companies with a flawed business plan.

Give me an example of a flawed business plan.

My favorite theme for a short is a one-product company because if that product fails, they have nothing else to fall back on. It's also much easier to check out sales for a one-product company. A perfect example is Milestone Scientific. The company manufactured a product that was supposed to be a painless alternative to dental novocaine shots. It sounded like a great idea, and originally we started looking at the stock as a buy prospect. One of our analysts went to a dentistry trade show and collected a bunch of business cards from attending dentists. The primary Wall Street analyst covering the stock assumed every dental office would be buying five of these instruments, and he projected unbelievably huge earnings.

I visited the company in New Jersey. There were three people sitting in rented offices who were outsourcing everything. We started calling dentists and found the product didn't work as well as advertised; it wasn't entirely painless, and it also took longer than novocaine to take effect. Another crucial element was that the company sold the product with a money-back guarantee. They booked all their shipments as revenues and left themselves out on a limb in terms of product returns.

We also talked to the manufacturer to whom the company was outsourcing their production and found out the number of units actually shipped as well as their future production plans. We could see that the orders were slowing down dramatically on the manufacturing side. The differences between reality and the Wall Street research report were about as far apart as I have ever seen.

What ultimately happened to the stock?

It went down below one dollar.

Wasn't it difficult to get the manufacturer to talk to you in that type of situation, let alone give you all that detailed information?

If you call, there's at least a chance the person will talk to you. One of things I tell my analysts is, "Make the calls. Maybe they won't talk to you, but I guarantee that if you don't call, they won't talk to you." In this case, the manufacturer was very helpful at the start, but then they wised up to what we were doing and stopped taking our calls. But by then, we had all the information we needed.

What do you say when you call a manufacturer in this type of situation?

I tell him the truth. I tell him that I am a fund manager and am doing research on the company and the industry. In some cases, when we call a company, we ask them to provide us with the names of some of their top customers to help us evaluate their product.

Does giving you this information sometimes work against the company because their customers don't like them as much as they believe?

When I first started doing this I thought that contacting customers supplied by a company would be like talking to references on a résumé—they would only say complimentary things. I was amazed when this frequently proved not to be the case. I have often wondered whether a company had any idea what their customers really thought about them. Sometimes we have found our best information this way.

Any other examples of how you pick your short positions?

A good example is Balance Bars. You could walk into any GNC store and see shelves loaded with competitive products and the price of Balance Bar items marked down. Yet the stock was trading at a multiple of thirty-five times earnings; it should have been trading at ten times earnings.

That sounds a lot like Peter Lynch talking about getting trading ideas by going to the mall with his family.

Peter Lynch has probably inspired me more than anyone else. I read his book *One Up on Wall Street* at least ten times. One question I ask people I interview is whether they've read his book. If they haven't, it tells me they are not as serious about the stock market as they claim to be.

What aspect of the book do you personally find so valuable?

The message that it is critical to do your own research rather than depending on Wall Street research.

What type of research?

Talking to companies and customers.

But the ordinary investor can't call up companies.

The ordinary investor may not be able to call up the company CFO, but as Lynch advises, the nonprofessional can call the investor relations office and still get valuable information by asking the right questions. The gist of Lynch's advice to the ordinary investor is: Invest in what you know—the company you work for (assuming it is doing well), companies in the same industry, or companies that make a product you can touch and feel. His point is that people would be much better off investing in companies they understand than listening to their broker and investing in companies they know nothing about. One part of Peter Lynch's philosophy is that if you can't summarize the reasons why you own a stock in four sentences, you probably shouldn't own it.

Did you ever meet Peter Lynch?

I never met him, but I interviewed at Fidelity on several occasions. I was obsessed with getting a job there because I wanted to be the next Peter Lynch and eventually run the Magellan fund. The last time I interviewed with Fidelity, which was right before I took the job at Friess Associates, I got as far as meeting with Jeff Vinik [Lynch's initial successor as manager of the Magellan fund]. He asked me only two questions, which will stick in my mind forever. First, he asked, "What is the bond rate?" I was a stock guy who never paid attention to the bond market. I subsequently learned that Vinik pays very close attention to interest rates because he trades a lot of bonds. His second question was, "You're twenty-nine years old; what took you so long?" The interview was over in less than five minutes.

Do you, like Peter Lynch, get trading ideas by going to the mall?

All the time. I love going to malls. Investing is not as complicated as people make it out to be. Sometimes it just requires common sense. Anyone can go to the mall and see that a store like Bombay is empty and the Gap is filled with people. If you go to four or five malls and see the same thing, there is a reason for it. Bombay hasn't had the right products to make people want to buy their stuff for years, whereas the Gap is continually changing with the times and getting in fresh inventories that meet their customers' needs.

Does that imply that you bought the Gap and shorted Bombay?

We don't trade the Gap because we only trade small cap stocks. We have been short Bombay from time to time.

What are examples of trades that were largely inspired by mall visits?

Last Christmas I went to Men's Wearhouse because I needed a suit. I hated the clothes, and I noticed the store was virtually empty. We did some additional research to confirm the trade, but we ended up shorting the stock.

How about on the long side?

One stock we bought is Claire's. I noticed that the store always seemed to be mobbed with teenagers. We also liked their financials and found their management very forthcoming.

We were talking about companies with flawed business plans. Any other examples?

Enamalon. The company's single product was a toothpaste that supposedly did a better job of whitening teeth. If they didn't spend a lot of money on promotion and advertising, they would never get a toehold in the highly competitive toothpaste market. On the other hand, if they did spend enough to get widespread consumer recognition, they would burn through most of their capital. It was a no-win situation from the start. The other problem was that the product cost a lot more than ordinary toothpaste but didn't work any better. We had everyone in our office try it, and only one person liked it.

You said the name of the company was Enamalon? I never heard of the toothpaste.

Exactly, that's my point.

What happened to the stock?

The last time I checked, it was trading for one dollar.

It sounds like an important element in your decision to short this stock was to have everyone in the office sample their product. Any other examples of short ideas that were derived by "consumer research"?

[He searches his memory and then laughs.] One of our shorts was Ultrafem. It was a one-product company that was trading at over a $100 million capitalization. The product was a substitute for feminine pads that used what the company termed "a soft cup technology." The company had put out press releases trumpeting the superiority of their product to conventional alternatives. I called the manufacturer and got them to send me five free samples, which I gave to five women friends. After they tried it, they all came back to me with virtually the same response: "You've got to be kidding!" I shorted the stock. The stock was trading in the twenties when I conducted my "market research;" it's now trading at three cents with a market capitalization of $260,000.

Where did you get out?

We covered our position recently.

You held it all the way down!

This was probably my number one short pick of all time, but unfortunately we had very few shares on the way down because we were bought in on a lot of our stock.

By "bought in" do you mean that the stock you borrowed was called back? [In order to short a stock, the seller must borrow the shares he sells. If the lender of those shares requests their return, the short seller must either borrow the shares elsewhere, which may not be possible, or else buy back the shares in the market.]

Exactly, and the stock was fully locked up [there weren't any shares available to be borrowed]. That's when I learned that the short game is very relationship dependent. If there is a scarcity of stock available for borrowing and I'm competing with a large fund manager who does more business with the brokerage firm than I do, guess who's going to get those shares. This occurred back in 1997; we were a lot smaller then.

Why would loaned shares be called back?

Because the investor requests the stock certificate in his name. [Unless an investor specifically requests the stock certificate, the stock will be held by the brokerage firm ("in the Street name") and loanable.]

Why would an investor suddenly request receipt of his stock certificate?

Companies whose stock price is very vulnerable because of weak fundamentals will often attract a lot of short selling. Sometimes these companies will encourage their investors to request their stock certificates in their name, in the hopes of forcing shorts to cover their positions when the loaned stock is recalled. Sometimes a few firms will buy up a large portion of the shares in a stock with a heavy short interest and then call in the shares, forcing the shorts to cover at a higher price. Then they will liquidate the stock for a quick profit.

Are you implying that large fund managers will sometimes get together to squeeze the shorts?

It is illegal for portfolio managers to get together to push the price up or down—that's considered market manipulation. Does it happen anyway? Sure, it happens all the time. During the past five months, just about every stock with a heavy short interest got squeezed at one time or another.

Do most stocks that are squeezed eventually come down?

I am a firm believer that if a stock is heavily shorted, there is usually a good fundamental reason. Most of the time, those stocks will end up much lower. In the interim, however, even a near-valueless stock can go up sharply due to an artificial scarcity of loanable shares.

How do you time your shorts? Certainly there are a lot of overpriced stocks that just get more overpriced.

The timing is definitely the tough part. That is why we spread our short position across so many stocks and use rigorous risk control on our shorts. I don't mind if I have a long position that goes down 40 percent, as long as I still believe that the fundamentals are sound. If a short goes 20 to 30 percent against us, however, we will start to cover, even if my analysis of the stock is completely unchanged. In fact, I will cover even if I am convinced that the company will ultimately go bankrupt. I have seen too many instances of companies where everything is in place for the stock to go to zero in a year, but it first quintupled because the company made some announcement and the shorts got squeezed. If that stock is a 1 percent short in our portfolio,

I'm not going to let it turn into a 5 percent loss. We've had a lot of short positions that we closed out because they went against us and that later on collapsed. But we are much more concerned about avoiding a large loss than missing a profit opportunity.

The discussion of the inherent danger of being short a stock that is subject to a squeeze leads to a conversation about Watson's childhood experience with poisonous snakes, which was described at this chapter's opening.

Did you feel any fear while you were holding those snakes?

No, I would describe the feeling as closer to excitement. I was a pretty hyperactive kid.

Is there anything that you are afraid of?

I'm going skydiving next week—*that* scares me.

Why is that?

I thought about that. I realized what scares me—things I can't control. When I held those snakes, I had control. I'm planning to learn race car driving in Italy this year, and that doesn't scare me because I'll have control of the car. But I have no control over the parachute. I just hope that the person who prepares my chute doesn't have a bad day.

Why are you going skydiving if you have no control?

I just had my birthday this past Saturday; it was one of my gifts. I don't have any choice. Maybe the person who gave me the present will forget—but I doubt it *[he laughs]*.

What do you look for when you hire an analyst?

For a number of reasons, everyone I hire is in their twenties. First, they will work eighty to a hundred hours a week. Second, they haven't made so much money that they will sit back and relax. Third, they won't think twice about calling up a CFO, distributor, or customer. I also hire people who want to win.

Picking stocks is as much an art as a science. There are some people who no matter how hard they work, how much research they do, or how many companies they call, will not succeed because they don't have the knack of figuring out what is and isn't going to work.

Did you ever hire anyone who didn't work out?

The first person I hired. He was one of the smartest people I have ever known. The problem was that he didn't have any intuition, and he didn't get the risk side. For example, he would say, "We have to short Yahoo at 10 because it is worth zero." He didn't have any instinctive feel for what was going on in the market.

So much of your approach seems to be tied to speaking to company management. If tomorrow you awoke in the financial Twilight Zone and found yourself to be an ordinary investor instead of a fund manager with hundreds of millions in assets, how would you alter your approach?

Well, first of all I would still have a telephone. I might not be able to call the CFO, but I could call other employees of the company, as well as consumers and distributors of their products. Also, the Internet today allows you to get a tremendous amount of information without speaking to anyone. You can get the company's 10-Qs and 10-Ks [the quarterly and annual company reports required to be filed by the SEC], company press releases, insider trading statistics, and lots of other valuable information. Also, I could still go to the mall and check out a company's product, which is a big part of what we do.

Anything stand out as your best trade ever?

[He thinks for a while.] I usually don't get excited about winners; I'm too busy looking for the next trade.

What lessons have you learned about investment?

Do the research and believe in your research. Don't be swayed by other people's opinions.

Anything else?

You have to invest without emotions. If you let emotions get involved, you will make bad decisions.

You can't be afraid to take a loss. The people who are successful in this business are the people who are willing to lose money.

★

One of the most common trading blunders cited by the Market Wizards is the folly of listening to others for advice—a mistake that proved very costly to some (Walton and Minervini for example). Steve Watson was lucky: He learned the lesson of not listening to others' opinions from a college course instead of with his own money.

Watson begins his investment selection process by focusing on stocks that are relatively low priced (low price/earnings ratio), a characteristic that limits risk. A low price is a necessary but not sufficient condition. Many low-priced stocks are low for a reason and will stay relatively depressed. The key element of Watson's approach is to anticipate which of these low-priced stocks are likely to enjoy a change in investors' perceptions. In order to identify potential impending changes that could cause a shift in market sentiment, Watson conducts extensive communication with companies and their competitors, consumers, and distributors. He is also a strong proponent of such commonsense research as trying a company's product, or in the case of a retailer, visiting its stores. Finally, Watson looks for insider buying as a confirmation condition for his stock selections.

Shorting is considered a high-risk activity and is probably inappropriate for the average investor. Nevertheless, Watson demonstrates that if risk controls are in place to avoid the open-ended losses that can occur in a short position, shorting can reduce portfolio risk by including positions that are inversely correlated with the rest of the portfolio. On the short side, Watson seeks out high-priced companies that have a flawed business plan—often one-product companies that are vulnerable either because the performance of their single product falls far short of promotional claims or because there is no barrier to entry for competitors.

Watson achieves risk control through a combination of diversification, selection, and loss limitation rules. He diversifies his portfolio sufficiently so that the largest long holdings account for a maximum of 2 to 3 percent of the portfolio. Short positions are capped at about 1.5 percent of the portfolio. The risk on long positions is limited by Watson's restricting the selection of companies from the universe of low-priced stocks. On the short side, risk is limited by money management rules that require reducing or liquidating a stock that is moving higher, even if the fundamental justification for the trade is completely unchanged.

Watson has maintained the pig-at-the-trough philosophy he was exposed to at Friess Associates. He is constantly upgrading his portfolio—replacing stocks with other stocks that appear to have an even better return/risk outlook. Therefore, he will typically sell a profitable long holding even though he expects it to go still higher, because after a sufficient advance, he will find another stock that offers equal or greater return potential with less risk. The relevant question is never, "Is this a good stock to hold?" but rather, "Is this a better stock than any alternative holding that is not already in the portfolio?"

★

Update on Steve Watson

Not long after our interview, Watson turned over the day-to-day management of his funds to two of the company's portfolio managers to allow him to pursue other interests on the West Coast. (He declined to discuss these new endeavors on the record.) Watson remains an investor in the funds and retains investment decision involvement through frequent phone consultations with his appointed portfolio managers. Insofar as Watson made his dramatic career shift near the end of the bull market, one has to wonder whether his innate market sense might have influenced the timing, at least on a subconscious level.

Why did you decide to shift away from active fund management?

I hired two guys I really respect, and I thought they would do well. It's like the old man passing on the torch.

But you're not an old man—you're a lot younger than I am!

I wanted to pursue new challenges.

What's your long-term view of the market?

I have never seen microcap stocks so cheap, but I also have never seen so many stocks that are lacking a catalyst to make them move higher. So the ingredients are there for a rebound, but the timing is not imminent. I just reviewed two hundred microcap stocks yesterday and was amazed by how many are trading at or below cash. Their businesses aren't great, but they're cutting costs. With their cost structures reduced, if the economy begins to improve and you get any increment in revenues, they'll be in position to put up good earnings. Although the market probably still has some more weakness ahead of it [this interview was conducted August 2002], I'm quite optimistic about the longer-term outlook—say, beginning in 2003.

DANA GALANTE

Against the Current

Imagine two swimmers a mile apart on a river who decide to have a race, each swimming to the other's starting point. There is a strong current. The swimmer heading downstream wins. Is she the better swimmer? Obviously this is a nonsensical question. An Olympic swimmer could lose to a novice if the current is strong enough.

Now consider two money managers: one only *buys* stocks and is up an average of 25 percent per year for the period while the other only *sells* stocks and is *up* 10 percent per year during the same period. Which manager is the better trader? Again, this is a nonsensical question. The answer depends on the direction and strength of the market's current—its trend. If the stock market rose by an average of 30 percent per year during the corresponding period, the manager with the 25 percent return would have underperformed a dart-throwing strategy, whereas the other manager would have achieved a double-digit return in an extraordinarily hostile environment.

During 1994–99 Dana Galante registered an average annual compounded return of 15 percent. This may not sound impressive until one considers that Galante is a pure short seller. In reverse of the typical manager, Galante will *profit* when the stocks in her portfolio go *down* and lose when they go up. Galante achieved her 15 percent return during a period when the representative stock index (the Nasdaq, which accounts for about 80 percent of her trades) rose by an imposing annual average of 32 percent. To put Galante's performance in perspective, her achievement is comparable to a mutual fund manager averaging a 15 percent annual return during a period when the stock market declines by an average of 32 percent annually. In both cases, overcoming such a powerful opposite trend in the universe of stocks traded requires exceptional stock selection skills.

Okay, so earning even a 15 percent return by shorting stocks in a strongly advancing market is an admirable feat, but what's the point? Even if the stock market gains witnessed in the 1990s were unprecedented, the stock market has still been in a long-term upward trend since its inception. Why fight a trend measured in decades, if not centuries? The point is that a short-selling approach is normally not intended as a stand-alone investment; rather, it is intended to be combined with long investments (to which it is inversely correlated) to yield a total portfolio with a better return/risk performance. Most, if not all, of Galante's investors use her fund to balance their long stock investments. Apparently, enough investors have recognized the value of Galante's *relative* performance so that her fund, Miramar Asset Management, is closed to new investment.

Most people don't realize that a short-selling strategy that earns more than borrowing costs can be combined with a passive investment, such as an index fund or long index futures, to create a net investment that has both a higher return than the index and much lower risk. This is true *even if the returns of the short-selling strategy are much lower than the returns of the index alone.* For example, an investor who balanced a Nasdaq index–based investment with an equal commitment in Galante's fund (borrowing the extra money required for the dual investment) would have both beaten the index return (after deducting borrowing costs) and cut risk dramatically. Looking at one measure of risk, the two worst drawdowns of this combined portfolio during 1994–99 would have been 10 percent and 5 percent, versus 20 percent and 13 percent for the index.

Galante began her financial career working in the back office of an institutional money management firm. She was eventually promoted to a trading (order entry) position. Surprisingly, Galante landed her first job as a fund manager without any prior experience in stock selection. Fortunately, Galante proved more skilled in picking stocks than in picking bosses. Prior to founding her own firm in 1997, Galante's fourteen-year career was marked by a number of unsavory employers.

Galante likes trading the markets and enjoys the challenge of trying to profit by going the opposite of the financial community, which is long the stocks that she shorts. But the markets are an avocation, not an all-consuming passion. Her daily departure from the office is mental as well as physical, marking a shift in her focus from the markets to her family. She leaves work each day in time to pick up her kids up at school, a routine made possible by her western time zone locale, and she deliberately avoids doing any research or trading at home.

The interview was conducted in a conference room with a lofty, panoramic view of the San Francisco skyline. It was a clear day, and the Transamerica building, Telegraph Hill, San Francisco Bay, and Alcatraz stretched out in front of us in one straight visual line. The incredible view prompted me to describe some of the palatial homes that had served as the settings for interviews in my previous two Market Wizard books. Galante joked that we should have done the interview at her home. "Then," she said, "you could have described the view of the jungle gym in my backyard."

Note: For reasons that will be apparent, pseudonyms have been used for all individuals and companies mentioned in this interview.

★

When did you first become aware of the stock market?

My father was a market maker in the over-the-counter market. When I was in high school, I worked with him on the trading desk during summer vacations and school breaks.

What did you do for him?

In those days, although we had terminals, we didn't have computers. Everything was done by hand. I posted his trades while he was trading.

Did you find yourself trying to anticipate market direction?

I don't really remember, but I was never really obsessed with the market, like a lot of the people that you have written about. I like the market, and I think it's exciting and challenging, but I don't go home and think about it.

What was your first job out of college?

I worked for Kingston Capital, a large institutional money management firm. I started out doing back office and administrative work. Eventually, I was promoted to the role of trader, and I did all the trading for the office, which managed one billion dollars.

By trader, I assume you mean being responsible for order entry as opposed to having any decision-making responsibility?

That's right, I just put in the orders.

What was the next step in your career progression?

In 1985, Kingston was taken over in a merger. The acquiring firm changed everyone's job description. They told me I couldn't do the trading anymore because it all had to be done out of New York. They wanted me to move into an administrative role, which would have been a step back for me.

Henry Skiff, the former manager of the Kingston branch office, went through an analogous experience. He was shifted to a structured job that he couldn't stand. He and another employee left Kingston after the merger to form their own institutional money management firm. Henry offered me a job as a trader and researcher. Although Henry was a difficult person to work for, I liked the other person, and I didn't want to go back to an administrative position.

I left with Henry and helped him start the office for his new firm. I did research and trading for him for two years. Although it was a good experience, I realized my future was limited, since Henry was not willing to give up much control over the portfolio. Around the time I decided that I had to leave, my husband got a good job offer in another city, and we decided to move. I found a job at Atacama Investment, which at the time was an institutional money management firm. I started out as a portfolio manager, comanaging their small cap fund [a fund that invests in companies with small capitalization], which had a couple of billion dollars in assets.

Had you had any experience before?

Not picking stocks.

Then how did you get a job as a portfolio manager?

I originally started out interviewing for a trading job. But the woman who had been managing the portfolio, Jane, was on maternity leave.

She only had about six months' experience herself, and they needed someone to fill the slot. Mark Hannigan, who ran Atacama, believed that anyone could do that job. He called us "monkeys." He would tell us, "I could get any monkey to sit in that chair and do what you do." He also used to tell me that I think too much, which really annoyed me.

Mark's philosophy was that if a stock's price was going up on the chart, earnings were growing by 25 percent or more, and if a brokerage house was recommending it, you would buy it. There was minimal fundamental analysis and no consideration of the quality of earnings or management. This is the origin of why I ended up trading on the short side of the market.

Did being a woman help you get the job because you were replacing another woman?

No, I probably got the job because they could pay me a lot less.

How little did they pay you?

My starting salary was twenty-five thousand dollars a year.

What happened to Jane?

After two months, she returned from maternity leave, and we worked together. She was a perennial bull. Everything was great. She was always ready to buy any stock. I was the only one who ever thought we should wait a minute before buying a stock or suggested getting out of a stock we owned before it blew up.

Were you and Jane working as coequals, or was she your boss because she was there before?

We were comanagers. I actually had more experience than she did, but she joined the company six months earlier. We worked as a team. Either one of us could put a stock in the portfolio.

Was it a problem having to comanage money with another person?

Not really, since neither one of us had much experience. I would pick a stock and say, "Look at this," and Jane would say, "Yeah, that looks good; let's buy 100,000." The real problem was the trading desk. Once we gave them a buy order, we had no control over the position. The trade could be filled several points higher, or days later, and there was nothing we could do about it.

Do you mean that literally? How could there be such a long delay in a trade being filled?

Because the trader for the company was front-running orders [placing orders in his own account in front of much larger client or firm orders to personally profit from the market impact of the larger order he was about the place]. If a stock we wanted to buy traded 100,000 shares that day and we didn't get one share, he would say, "Sorry, but I tried." Since I was a trader, I knew enough to check time-and-sales [an electronic log of all trades and the exact time they were executed]. If you questioned him, however, he would just rip you in front of everybody. (We all worked in one large room.)

Rip you in what way?

He would scream at me, "You don't know anything about fucking trading. Just go back and sit at your desk."

Did you realize he was crooked back then, or did you just find out later?

He was the highest-paid person there. He was probably making several hundred thousand dollars a year. But he lived well beyond even his salary. He had a huge house, and he was always taking limousines everywhere. Everyone suspected that something was going on. It turns out that there was; it all came out years later when the SEC investigated and barred him from the industry.

It's rather ironic that as a trader who was merely responsible for entering orders, he was making ten times what you were making as the portfolio manager. I assume this is fairly unusual.

Yes, it is. Normally, the traders always make much less.

When did you get your first inclination to start shorting stocks?

I sat close to Jim Levitt, who ran Atacama's hedge fund. I was very interested in what he was doing because of his success in running the fund.

Was Jim a mentor for you on the short side?

Yes he was, because he had a knack for seeing reality through the Wall Street hype. I jokingly blame him for my decision to go on the short side of the business. When things are going badly, I'll call him up and tell him it's all his fault.

What appealed to you about the short side vis-à-vis the long side?

I felt the short side was more of a challenge. You really had to know what you were doing. Here I was, just a peon going up against all these analysts who were recommending the stock and all the managers who were buying it. When I was right, it was a great feeling. I felt as if I had really earned the money, instead of just blindly buying a stock because it was going up. It was a bit like being a detective and discovering something no one else had found out.

When did you start shorting stocks?

In 1990 after Jim Levitt left Atacama to form his own fund because he was frustrated by the firm's restrictions in running a hedge fund.

What restrictions?

The environment wasn't very conducive to running a hedge fund. One of the rules was that you couldn't short any stock that the company owned. Since the firm held at least a thousand different stocks at any time, the universe of potential shorts was drastically limited. They also had a very negative attitude toward the idea of shorting any stocks.

When Jim Levitt quit, I was on vacation in Lake Tahoe. Mark called me and told me that I would be taking over the hedge fund because Jim had left the firm. Mark's philosophy was that anyone could short stocks. He ran computer screens ranking stocks based on relative strength [price change in the stock relative to the broad market index] and earnings growth. He would then buy the stocks at the top of the list and sell the stocks at the bottom of the list. The problem was that by the time stocks were at the bottom of his list, they were usually strong value candidates. Essentially you ended up long growth stocks and short value stocks—that approach doesn't work too often. But he had never been a hedge fund manager, and he thought that was the way you do it.

Did you use his methodology?

No, I really didn't.

How were you picking your shorts then?

I looked for companies that I anticipated would have decreases in earnings, instead of shorting stocks that had already witnessed decreases in earnings.

How did you anticipate when a company was going to have decreased earnings?

A lot of it was top down. For example, the year I took over the hedge fund, oil prices had skyrocketed because of the Gulf War. It was a simple call to anticipate that the economy and cyclical stocks would weaken.

Why did you leave Atacama?

In 1993 Atacama transformed their business from an institutional money management firm to a mutual fund company. Also, both my husband and I wanted to move back to San Francisco. I spoke to a number of hedge funds in the area, but none of them were interested in giving up control of part of their portfolio to me, and I didn't want to go back to working as just an analyst after having been a portfolio manager.

With some reluctance, I had dinner with Henry Skiff. It was the first time I had seen him in five years. He said all the right things. He assured me that he had changed, and he agreed with everything I said. He had formed a small partnership with about one million dollars. He told me I could grow it into a hedge fund, run it any way I wanted, and get a percent of the fees.

What, exactly, was it about Henry that you didn't like when you had worked with him five years earlier?

I didn't have a whole lot of respect for him as a portfolio manager. I'll tell you one story that is a perfect example. During the time I worked for him, junk bonds had become very popular. Henry had a friend at a brokerage firm who offered to give him a large account if he could manage a junk bond portfolio. We had no clue. Henry gave us all a book about junk bonds and told us to read it over the weekend. The following Monday we began trading junk bonds; Henry was the manager, and I was the trader. The book had said that the default rate was 1 percent, which turned out to be completely bogus. The whole thing ended up blowing up and going away. Also, although I didn't find out about it until years later, Henry had embellished his academic credentials in the firm's marketing documents, falsely claiming undergraduate and Ph.D. degrees from prestigious universities.

Anyway, Henry convinced me that rejoining him was a great opportunity. He offered to give me a large raise over what I had been making. He even offered to pay for my move. I figured the job would give me a way to move back to San Francisco and that if it didn't work out I could always find another job. Henry had a great marketing guy, and we grew the fund to $90 million. But Henry hadn't changed; he second-guessed everything I did.

Henry would see a stock go up five dollars and get all excited and say, "Hey Dana, why don't you buy XYZ." He wouldn't even have any idea what the company did. I would buy the stock because he wanted me to. The next day the order would be on the trade blotter, and he would ask me, "Hey, Dana, what is this XYZ stock?" That was another experience that turned me off to the long side of stocks.

There was tremendous turnover at the firm because Henry treated his staff so poorly. We had a meeting every morning where the managers talked about the stocks in their portfolio. Henry would just rip the managers apart. One of his employees, a man in his fifties, committed suicide. Henry would tear the confidence out of people, and this poor guy just didn't have it in him to take it. I had worked with him for a while, and he was a broken man. I can't say he killed himself because of the job, but I wouldn't be surprised if it was a factor.

Was Henry critical with you as well?

He was constantly second-guessing me and arguing with me every time I put on a trade he didn't agree with.

Then how much independence did you have?

I had independence as long as I was doing well, but every time the market rallied, he wanted me to cover all my shorts. We fought a lot because I didn't give in. One thing I did is that if Henry insisted I buy a stock, I would buy it, but then immediately short another stock against it. That way I would negate any effect he was trying to have on the portfolio. I did well, but after two years, I couldn't take it anymore and quit.

Did you start your own firm after you left Henry the second time?

No. After I quit, I was hired by Peter Boyd, who had a hedge fund that had reached $200 million at its peak. He told me that he'd heard a lot of good things about me and was going to give me a portion of his fund to manage. He said that I could run it any way I wanted. I told him that I thought I could add the most value by trading strictly on the short side because that was something he didn't do. He started me out with $10 million and gave me complete discretion. It was great for me because it was like having my own business without any of the administrative headaches.

Everything was fine for the first two years, but in the third year, the fund started to experience very large redemptions because of poor performance. Boyd had to take the money from me because his own portfolio wasn't very liquid. He had lost the money by buying huge OEX put positions, which expired worthless only days later. [He bought options that would make large profits if the market went down sharply but would expire as worthless otherwise.]

It almost sounds as if he was gambling with the portfolio.

It sure appeared to be gambling. Looking back, it seemed that he tried to hide these losses by marking up the prices on privately held stock in his portfolio. He had complete discretion on pricing these positions.

How was he able to value these positions wherever he wanted to?

Because they were privately held companies; there was no publicly traded stock.

Is it legal to price privately held stocks with such broad discretion?

Yes. In respect to private companies, the general partner is given that discretion in the hedge fund disclosure document. The auditors also bought off on these numbers every year. He would tell them what he thought these companies were worth and why, and they would accept his valuations. They were these twenty-two-year-old auditors just out of college, and he was the hedge fund manager making $20 million a year; they weren't about to question him.

Another hedge fund manager I interviewed who also does a lot of short selling said that the value of audits on a scale of 0 to 100 was zero. Do you agree?

Yes.

Even if it's a leading accounting firm?

Oh yeah.

How could hedge fund investors be aware whether a manager was mispricing stocks in the portfolio?

The quarterly performance statements are required to show what percent of the portfolio consists of privately held deals. His performance was so good for so long that people didn't question it.

What percent of his portfolio consisted of private deals?

In the beginning it was about 10 percent, but as he lost more and more money, the portion of the portfolio in privately held companies continued to grow. By the end, privately held stocks accounted for a major portion of the portfolio, and he was largely left with a bunch of nearly worthless paper.

It sounds as if he was gambling in the options market and hiding his losses by marking up his private deals. Wouldn't the truth come out when investors redeemed their money and received back much less than the reported net asset value?

Although I'm not sure, I believe the first investors to redeem received the full amount, but as more investors redeemed their funds, the true magnitude of the losses became apparent.

Did you know what he was doing at the time?

I knew about the option losses, but no one knew about the private deals. They were off the balance sheet.

It sounds as if you worked with quite a host of characters. You didn't do too well picking your bosses.

Yes, I know. You think that wouldn't be a good sign, but . . .

How did you start your own firm?

I had one account that I had met through Peter. He hired me to run a short-only portfolio. That was the account I took with me to get started.

What year was this?

1997.

Your track record shows your performance back to 1994.

To generate the early years of my track record, I extracted the short trades for the period until I started trading the short-only portfolio.

Do you use charts at all?

I use them for market timing. I think that is one of the things that has saved me over the years. If, for example, the stock I am short collapses to support, I will probably get out.

How do you to define *support*?

Price areas that have witnessed a lot of buying in the past—points at which prices consolidated before moving higher. Some dedicated shorts will still hold on to their positions, but I will usually cover. I'll figure the market has already gone down 50 percent. Maybe it will go down another 10 or 20 percent, but that is not my game. I look for stocks that are high relative to their value.

That is an example of how you use charts for profit taking. Do you also use charts to limit losses?

When a chart breaks out to a new high, unless I have some really compelling information, I just get out of the way.

How long a period do you look back to determine new highs? If a stock makes a one-year high but is still below its two-year high, do you get out?

No, I am only concerned about stocks making new all-time highs.

Have you always avoided being short a stock that made new highs, or have you been caught sometimes?

No, I have been caught sometimes.

Can you give me an example.

One stock I was short this year, Sanchez Computer Associates, went from $32 to $80 in one day.

In one day?

It's a company that makes back-office and transaction processing software for banks. Most of their clients are in underdeveloped countries and don't have their own systems. The business was slowing down, and the Street cut its annual earnings estimate from 75 cents a share to 50 cents. The stock was still trading at $25 at the time, and as a short, that news sounded great to me. I thought the stock would go a lot lower. Shortly afterward, the company announced that they would start an on-line banking software service. This was at a time when the on-line banking stocks were going ballistic.

What was the previous high in the stock?

It was in the low thirties. The stock just blew way past it.

Were you still bearish the stock when it went to 80?

Yeah, nothing had changed.

How do you handle that type of situation from a money management standpoint?

I had never been in that type of situation before—not even remotely. Our portfolio is relatively diversified. The most I had ever lost on a single stock in one day was one-half of one percent. That day, I lost 4 percent on the stock.

What portion of your portfolio was the stock?

Before it went up, about 2.5 percent. That is a fairly large position for me, but I had a lot of conviction on the trade.

Did you try to cover part of your position on the day the stock skyrocketed?

The stock was up almost $10 right from the opening. I started scrambling around, trying to figure out what was going on. Then it was up $20. Then $30. I tried to cover some of my shorts, but I only wound up getting filled on about one thousand shares out of a total of forty thousand that I held.

At the end of the day, you were still short thirty-nine thousand out of forty thousand shares, the stock had already exploded from 30 to 80, and you were still bearish on the fundamentals. What do you do in that type of situation? Do you decide to just hold the position because the price is so overdone, or do you cover strictly because of money management reasons?

This was a unique situation. I never had a stock move against me like that. I've also never been short an Internet stock. Initially, being the realist that I am, I just tried to get the facts. I checked out all the companies that did Internet banking to see what kind of software they used, and Sanchez's name was never mentioned.

The next day the stock dropped $15. I thought the stock would go up again, because typically these types of situations last more than one day. I covered enough of my position to bring it down to 2.5 percent of my portfolio. Because of the price rise, it had gone up to 7 percent of my portfolio, and I can't allow that. Then the stock went down some more. By the time it went back down to 50, I had reduced my short position to five thousand shares.

What was your emotional response to this entire experience?

I was almost in shock because I felt a complete lack of control. I had never experienced anything like it before. Most people are afraid to go short because they think the risk is unlimited. That never bothered me. I consider myself pretty disciplined. I always thought that I had a good handle on the risk and that I could get out of any short before it caused too much damage, which up to that point I had. But here, the stock nearly tripled in one day, and I didn't know what to do. I was numb.

I was struck by a horrifying thought: Could the same thing happen to any of the other stocks in my portfolio? I began worrying about which of my shorts would be the next company to announce an online Web page. I started combing my portfolio, looking for any stock that might become the next Sanchez.

What eventually happened to the stock?

It went back up again. But when Sanchez started to look like it was ready to roll over, I rebuilt my short position. Ironically, when it subsequently broke, I made more money on my new short position than I had lost being short when the stock exploded several months earlier.

How large is your organization?

There are just two of us. Zack works with me and is an integral part of Miramar. There is a lot of money out there, and interested investors call me almost every day. I tell them that I am closed to new investment.

Is that because your methodology can't accommodate any more money?

I don't want to grow. I don't want to manage people; I want to manage the portfolio.

Could you grow your size by just taking larger positions instead of expanding the number of shorts?

I have only run shorts in a bull market. It's a constant battle. I have to find the best way to fight the battle with the lowest amount of risk. I need to know that I can cover my short positions if I have to. The larger my short position, the more difficult that would be. I've seen what happens to people who grow too fast, and I have taken the opposite extreme. I want to be comfortable doing what I do. I don't want to be scouring for new shorts because I am managing more money. I have my family, and when I go home, I don't think about work. I don't read *Barron's* over the weekend.

I suppose to some extent your attitude reflects a difference between male and female perspectives. Maybe, as a generalization, men want to become empire builders, whereas women don't.

That's probably it.

How do you select the stocks you short?

I look for growth companies that are overvalued—stocks with high P/E [price/earnings] ratios—but that by itself is not enough. There also has to be a catalyst.

Give me an example of a catalyst.

An expectation that the company is going to experience a deterioration in earnings.

How do you anticipate a deterioration in earnings?

One thing I look for is companies with slowing revenue growth who have kept their earnings looking good by cutting expenses. Usually, it's only a matter of time before their earnings growth slows as well. Another thing I look for is a company that is doing great but has a competitor creeping up that no one is paying attention to. The key is anticipating what is going to affect future earnings relative to market expectations.

In essence, you look for a high P/E stock that has a catalyst that will make the stock go down.

Right, but there is another key condition: I won't short a stock that is moving straight up. The stock has to show signs of weakening or at least stalling.

Can you give me an example of a typical short?

Network Associates has been a stock that I have been short on and off for the past two years. The company was masking higher operating expenses by taking huge research and development charges related to acquisition each quarter. They were taking other expenses as one-time charges as well. The SEC eventually made them change their accounting procedures to take these expenses over time as opposed to one-time charges. After the SEC stepped in, the chairman came out and said something like, "It's just an accounting issue. We don't pay much attention to accounting." He also made statements berating the shorts, saying they would get buried.

When a company blames the price decline in its stock on short sellers, it's a red flag. A company's best revenge against short sellers is simply reporting good numbers. Decent companies won't spend time focusing on short sellers. "Our stock was down because of short selling." Give me a break. We represent maybe one billion dollars versus nine trillion on the long side.

What was Network Associates' product or service?

Their primary product was an antivirus software, a low-margin item whose price had been coming down over time. They also bought out a number of companies that were making similar products, usually paying a large premium. The companies they were buying were stocks that I was short. I was upset because once they bought out these companies, I couldn't be short them anymore. At one point, they were virtually giving away their antivirus product. All you had to do was look at the Comp USA ads. After adjusting for all the rebates, they were selling their software for only about five dollars. That told you that their product wasn't moving.

If they were so desperate in their pricing, didn't their sales show a sharp drop-off?

No, because they were stuffing the channels.

What does that mean?

They were shipping all their inventory to distributors, even though the demand wasn't there.

Why would a company do that if they know the product is just going to get shipped back?

To make the revenues look better. Once they shipped the product, they can book it as sales.

But they can't keep that up forever.

They did it anyway. But it did come back to haunt them; eventually, the stock collapsed.

You mentioned that it's a red flag when a company blames shorts for the decline in its stock. What are some other red flags?

A company that goes from its traditional business to whatever is hot at the time. For example, during the gambling stock craze, there were companies that went from having pizza restaurants to riverboat gambling. Right now, the same thing is going on with the Internet. One company we shorted recently went from selling flat panel displays to offering an Internet fax service, trashing their whole business plan in the process.

Other red flags?

Lots of management changes, particularly a high turnover in the firm's chief financial officer. Also, a change in auditors, can be a major red flag.

Can you give me an example?

One of my shorts was Pegasystems, which was a software company that caught my attention because of high receivables [large outstanding billings for goods and services]. The company was licensing its software for a monthly fee, typically in five-year contracts, and recognizing the entire discounted value of the contract immediately.

Is this a valid accounting procedure?

It was certainly contrary to the industry practice. Apparently, the original accountants didn't go along with the figures, because the company fired them and hired a new accounting firm. They said they were making the change because their previous accounting firm didn't understand the business and wasn't aggressive enough. But the incredible thing is that people ignored that red flag.

You mean the stock still went up even after they fired their auditors?

Yes.

When did you get short?

After they fired their auditors.

Any other examples of questionable accounting?

I've had a few shorts that turned into frauds. One example was a company that ran a vocational school that purportedly taught people computer skills. They were getting funding from the government, but they were providing very poor quality education. I became aware of this stock as well because of high receivables.

What are receivables for a training company?

Tuition fees. The students weren't paying the tuition they owed. That's what first drew my attention to the stock. Then I learned the company was being investigated by the Department of Education in response to student complaints that they were using old software and that the instructors were inept. I shorted the stock in the forties, and got out near 10. The stock eventually went down to 1.

It sounds as if high receivables is a major indicator for you.

Yes, it's one of the screens we look at.

What are some of the other screens?

We also screen for revenue deceleration, earnings deceleration, high P/Es, high inventories, and some technical indicators, such as stocks breaking below their fifty-day moving average.

Do you screen for these factors individually, or do you screen for multiple characteristics?

Usually multiple characteristics, but you can't screen for all these factors at one time, or else you won't get any stock that fits all the search requirements.

Although you have done fine as a 100 percent short seller, have you had any second thoughts about your choice since we have been in such a relentless bull market?

No, I find short selling more rewarding because of the challenge. You make a lot of money in this business, and I think you need to work for what you get. To just sit there and buy Internet stocks every day doesn't seem right. I can't relate to it. In fact, I wonder how I will do if we ever do get into a bear market because I am so used to a bull market, watching people ignore bad news and taking advantage of that.

But I would imagine that in a bear market, your job would be much easier.

In August 1998 when the market went down fast and hard, I was more stressed out than I am normally.

But you did very well during that period.

I did great, but I thought it was too easy. I wasn't fighting a battle. I felt as though I didn't have to work. Any stock I went short would go down. It was a weird feeling. That's what people do all the time on the long side; they just buy stocks, and they tend to go up.

And you didn't like that?

No, it was very uncomfortable. Maybe I am a little sick; I don't know what's wrong with me.

When a market suddenly breaks a lot, as it did then, do you reduce your short exposure?

I did in that instance because it happened so quickly. I made 30 percent in one month. That has never happened to me before. I covered about 40 percent of the portfolio.

What kind of risk control strategies do you use?

If I lose 20 percent on a single stock, I will cover one-third of my position. I limit the allocation to any single stock to a maximum of about 3 percent of the portfolio. If a stock increases to a larger percentage of the portfolio because of a price rise, I will tend to reduce the position. I also control risk through diversification: There are typically fifty to sixty names in the portfolio spread across different industry sectors.

Do you know other short sellers?

Yes. With the exception of a couple of short sellers that have become my friends, most short sellers tend to be very pessimistic on the world and life. They tend to be very negative people.

But you're not?

I don't think I am. I think I am just a realist. One thing that differentiates me from other short sellers is my experience on the long side.

Why is that important?

Because it's all about why people buy and sell. My experience in working with momentum-type managers gives me a sense of their thought processes, which helps me know when to get out of the way and when to press my bets. I have some friends who are short sellers that have never worked on the long side. They would call me up and ask, "Dana, why are they buying this stock? It has negative cash flow, high receivables, etcetera." They look at the raw numbers, and they are realists. They don't understand that a lot of people just buy the stock because it's going up or because the chart looks good. We've gone to the stratosphere now. Most of the people I know who were short sellers have been blown away. They don't even ask me those questions anymore.

What advice could you give to the ordinary investor who trades only on the long side?

A good company could be a bad stock and vice versa. For example, Disney is a good company—or at least my kids love it. But during the past few years we were able to make money on the short side because the company had become very overpriced on overly optimistic expectations that its business would grow robustly forever.

Although Galante is a 100 percent short seller, her ideas are still relevant to the long-only investor. Galante's methodology can be very useful as a guideline for which stocks to avoid or liquidate. The combination of factors Galante cites include:

- very high P/E ratio
- a catalyst that will make the stock vulnerable over the near term
- an uptrend that has stalled or reversed

All three of these conditions must be met. Investors might consider periodically reviewing their portfolios and replacing any stocks that meet all three of the above conditions with other stocks. By doing so, investors could reduce the risk in their portfolios.

In addition, Galante cites a number of red flags that attract her attention to stocks as potential short candidates. By implication, any of these conditions would be a good reason for investors who own the stock to seriously consider liquidating their position. These red flags include:

- high receivables
- change in accountants
- high turnover in chief financial officers
- a company blaming short sellers for their stock's decline
- a company completely changing their core business to take advantage of a prevailing hot trend

Update on Dana Galante

After a career spent fighting a long-term uptrend, Galante in recent years finally found herself trading in the market direction. Therefore, it should come as no surprise that Galante has done quite well during the bear market. During the 2½-year period since the first month of the bear market (April 2000), Galante's fund was up an imposing 89 percent (119 percent before fees).

This is a rather unusual experience for you: shorting stocks in a bear market. After all the years of trading against the broad market trend, what does it feel like trading with the trend in your direction?

The first year of the decline [2000], it felt pretty good because there were so many overvalued shorting opportunities. The second and third years of the decline, however, were just as difficult as the upmarket years because of the sporadic, sharp bear market rallies. Also, the lower valuations, especially now, make it difficult to find shorting opportunities.

How do you compare the differences and similarities in being a short seller in a bear market versus a bull market?

Previously, there was a lot more downside in stocks. Now, many stocks are getting to real value levels. As a result, our exposure levels are much lower now than they were during the bull market. In 1999–2000 we were 100 percent invested. This year [2002], our highest exposure was 70 percent, and right now we are only 20 percent invested.

Are you concerned about having so much more company on the short side, particularly from other hedge funds (not just short funds)?

In the twenty years I have been trading the markets, there has always been some new angle that affects what I do. I try to look at how I can capitalize on a new situation rather than worrying about how it may hurt me. In the case of new participants on the short side, I actually think it creates more opportunities because you get these short-term run-ups in certain stocks triggered by short-covering from people who don't know what they are doing. There are a lot of former long-only managers who have decided to become hedge fund managers by also trading the short side, despite their lack of experience.

Do you see short sellers being made scapegoats for the market decline? What is your opinion about such criticism?

The people who are saying that should be happy there are short sellers out there because they are the ones who are buying. Short sellers are the ones who have the reason to buy and the power to buy, and the rallies we have seen in this bear market have been driven by short-covering. The only time in my life I felt bad about short selling was after September 11; I would have felt guilty shorting then, so we didn't do much of anything at the time.

Identifying companies that employ overly aggressive accounting is an important element in your approach. Has the recent spate of highly publicized accounting scandals meaningfully changed the situation?

In the past, as long as a company reported good earnings, even if it was just beating the street estimate by a penny, no one looked at how they got that number. The market frequently all but ignored the red flags we look for such as negative cash flow, excess receivables, excess inventories, and aggressive revenue recognition. The good thing for us is that now if people see these factors in a company, it's an issue.

What other changes do you anticipate as a result of the market's much closer scrutiny of accounting issues?

One issue I expect will garner increasing attention is the still widespread use of pro forma accounting instead of GAAP accounting.

Please define pro forma accounting.

Pro forma accounting is an artificial creation of the late 1990s, which takes out all sorts of charges that the company claims are nonoperating charges, when in reality they often are. There are some companies that even take out costs that occur every quarter, which is the very essence of an operating charge. The SEC requires GAAP reporting, and that is the number a company lists in its annual report; but a company can report any number it wants to the street. The biggest culprit is First Call because they accept pro forma earnings as the company's earning estimate, so that's what the street looks at. Some brokerage companies—Merrill Lynch was the first—are now reporting earnings both ways. For a lot of companies, there are huge deviations between the GAAP and pro forma numbers.

Even for the S&P 500 index as a whole, pro forma earnings are about 20 to 30 percent higher than GAAP earnings—the difference is that large! One of the things we are doing to identify possible shorts is to look for companies that have a large gap between pro forma earnings and GAAP earnings.

Are frauds likely to become less prevalent because of all the publicity and legislative actions (both enacted and pending)?

Greed is something that never goes away. Maybe the types of frauds we've seen will change, but there will always be some new scheme to take advantage of investors.

MARK D. COOK

Harvesting S&P Profits*

Mark D. Cook drives his pickup truck off the road, up the hill overlooking his father's farm on the outskirts of East Sparta, Ohio. The weather is unseasonably warm and feels very much like a day in late spring, but it is still late winter. The rolling fields stretch out before us in various shades of brown. "I wanted you to see this," Cook says. "When it greens up in spring, there is no more beautiful sight in the world."

I paint the scene in my mind and visualize easily enough how it could appear quite pleasant with the renewal of spring. But to see this landscape with the sense of majesty implied by Cook's voice, you have to look at it through the eyes of someone who has worked the land and sees it as a provider of sustenance and a link between generations.

"When my dad bought this farm nearly sixty years ago," Cook says, "the land was so poor you couldn't grow ragweed a foot tall on it. Whenever my trading is going badly and I feel stressed out, I come up here. When I look out at all that has been accomplished through hard work, despite the difficulties that were encountered, it gives me a sense of serenity." Cook is passionate about trading, but his love for his market career still comes in third place after family and the land.

The first time I saw Mark D. Cook he was a fellow speaker at an industry conference, and he made an impression before he uttered a single word. He came up to the podium dressed in bib overalls. He did this to make a point about his roots, but his choice of dress was not merely

*This chapter contains some references to options. Readers completely unfamiliar with options may find it helpful (although not essential) to first read the four-page primer in the appendix.

show, there was also substance to it. Even though he has made millions trading, Cook continues to do some farmwork himself. It is difficult to justify his manual labor in any economic sense. Cook rationalizes his part-time farmwork, which is in addition to the fifty to sixty hours per week he puts in as a trader, by saying that he is a workaholic. This is true enough, but I also believe that Cook would feel a tinge of guilt if he worked "only" as a trader while his eighty-one-year-old father continued to farm full-time.

Cook had brought me to his father's farm as part of a tour of the local area. As we drove along, Cook pointed out various tracts of land, which he identified by a year number. "There's 1997," he said, referring to the farm he had bought with his 1997 trading profits. "There's 1995," he said a few moments later, and so on. He apparently has had a lot of good years. Cook is almost zealous about converting his trading profits into real assets—and for Cook farmland is the ultimate real asset.

The highlight of the tour was linked to another outlet for Cook's trading profits: rare farm tractors. Cook shares his father's enthusiasm for collecting antique tractors, a mutual hobby that led to the creation of the Cook Tractor Museum. You won't find this museum, which is situated next to Cook's farmhouse trading office, in any guidebook. The museum's exhibits are displayed in a large metal shed structure that was built in 1996 to house the burgeoning rare tractor collection.

Cook picked up his father, Marvin, so that he could accompany us on the museum visit. Marvin Cook, who is the epitome of the taciturn farmer, turned into Mr. Tour Guide as soon as we entered the metal shed. He described the unique characteristics of each tractor model on display and the history of its manufacturer, who in most instances had disappeared from the American scene long ago. The museum contains some real rarities, including two of only five American tractors (only one other is known to still exist), built by an Ohio company that went out of business before the line went into full production.

Cook next took me to the farm he had bought with his 1994 trading profits. Cook currently leases the land for coal mining, and we hiked across the rolling fields and scrambled down a scree-strewn slope to view the open-pit mining operation. Buying this land gave Cook particular satisfaction because it was the alternative property his great-grandfather had considered purchasing before settling on the original family farmstead in 1890.

I had begun my interview with Cook the previous evening at Tozzi's, an eighty-five-year-old, family-owned establishment that is the best restaurant in Magnolia, Ohio. It is also the only restaurant in Magnolia (population: 1,000). The lack of competition, however, apparently hasn't had any adverse influence; the food was very good and the service attentive. After the two-hour dinner, Cook was only getting warmed up in talking about his career. We continued the interview at Cook's 125-year-old farmhouse office, a dark walnut-paneled room, unadorned except for a cow painting (Cook's wife, Terri, was the artist). At around 1 A.M., we were still not finished. Knowing that Cook wanted to get an early start the next morning, I decided to leave the remainder for the next day. We continued the interview the next morning at breakfast and finished it later that day in the airport parking lot, seated in Cook's pickup truck.

Cook's early attempts at trading were marked by repeated setbacks, experiences he relates in the interview. Cook, however, never gave up. Each failure only made him work harder. Finally, after many years of carefully tracking the stock market, filling volumes of market diaries, and assiduously recording and analyzing every trade he made, his trading became consistently profitable.

Once Cook became confident in his trading abilities, he entered several market contests, registering an 89 percent gain in a four-month competition in 1989, and 563 percent and 322 percent returns in back-to-back annual contests beginning in 1992. His annual returns in the six years since then have ranged between 30 percent and a stratospheric 1,422 percent. These statistics are based on defining percent return as annual dollar profits divided by beginning year equity, a conservative definition that understates Cook's true performance, because he frequently withdraws profits from his account but never adds funds. For example, in his low-return year (based on our definition of percent return), his withdrawals during the year exceeded his starting capital. Cook provided me with his account statements for his most recent four years. During this period, he was profitable on 87 percent of all trading days, with one-third of the months showing only winning days.

How does a farm boy end up trading the S&P?

I started trading because of a cow.

You'll have to explain that one to me.

In 1975, while attending Ohio State University as an agricultural business major, I was on the national cattle judging team for Ohio. That experience helped me get a summer job as one of the two cowboys that took Elsie the Cow around the country as publicity for Borden.

Was this like Lassie? When Elsie died, did they replace her with another Elsie?

They changed Elsies after the tour was over, which lasted about thirteen weeks.

Where did you go on this tour?

All over. We even received the key to the city from Mayor Daley in Chicago because the city's mascot was a cow. I was also interviewed on several TV and radio shows.

What kind of questions would they ask you about a cow?

Oh, how much milk did she produce? What kind of cow was she? How much crap did she produce in a day? How old was she? What did she eat? Does she kick? How come she doesn't have any flies? Whenever I got that last question, I said, "We give her a bath every day; she's cleaner than you are."

One night we were on a radio show in Chicago. The host was Eddie Schwartz who had an all-night talk program back in the 1970s before talk programs became big. We were on for hours. At about 3 A.M. he asked us, "Hey, what would you guys like to do now?"

"We've been on the road constantly," I answered. "We haven't gone out with any women for a while."

"No problem," he said. "What kind of girls would you like?" he asked us.

I was a bit of a ham, so I said, "The first two girls who get down here in bikinis, we'll show them a night on the town."

"Girls out there," he announced, "did you hear that?"

"I wasn't serious," I quickly added.

"No problem," he said. "You heard them out there," he told his audience. It wasn't fifteen minutes before two girls wearing bikinis showed up at the studio.

Before we left, he said to us, "I get a lot of obnoxious calls. I'd love to get a tape of your cow mooing so that I could turn it on whenever I have an annoying caller." We always kept Elsie on a local farm when we traveled. We arranged to meet Eddie at the farm the next morning.

Wait, wait, not so fast. What happened to the bikini girls?

Nothing happened, because my wife may read this *[he laughs]*.

The next morning when Schwartz arrived at the farm, he said, "Are you sure you can get her to moo, Mark?"

"Oh sure, I can get her to do anything." I tied her up to a wagon and placed the tape recorder inside.

"She isn't mooing," he said.

"No problem," I said. "Just move everybody out of the way. I'll calm her down, and as soon as I walk away, she'll start crying. She'll cry because she is a celebrity, and celebrities need attention."

"You're just pulling my leg," he said.

"No, I'm serious," I said, "just watch." I walked away, and it wasn't long before Elsie started bellowing at the top of her lungs. He used that tape on Chicago radio for years.

Being Elsie's cowboys also helped us get into the Playboy Club. One night while I was in Chicago, my boss joined us. I said, "We should go to the Playboy Club."

"Oh sure, Mark," he said. " How are we going to get in?" You could only get into the Playboy Club by invitation.

"Don't worry," I told him, "I can get us in."

"And how are you going to do that?" he asked.

"Just wait and you'll see," I told him. When we arrived at the club, I walked up to the imposing guard at the door and said, "You allow celebrities in, right?"

"Oh yeah," the man said, "we like celebrities. Who are you?"

"It isn't who I am," I answered, "but whom I represent." I pulled out my Elsie the Cow identification card. This was just after we had done the Mayor Daley ceremony.

"Oh sure," he said skeptically. He no doubt had heard every type of story by people trying to get in, although this was probably the first time someone had tried to use his pet cow to gain admittance.

"I have my girlfriend right here with me," I said as I pulled out a photo of Elsie standing next to me.

"Just a minute," he said as he went behind the padlocked door. He came back out with a celebrity key and let us in.

This is all very interesting, but what does it have to do with your becoming a trader?

After graduating college, I wanted to get a job as a stockbroker. I couldn't get hired. Nothing in my résumé seemed to help—not my grades, nor the fact that I played college basketball. Finally, I rewrote my résumé, prominently mentioning that I had been Elsie's cowboy. Shortly thereafter, I received a call to interview at a local brokerage office in Canton, which ultimately led to a job offer. The woman who screened résumés for the firm later told me, "I get hundreds of résumés. When I saw yours I said, 'Hey, this is the guy who took care of Elsie the Cow.'" I had been in Canton when I did the tour, and she had remembered seeing the picture in the local newspaper. That's how I got into the business, because of a cow.

Why did you want to become a stockbroker? Were you trading stocks?

I started trading stocks after I graduated college. By buying and selling cattle, I was able to build up a $20,000 stake.

Had you done any research? Did you have any methodology?

No, I just plunged right in. I still remember my first two trades: I bought Columbia and Sambo's. Columbia got bought out; and Sambo's went bankrupt. Starting out, I experienced the best and the worst and was hooked.

Do you remember why you bought those two specific stocks?

Yes, a lot of the research went into it. I bought Columbia because I had seen a documentary on the making of *Close Encounters of the Third Kind*, which Columbia was going to release, and I thought the movie was going to be a big hit. Columbia was bought out before the movie was released, so it didn't end up making any difference.

What about Sambo's?

When I went to the Rose Bowl with my fraternity brothers, we went out to eat at a Sambo's. I had never heard of the chain before and thought it was neat, so I bought the stock. That's a summary of my total research. I didn't know anything more about either of the two companies. Then the stockbroker I was dealing with said, "Mark, you like action. Why don't you try stock options?"

"I don't know anything about options," I told him. He gave me a booklet to read. After reading it from cover the cover, I called my broker and said, "It sounds pretty risky me."

"Oh no, it's just like trading stocks," he said.

In April 1978, I made my first option trade: I bought two Teledyne calls at $9 apiece for a total premium of $1,800. I sold the options two days later for $13, earning a total profit of $800 on my $1,800 investment. I said to myself, "Boy, this is a lot easier than shoveling manure and milking cows." For my next option trade, I bought Teledyne calls again, and again I made money. I thought I was going to be a millionaire in no time flat. I was doing so well that I thought, "Why trade with only a small part of my capital; I might as well use all of it." I kept trading Teledyne options. Finally, I put on an option position that went down. I thought I would hold it until it came back. It went to zero and expired on me. I lost all the money I had.

The whole $20,000?

That plus the approximate $3,000 I had been ahead before that trade. I remember filing my income tax for that year. I had made $13,000 in income and lost $20,000 in stock option trading. The worst thing was that I was only able to deduct $3,000 of losses against my income. So I had to pay income tax, even though I had a negative income.

Did you learn anything from that experience?

Yes. I learned that I wanted my money back. I'm not a quitter in any shape or form. I was determined to learn everything I could about stocks and options. That was the beginning of my pursuit to become a stockbroker. The only reason I wanted to become a stockbroker was to get my money back.

Did your parents know you had lost all your money?

Oh no, they probably thought I had my money in a CD.

Well, you did have your money in a CD.

Pardon?

A call debacle.

That's exactly right. My goal was to make $100,000 a year. By the time I was hired as a stockbroker in 1979, I had studied options quite thoroughly. I started trading options again, but I still kept losing money steadily. I analyzed my trades and found that I was losing money because I was holding on to options for several weeks or longer, and they would end up going to zero. I realized that the money I had lost had been made by the traders who sold the options that I bought. I decided from that point on, I would only sell options. I adopted a strategy of simultaneously selling both the calls and puts in high-volatility stocks.

The margin on short-option positions at that time was sometimes less than the premium I collected from the sale of the options. In 1979 when gold prices exploded, I sold options on gold stocks. I figured out that I could sell a combination [the simultaneous sale of a call and put] on ASA for more money than the margin I had to put up for the trade. At that time, the margin department hadn't figured this out. As a result, I could put on any size position and not get a margin call. There was only one slight problem—the stock took off on me. I made a little bit on the puts, which expired worthless, but lost a lot on the calls, which went way in the money. It was back to the drawing board again.

How did you have enough money to cover your losses?

Oh, I was a very good broker. I was the second from the top first-year broker nationwide for the firm. In 1981 I worked out a system for selling options when their premiums seemed too high and found someone to program the rules for me. Every week, the program would spit out a list of potential trades. Since I was selling options that were well out-of-the-money, they almost always expired worthless. Every Friday after the close, I would run the program, and every Monday morning, I would put on the trades. I was rolling along making several thousand dollars a month.

By May 1982, I had built my account up to $115,000. I reached greater depths of greed. I thought that I'd perfected this and it was working great. I stepped up the trading in my account and my family's accounts. That month I made an additional $50,000 using the same strategy.

In June 1982, I decided to step up my trading even more. One week that month I ran my program, and the computer printed out a list of trades involving Cities Service. The stock was trading at $27 at the time, and the 35, 40, and 45 call options were selling for premiums far above the model-implied prices, with only about a week left before expiration. [Options with these strike prices would go to zero unless the stock price rose above these respective levels in the remaining week before their expiration.] I couldn't believe the prices; I felt as if they were giving me the money. I sold hundreds of these options. I still remember that on June 16, 1982—one day before the day that will live in infamy for me—I tried to sell an additional hundred options at a specific price right before the close, but I didn't get filled.

The next day, they announced that Cities Service was going to be bought out for $20 more than my highest strike price option. They shut down trading in the stock and options for the rest of the week and didn't resume trading until after the option expiration. Of course, the options got exercised [leaving Cook short one hundred shares for each option he had sold], and by the time the stock started trading again, I was down $500,000.

Did that include your family's accounts?

No, that was just my account. I had gone from $165,000 at the start of June to a deficit of over $350,000. In addition, I had lost over $100,000 apiece in accounts I had for my mother, father, and aunt. I still have the trade slips right here in my desk drawer. It wasn't until last year—seventeen years after this happened—that I was able to pull them out and look at them. I had a margin call in excess of one million dollars on my account, which is what I would have had to put up if I wanted to hold the short stock position instead of buying it back. Technically, you are supposed to have five days to meet the margin call, but the firm was on me to cover the position right away.

That night I called my mother, which was the hardest phone call I ever had to make. I felt like a complete failure. I felt like I should be put in shackles and hauled away. "Mom," I said, "I need to talk to you."

"What is it?" she asked.

"I think you need to come over to the house tomorrow morning to discuss it."

"It'll have to be pretty early," she said, "because I have to get to the college." [At the time, Cook's mother, Martha, was chairman of the education department at Malone College in Canton, Ohio, where she still teaches a course in English grammar.]

"That's okay, Mom, the earlier, the better." The next morning, around 6:30 A.M., I looked out my window and saw my mom dragging up the walk at a snail's pace, which was very uncharacteristic for her.

She came in and asked, "Mark, what is the problem?"

"Sit down on the couch, Mom," I said solemnly.

She sat down and asked, "What's wrong, Mark? Is it something serious?"

"Yes, I'm afraid it is," I answered. "Mom, I lost $100,000 of your money."

She didn't flinch at all. She looked me straight in the eye and asked sympathetically, "How much did you lose, Mark?"

"I lost half a million dollars," I said.

"But you don't have half a million dollars."

"I know, Mom."

"What else?" she asked.

"What do you mean, 'what else'?" I asked.

"Besides losing all this money, what else is wrong?"

"That's it, Mom," I answered.

"Oh, is that all! I thought you had cancer."

Did that ever put things in a different light. Her next sentence to me was unbelievable: "How long will it be until you make it back?" she asked.

If she would have said anything else, I would have quit. But she had said just the right thing, at the right time. I straightened myself up a bit and said, "Five years," picking a number out of the air because I had no clue how I would make the money back.

"If you make the money back in ten years, that's okay," she said. "Now go ahead and do it."

From that point forward, I never again sold any naked options [option positions that have an open-ended loss if the market goes up or down sharply].

What eventually happened to Cities Service after the brokerage firm liquidated your account?

That's the ironic thing. The deal fell through. If I had been able to meet the margin call, within a month, I would have made back all my money and even had a profit. The takeover offer was made just before expiration and then retracted afterward. There should have been an investigation, but there never was. On the positive side, though, if I had been filled on the last hundred options I was trying to sell the day before the takeover announcement, I would have been forced into bankruptcy.

How were you able to cover the $350,000 deficit you had in your account?

My parents gave me $200,000, and I borrowed the remaining $150,000, using my farm as collateral. There is nothing more debilitating than borrowing money to put into a brokerage account to bring it up to zero. I was only twenty-eight years old at the time, and I was determined to claw my way back. I worked fourteen-hour days. I would get up at 5:30 A.M., milk cows until 9 A.M., clean up, go into the office, and work as a broker until 5:30 P.M. When I came home, I changed clothes, went out into the barn to do the milking, and then came back in at 9 P.M. to eat dinner and go to bed. In essence, I was working two full-time jobs. I kept this routine up for five years until I sold the dairy operation.

Did you maintain this grueling schedule because you were trying to make your money back as quickly as possible?

I had to keep the farming operation going because I had borrowed against it. Also, remember that this was 1982, which was the virtual peak in the interest rate cycle. My monthly interest-rate payment alone was $8,800. My net worth was probably a negative $200,000. A number of people advised me to declare bankruptcy, but I wouldn't do it. When I look back at it now, I realize that declaring bankruptcy would probably have been the right business decision. But I wouldn't be the trader I am today if I had done it, because that would have been admitting defeat.

Did you also feel that this self-imposed servitude was just punishment?

I really did.

How did your wife respond to this whole situation?

She was actually quite supportive. When I started digging myself out of it, she said, "I've never seen anyone who can make money like you can when you're backed into a corner." She's right. Even now, whenever I have a losing month, I just claw like a tiger to make it back. That's when I work my hardest. When I work fifteen-hour days, my wife knows that my trading is not going well. Conversely, when I'm home early, she'll say, "Your trading must really be floating along."

Most traders that I've talked to about losing periods say they ease up or even take a break during those times.

I do just the opposite. Whenever I am down, the frequency of my trading steps up.

But aren't you afraid that you will aggravate your losses by doing that?

I increase my activity, not my exposure. In fact, the first thing I do when I'm losing is to stop the bleeding. That's why I have this sign on my computer. [He points to a sheet that reads GET SMALLER.] I don't get out of the trade that is hurting me completely; I just reduce the position size. Then the next trade that I do, I feel compelled to make money. It doesn't matter how much. The point is to rebuild my confidence. Even if I only make a few hundred dollars on that trade, it shows that I can still make money. Once I have a winning trade, I'm ready to go again.

What advice would you give to other traders about handling losing situations?

Hope should never be in your vocabulary. It is the worst four-letter word I know. As soon as you say, "Boy, I hope this position comes back," you should reduce your size.

What about the flip side—winning streaks—any advice there?

Never increase the size of your positions on a winning streak. Otherwise you guarantee that you will have your largest position on a losing trade.

How long was it until you started trading again after the Cities Service disaster?

Almost two years. The first trade I put on was in April 1984, right after the birth of my first daughter.

Were you profitable when you resumed trading?

I was approximately breakeven for 1984 and 1985. My first big profitable year was 1986.

Did something change then?

Yes, I had developed my cumulative tick indicator. In 1986, I began keeping a daily trading diary. Every day I wrote down recurrent patterns that I noticed in the market. One indicator that appeared to be useful was what is called the *tick*, which is the number of New York Stock Exchange stocks whose last trade was an uptick minus the number whose last trade was a downtick. When the market is going up, the tick will be positive, and when it's going down, it will be negative. I noticed that whenever the tick became very negative, the market would tend to snap back on the upside. Conversely, strongly positive tick readings seemed to be followed by sell-offs.

I asked a broker who had been in the business for thirty years what it meant when the tick got very positive or negative. He said, "A negative tick means the stock market is going down, and a positive tick means it is going up."

"Yeah, I know that," I said, "but what do I do when the tick is very positive or negative?"

"Well, if it's a high plus, you buy, and if it's a high minus, you sell," he answered. I asked a number of other brokers the same question, and they gave me the same advice.

Since this advice contradicted my observations, I did just the opposite: When the tick went above plus 400, I would sell, and when it went below minus 400, I would buy. I recorded the results in my diary and confirmed that this strategy was making money. I noticed, however, that the more minus the tick became, the more the market would snap back, and the more positive it became, the more the market would sell off. That's how I got the idea of keeping a cumulative count on the tick, which evolved into my cumulative tick indicator. I have never had this indicator fail, but you need nerves of steel to trade with it because the market is always in a panic situation—usually because of an external news event—when the readings get extreme.

I know your cumulative tick indicator is a proprietary measure, but what can you tell me about it?

The calculation ignores periods when the tick is in a neutral band, which I define as a reading between –400 to +400. When the tick is beyond these thresholds, a reading is recorded at fixed time intervals and added to a running total. When this total gets below the historical 5th percentile, it signals an oversold situation [a buying opportunity], and when it gets above the 95th percentile it signals an overbought situation [a selling opportunity].

How long did it take you to recover the $350,000 trading deficit that was left over from the Cities Service trade?

Five years, measured from the Cities Service trade, which was three years after I resumed trading. The big year was 1987. When I say that, people automatically assume that I must have been short during the October crash, but I actually made most of the money during the bull market earlier that year.

At that time I wasn't day trading yet. In May 1987 I saw what I believed was a phenomenal buying opportunity in stock index call options. Two factors had converged: my cumulative tick indicator was giving extremely bullish readings, and the decline in volatility had made the option premiums very cheap. My grandfather used to tell me, "Buy things when people don't want them, and sell things when people want them." I put $55,000 into long-term, out-of-the-money stock index calls that were trading at ½ to ⅝. [In this type of option position, the trader can make multiples of the initial outlay if there is a *huge* price advance, but lose the entire investment in any other price scenario.] I bought well over a thousand options. During the next few months, stock prices exploded and the volatility shot up—a combination that caused the value of my options to soar.

Ever since the Cities Service disaster in 1982, I had wanted to demonstrate to my parents that I wasn't a failure. On August 7, 1987, I went over to see them. I told them, "I'm trading options again."

"Oh no!" exclaimed my dad. "What is the bad news this time?"

"Well, Dad, that is why I'm here," I answered.

"Why do you trade those things, Mark? Didn't you learn your lesson? Do you have a problem again?"

"Yes, I have an income tax problem," I answered. "The calls I bought are worth $750,000."

"How much did you invest?" my father asked.

"Fifty-five thousand dollars," I answered.

"Gosh, take it!" he said.

"No," I said, "they are going up more tomorrow." The next day I cashed out the position for a $1.4 million-dollar profit.

What else do you base your trading decisions on besides the cumulative tick indicator?

The cumulative tick indicator is an intermediate tool that only sets up about two to four times a year; the rest of the time, it's in a neutral reading. I have a variety of different trades I use.

Can you give me an example of some of them?

One trade I do I call a "conjunction trade" because it requires two simultaneous conditions for a buy signal: the tick going below –400 and the *tiki,* which is a tick indicator based on the thirty Dow Jones stocks, going below –22. I give this trade only twenty-one minutes to work. Whenever I get a signal, I set my egg timer. [*He winds up the egg timer on his desk, which ticks audibly as it unwinds during the ensuing conversation.*] I picture the egg timer as a bomb, and I have to be out of the position before it goes off. I will liquidate the position when any of the following three things happen: I get my 3-point profit objective, my 6-point stop-loss is hit, or the twenty-one-minute time limit is running out.

Why twenty-one minutes?

Because of the trading diaries that I keep. I've recorded these trades time and time and time again. The best trades work the quickest. I found that you should make three points within the first ten minutes. After ten minutes, the trade could still work, but the odds are much lower. Once you get to fifteen minutes, the odds are so reduced that all you want to do is get out the best you can. The more time that goes by, the lower the probability that the objective will be reached.

I note that you are using a risk point that is twice as large as your objective. That's fairly unorthodox.

It's all a matter of probabilities. I like high-probability trades. This trade, as many of the other trades I do, works approximately seven out of eight times on average. If I make 3 points seven times and lose 6 points one time, I still come out ahead 15 points across eight trades.

Another trade I do involves watching the ratio between the S&P and Nasdaq. I use this information to decide which market I will trade if I get a signal. If I get a buy signal on one of my other indicators, I will buy the index that is relatively stronger that day. And if I get a sell signal, I will sell the index that is relatively weaker.

What would be an example of a signal?

I have a trade that I called a "tick buy," which means that if the tick gets to −1000, I will buy because the market will tend to snap back after that point.

In other words, if you get a tick buy signal, which implies a sharply declining market, you'll buy the index—S&P or Nasdaq—that is less weak.

That's right.

Can you give me any other examples of trades that you do?

One trade I call a "catapult trade" because it's just like a catapult, which gets bent back until it springs and then the projectile flies over a threshold. For example, if the S&P is trading back and forth in a range between 1350 and 1353, and each time it pulls back, it holds a little higher, then I'll expect it to catapult above the top of the range by the width of the range, or to 1356. The reason the trade works is because stops tend to build up right above the catapult point.

Another trade I do is the bond ratio trade. The bonds and S&P are like a couple. The bond market always leads, so it is the female, because the male always follows the female. When a couple first start to date, they don't know each other yet, and they will be a bit out of harmony. On analogous markets days, when the bonds go up, the S&P may also go up, but it won't follow very tightly. Then they get engaged, and the relationship becomes closer. Then they get married and go on a honeymoon. When they are on a honeymoon, everything they do is synchronous. On "honeymoon days" in the markets, when I see the bonds go up a few ticks, I know the S&P will immediately follow, and I will buy the S&P for a quick trade. After the honeymoon, when they settle into married life, the bonds will drag the S&P husband along, but they are not quite as joined as they once were. Then the couple gets estranged, or in market terms, whenever the bonds go up, the S&P will likely go down. Then comes the bitter divorce. On "divorce days" the bonds and S&P will move in exactly opposite directions. Every day, I make a determination of what type of day it is. Today, for example, the bonds were going up, and the S&P was selling off. The Street called it a "flight to quality," but to me it was just a "divorce day."

Did you ever manage money, or have you always traded just your own account?

In 1989, I decided to get into money management. I asked people I knew in the business what I needed to do as an unknown in the middle of nowhere to attract investors. One person suggested that I enter the U.S. Investing Championship [a now defunct real money trading contest] to attract greater public visibility. That was the first time I had ever heard of this trading competition. Back in 1989, the contest was held for four-month intervals. I entered the options division category and finished second, making 89 percent for the four months. That gave me enough confidence to think that I could do this. I decided to give up my brokerage business and concentrate just on my own trading.

Why couldn't you continue to do both?

It seemed to me that just about every time I was in a trade and had to do something quickly, a client would call and want to talk about utility stocks or something equally urgent.

I opened a personal account with a clearing firm in New York that also did business with other money managers. After my account had been active for about three or four months, I received a call from compliance [the company department responsible for making sure that all accounts are traded in accordance with government and industry regulations]. My immediate thought was, "Oh no, what's the problem now?"

"I've been looking at your account," the caller said, "and it appears that you only trade options."

"That's right," I answered warily.

"It also looks like you only buy options," he said.

"That's right," I answered. "I don't believe in selling options."

"Why not?" he asked.

"Too much risk," I said.

"I reviewed all your trades since you opened your account with us," he said.

"Is there a problem?" I asked.

"No, as a matter of fact, I have never seen anybody who can trade like you do."

"What exactly does that mean?" I asked.

"Well, for starters, you are the shortest-term trader I have ever seen. In fact, it seems like you never hold a position for more than three days. Why is that?" he asked.

"That's because after years and years of trading experience, I have learned that if I hold positions for more than three days, it diminishes my return. When you buy an option, the premium steadily evaporates over time. It's like holding an ice cube in your hand: the longer it's there, the more it diminishes until finally it doesn't exist at all. You are in the compliance department," I said. "Is there a problem?"

"We have been looking for someone like you for a long time. We are waiting for you to get a one-year track record before offering you as a money manager to our clients. I wasn't supposed to contact you until this point because we thought it probably would change your trading pattern if you knew you were being watched."

"You don't know me," I said. "That's not going to happen."

"We'll see," he said.

Had he been tracking your account because he was looking for potential in-house money managers?

Oh no, he started following me from a compliance standpoint to shut me down. I assume the fact that I was trading only options and turning over my trades very quickly must have sent up all sorts of red flags.

He continued to monitor my account, and after the account reached the one-year mark, he called again. "You actually did better after you knew I was watching you," he said.

"I guess you gave me a bit of incentive," I answered.

"I can't sell this, though," he said.

"Why not?" I asked.

"You did too well. No one is going to believe these numbers. But don't worry, I'm going to raise money for you anyway. I don't have to show your track record. People will just invest with you based on my recommendation."

He pulled together a number of small accounts into a single million-dollar account, which I started trading at the beginning of 1991. If you recall, that was right at the brink of the United States' launching an attack on Iraq, and the stock market had been selling off precipitously. The cumulative tick indicator was signaling that the market was heavily oversold. On January 4, I started buying S&P index calls [an option position that bets on a rising market]. I continued to add to the position over the next few days.

Wait a minute. I thought you held positions only for a maximum of three days.

That's true for most of my trades. There is one major exception: if my cumulative tick indicator, which only sets up a few times a year, is still telling me to buy, then I will hold a position beyond three days. When the tick indicator sets up, the market sometimes responds immediately, but I've also seen it take as long as seven weeks. As long as the indicator is still providing a signal, I will only trade in the same direction. If it's oversold, I will only buy calls, and if it's overbought, I will only buy puts. [Puts are option positions that give the buyer the right to *sell* the stock or index at the strike price and will therefore make money in a declining market.] I still traded in and out of the market, but I kept a core position of long calls. This core position was down about 25 percent. Since for this account I used a money management plan that limited my total investment to one-third of the equity, I was down about 8 percent in terms of total equity.

On January 7, for the first time, I received a call from the president of the company. I had only been trading the account for one week. "What do you think about the market? he asked.

I knew what was happening. He was getting worried calls from the investors who were faceless people to me. "Well," I said, "my cumulative tick indicator is very oversold." I explained to him that whenever my index was deeply oversold, it signaled a major buying opportunity.

"How soon until the market goes up?" he asked.

"It can spring at any time," I said. "We need a catalyst, but I can't tell you exactly when that will be."

"Your indicators don't work at all," he said. "The market is going straight down."

"You can pull the plug," I said, "but I want you to understand that if you do, the investors are going to know that you were the one who closed out the positions, not me."

My secretary had been sitting there, listening to my end of the conversation. When I hung up, she said, "Gosh, you were pretty rough with him."

"Don't worry," I said, "he is not going to close the account and take responsibility. He's going to leave me out there to hang."

On the night of January 10, the United States began its air attack on Iraq, and the next day the market exploded on the upside. Not only did the market go up tremendously, but the sharp increase in volatility also caused option premiums to expand. On January 12, the president of the company called me back.

Where was the account at this point?

The option position I held had nearly quadrupled. [Since Cook had invested one-third of the equity, this implies that the account equity had nearly doubled.] By this time, I had already started to take profits on my position. Of course, he knew that I had started liquidating the position when he called.

"What do you plan to do?" he asked.

I plan to continue to scale out of the position," I answered.

"But it's really going up now," he said. "Do you think it will continue?"

"Yes I do," I answered, "because my cumulative tick indicator is still oversold."

"Then why don't you hold the position?" he asked.

"You don't understand," I said. "One reason the option premiums have gone up so much is because of the explosion in volatility. [Option prices depend on both the underlying market price *and* volatility.] Once the volatility starts to ease, option prices may not go up much even if the market continues to rise. Also, I realize now, which I didn't before you called me last week, that your investors are pretty nervous, and they probably want money in their pockets. Isn't that right?"

"That's true," he answered.

"Fine," I said, "we'll continue to liquidate the position and take it from there."

"Mark," he said, "that's why you are the trader you are." Those were his exact words.

"Thanks for telling me I'm a good trader," I said for my secretary's benefit, who had been listening to the conversation intently. "Now you realize that my indicators work—don't you?"

"Oh yes," he answered, "your indicators work."

After I hung up the phone, my secretary said, "Wasn't that nice of him to call and compliment you."

"Just watch," I said. "He will jerk this money just as soon as he can."

"Why would he do that?" she asked in disbelief.

"Because he can't stand the volatility, and he can't handle the clients. He also doesn't understand what I am doing, which makes him a terrible intermediary. His involvement will only lead to doubt and skepticism among the clients. It would be different if I were talking to the clients directly and they could hear the confidence in my voice." Ironically, I had chosen this type of structure because I wanted to be at arm's length from the investors so that I wouldn't be influenced by their emotions. Instead, I ended up with someone in the middle who was just aggravating the situation. "He'll find some excuse to pull the account," I told my secretary.

"How could he find an excuse," she asked, "when you have nearly doubled their money?"

"I don't know," I said, "but he will find something."

By that point, the option premiums had expanded so far that it virtually eliminated any profit opportunities if you were only a buyer of options, as I was. Buying options then was like paying Rolls-Royce prices for a Yugo.

Did you stop trading?

Yes, I had to back off. I have to believe a trade has at least a 75 percent chance of being right or else I won't put it on. I continued to trade very lightly over the next few months, and the account drifted sideways.

At the end of April, the president of the company called again. "How come you're not trading anymore?" he asked. "Are you afraid?" he sneered.

"Yes, I'm afraid, but not of what you think. I'm afraid of the marketplace. I don't see trades that will give me my 75 percent probability of winning, and I'm not going to do any coin-flip trades."

"Well, my investors are expecting you to trade," he said. "Why can't you do the same thing you did in January?"

"Because the market is not the same," I said. "We could do nothing for the rest of the year and still have a good year."

"Yeah, you're still up 85 percent for the year," he admitted.

"And the investors aren't happy with that?" I asked.

"They saw you double their money in January, and they want you to really go for it. You better do some more trades, Mark," he said.

"What does he want now?" my secretary asked after I hung up the phone.

"Now he wants to force me to trade. Isn't that interesting. In January he wanted me to shut the account down, and now, when I shouldn't be trading, he wants me to trade more."

What did you do?

I thought I would put on one trade to keep him happy. Then if it didn't work out, I could talk him out of pressuring me to trade. But as soon as I put on the trade, I thought to myself that this is stupid; I'm putting on a trade that I think may lose money to prove a point. Sure enough, the trade lost money—not much, maybe 5 percent of the equity. I backed off and stopped trading.

How were you getting compensated for these accounts?

I was supposed to get a percent of the profits.

The standard 20 percent of profits?

This will give you an idea of how naive I was at the time. They told me, "Don't worry, we will make it right by you." I had nothing in writing. I went along with that because I was mainly interested in getting a track record rather than earning anything on this account. I was so hungry to get started that I would've taken virtually any deal.

At the end of May, the president called again. He told me that two of the accounts were pulling their money. "Oh, I guess they have some pressing financial needs," I conjectured.

"I'll be honest with you, Mark," he said, "there are more investors that are right at the cusp of closing their accounts."

"Why?" I asked.

"Well, you haven't done anything for us lately," he answered.

"Do you realize how much the account is up?" I asked. "If you had told these investors at the beginning of the year that they were going to make 80 percent on their money, don't you think they would've been ecstatic?"

"Yes, but you did more than that in the first month," he replied. "During the past four months, you haven't made anything."

"Wait a minute," I said. "What expectations did these investors have?"

"I showed them your track record for last year."

"You did what!" I exclaimed. "That track record was based on my own account, which trades up to 100 percent of the equity. My account will make three times as much as this account because of the leverage, but the drawdowns will also be three times as large, and I don't think your investors could handle 40 percent drawdowns."

Ten minutes later he called back and said, "We're shutting the account down."

I was so mad, I could have spit blood. I don't know what he told the investors to make them all pull their money simultaneously. That was my first and last experience in managing any pooled money.

Did they ever pay you anything on the profits you had made?

Not a cent.

As Samuel Goldwyn said, "A verbal contract isn't worth the paper it's written on." What happened after they closed the account?

I was basically flat for the rest of the year because the environment wasn't conducive to buying options. In November 1991, I signed up for the 1992 U.S. Trading Championship, which by that time had expanded from a four-month to a one-year contest. In preparation, I researched all my past trades back to the 1970s to find out why I had made money and why I had lost money. I found that Tuesdays were my best day and Fridays my worst.

Why is that?

Because it takes me a little while to get warmed up. Mondays I am just getting back into gear, and by Tuesday I'm ready to roll. By the time I get to Friday, I've exhausted my energy, and if I have done well for the week, I just don't have the drive and zeal. So what did I do in 1992? I didn't trade on any Fridays, and I traded more aggressively on Tuesdays.

Did your trading change forever because of this analysis?

Oh yes, it was the best thing that I ever did. That's when I became a very proficient trader.

What advice do you have for people who want to follow in your footsteps and trade for a living?

If you decide to trade for a living, you have to treat it just like any other business endeavor and go into it with a plan. If you want to start a business, and all you do is walk into a bank, smile pleasantly, and ask for a $200,000 loan, do you think you'll get it? Are they going to say, "You have a really nice smile; here's the money." I don't think so. You need to have a solid business plan. The trouble is that most people start trading without any definitive plan.

What would a business plan for traders include?

It should contain specific answers to all of the following questions:

- What markets are you going to trade? You need to select a market that fits your personality because a market is a reflection of the people who trade it. People who trade Internet stocks are definitely different from people who trade utility stocks.

- What is your trading capitalization? On the one hand, you should honestly be able to say, "If I lose all this money, it won't change my lifestyle." On the other hand, you need a large enough account so that making at least as much as you do from your current job is a feasible goal. Otherwise, you will think that you are a failure because you will work harder as a trader than you do at the job you are in now.
- How will orders be entered? Will you scale into positions or put them on all at once? How will you exit losing trades? How will you exit winning trades?
- What type of drawdown will cause you to stop trading and reevaluate your approach? What type of drawdown will cause you to shut down trading?
- What are your profit goals, measured on as short a time frame as is feasible for your trading approach?
- What procedure will you use for analyzing your trades?
- What will you do if personal problems arise that could adversely impact your trading?
- How will you set up your working environment so that it is conducive to trading and maximizes your chances for success?
- How will you reward yourself for successful trading? Will you take a special vacation, buy yourself a new car, etcetera?
- How will you continue to improve yourself as a trader? What books will you read? What new research projects will you do?

What other advice would you give to people who want to become traders?

Approach trading as a vocation, not a hobby. I periodically give seminars for traders. I once had a tennis pro who attended my four-day seminar. On the third day, I asked people what they had learned so far and how they were going to apply it. When it was his turn, he said, "I'm not going to give up my tennis career. I give lessons on Tuesdays and Thursdays, so I'm going to trade on Mondays, Wednesdays, and Fridays."

"If you do that," I told him, "I guarantee that Tuesdays and Thursdays will be the days when you will need to be watching the market. You'll be making a hundred dollars giving a lesson and losing a thousand dollars in the market."

"I'm not going to have that problem," he said, "because I'm going to close out my positions every day." Six months later, he gave up trading. He did two things wrong: First, his primary passion was tennis. Second, trading wasn't a vocation to him; it was a hobby, and hobbies cost you money.

What are some other reasons people fail as traders?

People underestimate the time it takes to succeed as a trader. Some people come here and think they can sit with me for a week and become great traders. How many people when they went to college would've thought to walk up to the professor and say, "I know the course is for a semester, but I think a week should be enough for me to get it." Gaining proficiency is the same in trading as in any other profession—it requires experience, and experience takes time.

A man who attended one of my seminars a number of years ago asked me, "How long will it take me to become a professional trader so I can quit my job and support my family?"

"Three to five years," I said.

"What! I'm going to do it in six months," he answered.

"Well, you're probably a lot smarter than I am," I said. "I didn't make any money in my first five years."

It's seven years later, and he's still not profitable as a trader. You can't expect to become a doctor or an attorney overnight, and trading is no different. It is a vocation that takes time, study, and experience. Wisdom is a product of knowledge and experience. If you have more knowledge, you can get away with less experience and vice versa. If you can get both, the learning curve is very steep.

Why else do people fail as traders?

Another common reason is undercapitalization. Sometimes I get people at my seminars who want to start trading with $10,000. I tell them that they should convert the $10,000 into hundred-dollar bills and then flush them down the toilet one at a time because if they try trading with $10,000, the result will be the same, but it will only prolong the agony. Ten thousand dollars is not enough money to trade.

All the reasons for failure you have mentioned so far relate to the attitude with which people approach trading: a lack of commit-

ment or funds going in. What flaws besides attitude cause people to fail as traders?

It's not a matter of intelligence, or even market knowledge. I've seen people with good trading skills fail, and those without any previous experience succeed. The main thing is that every trader has to be honest about his or her weakness and deal with it. If you can't learn to do that, you will not survive as a trader.

Several years ago, an option trader who had scheduled to come visit me at my office asked whether I would be willing to review his trades for the past year before he came. I agreed because I genuinely want to teach people how to trade.

He said, "I had 84 percent winning trades last year."

"Good," I said, "did you make any money?"

"Well, no," he answered, "I lost money for the year."

"Then the 16 percent is what we need to focus on," I said.

"That's why I wanted to send you my trades."

He sent me his trades, and I found that out of about four hundred trades he did that year, five trades accounted for almost all his losses. At first I didn't notice any common denominator. Then I checked the dates and discovered that four out of five of these trades had been done on expiration Fridays. I called him up and said, "I found your problem."

"Oh good," he said. "What did you find?"

"Four out of five of your big losing trades were done on an expiration Friday."

"Oh, I knew that," he answered.

"Well, there is a way to fix this problem," I told him.

"Good, good," he said. "I knew you would have the answer."

"Don't trade on expiration Fridays."

"Mark, what are you talking about? Those are the most exciting trading days."

"You have to decide whether you want excitement or you want to make money. Quit trading on expiration Fridays. Go out and do something else on those days."

"Oh no, I can't do that," he said. "I can't give up the action on that day. I'll figure out how to fix the problem."

"If you don't fix this problem by quitting," I told him, "it's going to quit you."

Six months later, he was bankrupt. He knew indicators inside and out. He was a workaholic and very intelligent. He even knew how to take losses most of the time. But he just couldn't stand aside on that one trading day. He had identified his problem, but he couldn't fix it.

Any other stories come to mind about traders you tried to help, but who ultimately failed?

A few years ago, a man who attended one my seminars called me for advice. He told me that he wanted to become a full-time trader but had been unsuccessful so far. I gave him some advice about devising a business plan for his trading. He called a couple more times for additional advice. On one such call, his voice suddenly dropped. "I can hardly hear you," I said. "We must have a bad connection."

"No," he whispered, "my wife just walked into the room."

"She doesn't know how much money you have lost, does she?" I asked.

"No," he admitted.

"You have to tell her the truth. If she doesn't support you, and you are fearful of her, nothing I teach you will help. If you keep trading secretly, one of two things will happen: you will lose all your money, or you will lose your marriage." He didn't listen to me, and he ended up losing both.

What happened during September–December 1997? It was the only sustained losing period I saw in the statements you sent me and completely uncharacteristic in terms of your other trading. I believe you lost over $300,000 during a four-month period.

I find that as the year progresses, I tend not to do as well. I just chalk it up to my getting tired or sloppy toward the end the year.

But that doesn't explain it. This period was so much worse than any other period, including the latter part of other years, that there must be some other explanation.

[Cook rambles on further, trying to explain in general terms why he may have done poorly during that period. Then finally, a memory clicks.] Ah, you're absolutely right! I had forgotten about it. In July 1997, I fell and severely tore the ACL in my knee [a ligament in the center of the knee]. I wore a brace and was on pain medication. I finally had an operation in December.

Did the pain medication make you drowsy?

It threw my focus off. I wasn't as sharp. I felt as if I were moving in slow motion. I was also worried that I might never be able to play basketball with my kids again.

It sounds like you were depressed during that period.

Yes, I had gone from being physically active, both in sports and on the farm, to barely being able to walk. I put on over thirty pounds during those few months.

If your operation was in December, then your trading seemed to recover immediately afterward.

Yes it did. I felt so much better. I threw myself into rehabilitation, although I probably overdid it. I'm a gung ho type of guy. Two weeks after my operation, the physical therapist came over to me while I was on the weight machine and said, "We do lots of rehabilitation on ACL injuries. I will tell you just one thing, and maybe it will hit home: No one we had in here after ACL reconstructive surgery ever lifted as much weight as you are now. Do you get my point?" I backed off immediately.

[About a week after the interview, I spoke to Cook on the phone, and he told me he had asked his assistant, Stacie, about her impression of him during this injury period. She told him, "You couldn't walk. You even had trouble sitting because you were in such discomfort. You had pain in your face. You were just a shell of yourself, and it poured over into your trading. Once you had your operation, you were like a different person."]

Were there any other periods where personal turmoil interfered with your trading?

In September 1995, my father had a heart attack. He was in intensive care for eight days. During that period, I punished myself by doing every damaging trading mistake in the book.

Why did you feel responsible for your dad's heart attack?

He worked so hard. On the day he had his heart attack, it was over ninety degrees, and he was baling hay. My mom told me that he felt a little sick during the middle of the day, came back in, and then went back out to work. He baled four hundred bales of hay on the day he had his heart attack. I thought, "He's out there doing all that work for $700 or $800, and I'm sitting in an air-conditioned office, making $7,000 or $8,000." It didn't seem right to me, so I had to punish myself. When I look back on the trades I did during that period, it almost seems like temporary insanity.

Then you weren't doing your regular trades.

Oh no, I was doing almost the exact opposite.

Were you aware of what you were doing at the time?

I didn't care; I was totally despondent. I think I really wanted to lose money.

For your style of trading, you have to watch the market closely all day long. Have you had any situations where interruptions cost you money?

The trade that sticks in my mind most was in January 1987. It was my secretary's birthday. I never leave the office during the day when I have a position on. But on that day, trying to be a nice guy, I took her out for lunch to celebrate her birthday. When I left the office, the option position I had on was up $30,000. When I came back after lunch, the position was down $40,000. I couldn't believe the quotes. I always remember that trade. Now I give my secretary a card for her birthday *[he chuckles]*.

It sounds like a very expensive lunch. Are you sure you would have covered the position if you had stayed in the office?

Absolutely. That's one of my cardinal rules. I never let a profit turn into a loss.

I've exhausted my questions. Any final words?

I represent the average guy out here in rural America, in the U.S. Midwest. I sit in my great-grandfather's farmhouse, staring at a computer screen, and I can make a living trading. That's why I believe there is hope for people anywhere to do this. But you have to be willing to work hard and pay your tuition, which is the money you lose while you're learning how to trade. People ask me all the time, "How long do you think it will take for me to succeed?" I tell them, "three to five years of twelve-hour days and losing money." Very few people want to hear that.

It's not over until you give up. Mark D. Cook didn't just encounter initial failure, he failed repeatedly and spectacularly, losing his entire trading stake several times, and on one occasion, more than his entire net worth. Yet despite that inauspicious beginning and nearly a decade of false starts, Cook never gave up and ultimately triumphed, developing the methodology, business plan, and discipline that allowed him to extract triple-digit returns from the market with astounding consistency.

In contrast to the conventional wisdom, which advises looking for trades that offer a profit potential several times as large as the risk, most of Cook's trading strategies seek to make one dollar for every two dollars risked. This observation provides two important lessons, neither of which is that using a wider risk level than the profit objective is a generally attractive approach.

First, looking at the probability of winning is every bit as essential as looking at the ratio of potential gain to risk. As Cook demonstrates, a strategy can lose more on losing trades than it gains on winning trades and still be a terrific approach if its probability of winning is high enough. Conversely, a strategy could make ten times as much on winning trades as it gives up on losing trades and still lead to financial ruin if the probabilities are low enough. Consider, for example, betting continuously on the number seven in roulette: when you win, you will win thirty-six times what you bet, but if you play long enough, you are guaranteed to lose all your money because your odds of success are only one in thirty-eight.

Second, in choosing a trading approach, it is essential to select a method that fits your personality. Cook is happy to take a small profit on a trade but hates to take even a small loss. Given his predisposition, the methodologies he has developed, which accept a low return/risk ratio on each trade in exchange for a high probability of winning, are right for him. But these same methods could be very uncomfortable, and hence unprofitable, for others to trade. Trading is not a one-size-fits-all proposition; each trader must tailor an individual approach.

Personal problems can decimate a trader's performance. Consider, for example, Cook's uncharacteristic large losses during his knee injury and his father's heart attack. The moral is: If you are experiencing physical or emotional distress, either stop trading altogether, or reduce your trading activity to a level at which you can't do much damage. If Cook himself is guilty of any serious trading sin during the past decade, it is failing to heed this advice—a mistake he is determined not to repeat.

Most aspiring traders underestimate the time, work, and money required to become successful. Cook is adamant that to succeed as a trader requires a complete commitment. You must approach trading as a full-time business, not as a part-time interest. Just as in any entrepreneurial venture, you must have a solid business plan, adequate financing, and a willingness to work long hours. Those seeking shortcuts need not apply. And even if you do everything right, you should still expect to lose money during the first few years—losses that Cook views as tuition payments to the school of trading. These are cold, hard facts that many would-be traders prefer not to hear or believe, but ignoring them doesn't change the reality.

★

Update on Mark D. Cook

Cook has continued to roll along in his trading. Given his methodology, it makes no difference to him whether stocks are in a bull market or a bear market. For comparison, though, during the April 2000–September 2002 period when the S&P 500 declined by 45 percent and the Nasdaq by 75 percent, Cook's trading account realized a cumulative 114 percent profit compounded (84 percent if measured as cumulative dollars profit divided by the average account equity level).

In our first interview, we talked about the pattern of your trading showing dramatic deterioration in times when you faced personal stress. I know during the past two years you have had to deal with serious illness of a family member, but trading-wise you seem to have handled it better. Did you change what you do under such circumstances?

The main thing I did was scale back on my size. I knew from past experience that I couldn't be at 100 percent when I had personal problems. I realized that one of the reasons I traded poorly when I was under stress in my personal life was that if something went wrong when I was already in a weakened emotional state, it pushed me over the edge. I wasn't rational anymore, and I always ended up giving back too much money. I thought that instead of not trading at all, I could just cut back my position size, and still keep my rationality.

When everything is normal, and I'm not dealing with outside stress, I know what my appropriate position size should be, and I adjust it for market volatility. But when I have external problems gnawing at me, I'm not in the right mode to be trading that size. I never adjusted for that before, but in the past two years I have.

I not only reduced my position size, but I also traded fewer days. I was going over my monthly summary sheets before you called, and I noticed that many months I traded on only eleven or twelve days instead of my normal eighteen to twenty days. By trading less, I was picking my best spots. If I didn't get what I considered a concrete signal, I didn't trade that day.

Has your trading methodology changed at all during the past two years?

Yes, it has. In the past, I used to let some trades get away from me, which would lead to a large drawdown. Now, I use what I call an "insurance stop" on my initial trade each day. It's just like fire insurance on your house: You hope you never need it, but you need to have it just in case you do. The insurance stop is not based on any technical point or any analysis; it is simply used to limit my maximum daily loss to a given dollar amount.

When I wrote my business plan at the start of the year I arbitrarily picked a $25,000 maximum loss on my first trade of the day because I know I can get that back pretty easily. If I get hit on one of these insurance stops, the market is doing something that I don't understand, and I shouldn't be trading. For example, two weeks ago when the S&P 500 broke below the 900 level, my insurance stop was triggered. Initially, I felt sick about being hit with that loss, but then the market immediately went down another 30 or 40 full points, and I felt a lot better about it.

How much would you have lost on that trade if you didn't have the stop?

It probably would have cost me $100,000.

You only put your insurance stop in on the first trade of the day?

Yes.

But aren't you then leaving yourself vulnerable to a large loss on a subsequent trade?

No, because I actually give those trades a lot less latitude. The insurance stop is a much wider stop. It would be meaningless on trades later in the day because I become much more selective in my trades as the day goes on. After my first trade, I only put on what I consider very high probability trades, and I'm not willing to give those trades much room.

I'm different from most people in this respect. For example, I've noticed that most people I train will tend to take more risk when they are playing with the market's money. I'm just the opposite: Once I make a profit, I consider it my money, and I'm not about to let the market take it out of my pocket. So once I'm ahead on the day, I try to make sure I don't give back much of it.

One of the side benefits of having the insurance stop is that it has allowed me to go for bigger profits because I know I have a safety net if the trade turns around. It's like the trapeze artist that might try a triple instead of double somersault when he knows he has a net beneath him.

I assume that most of the people you train must have a bullish bias, which would have been problematical during the past two years. Have you found that to be the case, and if so what advice have you given them?

You're absolutely right. The strong bull trend in the stock market during the late 1990s bailed out a lot of people who were basically just long traders. During those years, if you held a position that went against you, it would eventually come back. I try to teach people not to have any preconceived notion about the market direction—to react to the market, not to anticipate it.

One hedge group that I worked with would wait for a trade to set up before taking a long position. If it didn't set up, they wouldn't do anything. So they were either long or on the sidelines. I finally got them to change, so that when conditions were unfavorable for a long position, they would go short instead of staying neutral. It worked, and they made a lot of money, but they couldn't stand being short. In their minds, the market went down, so it must be a buying opportunity. Well, guess what—they reversed to long, and the market just kept on going down. Even their language reflected their bias. When they referred to the market decline, they used the word "correction," not "downtrend." It never occurred to them that we might actually be in a bear market.

Has the bear market affected your trading at all?

Not at all; as long as I have volatility, I'm fine. A true trader can make money in any environment as long as he reacts and doesn't anticipate. He must feel the markets flow and never fight. He may often be wrong, but never inflexible.

ALPHONSE "BUDDY" FLETCHER JR.

Win-Win Investing

Every investment expert knows that you can't achieve high returns, say an average of 40 or 50 percent per year, without taking on significant risk. Apparently, no one ever bothered to explain this basic concept to Alphonse Fletcher Jr. Otherwise he would have known better than to try to generate consistent high returns, with hardly any losing months, as he has done since placing his first trade thirteen years ago.

Fletcher began his financial career at Bear Stearns as a researcher and trader of the firm's own funds. After two very successful years, he was lured away to a similar position at Kidder Peabody.* Although he loved working at Bear Stearns and was very reluctant to leave, Kidder's job offer was just too lucrative to turn down. In addition to his salary, Kidder promised Fletcher a 20 to 25 percent bonus on his trading profits.

In his first year at Kidder, Fletcher made over $25 million for the firm. Instead of the $5-million-plus bonus he had anticipated, however, Kidder paid him $1.7 million, with a promise to make additional deferred payments over the next few years. When Fletcher protested that the company was reneging on its deal with him, he was told he shouldn't complain because he was "one of the highest paid black males" in the country. One company officer is alleged to have commented that the bonus Kidder was obligated to pay Fletcher was "simply too much money to pay a young black man." These quotes were taken from the court transcripts in the suit that Fletcher brought against his former employer with

*The facts related to Fletcher's employment at Kidder Peabody were obtained from court-case summaries and articles appearing in *Business Week* (October 24, 1994), *The New Yorker* (April 29 and May 6, 1996), and *Fortune* (July 5, 1999).

other specifics derived from published articles; Fletcher himself was very reluctant to discuss the details of the episode. Fletcher was ultimately awarded an additional $1.26 million by an arbitration panel. After leaving Kidder, Fletcher founded his own firm, Fletcher Asset Management.

I visited Fletcher on one of those brutally hot, humid New York City summer afternoons. I always prefer to walk in cities whenever possible as opposed to taking taxis or public transportation. But I was running a bit late for my scheduled interview with Fletcher, so I hopped a cab. The midtown traffic was horrendous. After going two short blocks in five minutes, about one-third of my normal walking pace, I handed the driver a $5 bill and jumped out, still a mile and a half from my destination.

By the time I arrived at Fletcher Asset Management, I must have looked as if I had walked through a shower. The offices are located in a 120-year-old limestone townhouse on the Upper East Side. I stepped through the large, heavy wooden door, moving from the heat and noise of the modern city into a cool, quiet, and elegant interior. The entranceway led to a large circular reception area with soaring ceilings and a handcrafted spiral wooden staircase that rose to the offices on the four upper floors. The walls were painted in warm, rich complementary colors, which when combined with the lofty ceilings, wide ornamental moldings, and antique furniture created an atmosphere of a different time and place, far removed from New York City circa 1999. If I were filming a movie with a scene at an old-line Swiss investment firm catering to clients with tens or hundreds of millions of dollars, this would be the perfect set.

I was led into a library that served as a waiting room and was offered a large pitcher of ice water, which I rapidly gulped down as soon as the attendant left the room. After about ten minutes, I was escorted up the staircase to Fletcher's office.

It is clear that Fletcher has deliberately created an environment that is in striking contrast to the typical modern Manhattan office. The result is very effective in creating a tranquil sanctuary from the frenzy of the city outside, with a sense of style that must send a subliminal message to investors: your money will be safe here.

Fletcher, however, doesn't need impressive offices to attract investors. His performance results almost defy belief. That is not to say that he has the highest returns around—not by a long shot. However, those who look only at returns suffer from extreme naïveté. It is not return that matters, but rather return relative to risk. Here Fletcher shines. The Fletcher Fund, his flagship fund, founded in September 1995, has realized an average annual compounded return of 47 percent. Although this is quite impressive on its own, here is the kicker: He has achieved this return with only four losing months, the largest of these being a minuscule 1.5 percent decline.

Fletcher's track record prior to launching his fund is, if anything, even more astounding. During the first four years of its existence, Fletcher's firm, which was founded in 1991, primarily traded its own proprietary account. This account, which was traded at much higher leverage than his fund, garnered an incredible average annual compounded return of 380 percent during that period. (Although returns in these earlier years are not published or reported in any way because they represent a proprietary account, the figures have been audited.)

When I first saw Fletcher's track record, I couldn't conceive how he could achieve such a substantial return with virtually no risk. In our meeting, he explained exactly how he does it. Yes, in reading this chapter, you will find out as well. However, so as not to create false expectations, I will tell you at the outset that his methods are not duplicable by ordinary investors. Even so, why would he reveal what he does? The answer is explained in the interview.

★

When did you first develop an interest in the markets?

It probably started when I was in junior high school and my father and I worked on developing a computer program to pick winners at the dog racetrack. *[He laughs robustly at the memory.]*

Did you have any success trying to forecast dog races?

Oh yes. The computer would eliminate one set of races it couldn't predict. In the remaining races, the program had an 80 percent accuracy rate in picking a dog that would place in the money [win, place, or show].

That's pretty impressive. How much money did you make?

I learned an interesting lesson about odds: winning 80 percent of the time may not be enough if the odds are not right. I forget the exact number, but the track takes about 40 percent or more off the table.

Wow, that's incredible—that even makes slot machines look good!

So even though we won 80 percent of the time, it still wasn't enough to make any money.

What information were you using to predict the race outcome?

All the information that comes in the racing program—finish times for the dogs in different races, positions at different poles, weather conditions, etc.

How did you try to solve this problem? Did you use multiple regression?

Hey, remember I was only in junior high.

When did you actually get involved with stocks?

When I was in college, I had a summer job with Pfizer, and they had an employee program that allowed you to buy stock in the company for a 25 percent discount. That sounded like a great deal to me. Ironically, as we fast-forward to the present, both of these principles—the computerized analysis of odds and buying stock at a discount—are hallmarks of what we do today. Of course, I don't mean this literally, since we don't buy stocks at a discount, and we don't make bets on who's going to be the winner. Nevertheless, those concepts tie into our current strategies in a remarkable way.

Let's go back to your origins. How did you actually get involved in trading the market?

I graduated Harvard with a math degree. At the time, everyone was going into M.B.A. programs or Wall Street.

As a math major at Harvard, I assume that you must have had phenomenal SAT scores.

Let's just say that I did very well. The funny thing is that I didn't take any of the SAT preparatory courses. I prefer to figure out things for myself rather than learn the tricks of the trade. I'm still like that today. Sometimes I play word or math games for fun.

For example.

This is my latest thing. *[He picks up an abacus.]* I have no interest in reading instructions on how to use it, but I am intrigued by the idea of trying to figure it out for myself. I want to work out what algorithm you would use to do addition, subtraction, multiplication, and division on this instrument.

Did you plan to go to Wall Street when you finished college?

No, actually I planned to go into the air force

Why the air force?

I had been in air force ROTC in college, and the idea of becoming a weapons officer and being responsible for all the new high-tech equipment appealed to me.

Did you join the air force?

No. In the late 1980s, there were significant cuts in the defense budget. In order to reduce the number of personnel, the air force encouraged us to go into the reserves. A good friend convinced me to look for a job on Wall Street. I was offered a position at Bear Stearns and fell in love with the place. They in turn virtually adopted me. I don't know what the magic was, but Elliot Wolk, who was a member of the board of directors and the head of the options department, took a liking to me.

Were any of your courses at Harvard helpful in preparing you for the real world?

In my senior year, I took a graduate-level course in financial engineering. I did my project on the options market and found it fascinating. I tried to model what would happen if an option price was forced away from its theoretical value, say because someone placed a large buy or sell order that moved the market. My results convinced me that I had found a way to consistently capture profits in the options market. The idea that I could develop a model that would consistently make money in options, however, went against all the theory I had learned about the markets.

From that comment I take it that, at the time, you believed in the efficient market hypothesis, as it was taught at Harvard.

Yes indeed *[he laughs loudly]*. In many respects, I still believe it, but as you'll see, there is an interesting other side.

You believe it—in what sense? After all, your own performance seems to belie the theory that markets are perfectly efficient.

If IBM is trading at $100 right now, it's probably worth $100. I think it is very difficult to outsmart liquid markets.

You mean by using a methodology that depends on getting the future price direction right?

That's correct.

So where doesn't the efficient market hypothesis apply—say in your own case?

My analysis implied that it was possible to implement offsetting trades, in which the total position had little or no risk and still provided a profit opportunity. In the real world, such discrepancies might occasionally occur because a large buy or sell order might knock a specific option or security out of whack with the rest of the market. In a theoretical model, however, it should be impossible to show a consistent risk-free opportunity if the efficient market hypothesis is correct. As it turned out, my model was right. In fact, it was the basis for the very first trade I did for Bear Stearns, and it was very lucrative for them.

What was this virtually risk-free market opportunity that you say was consistently available?

The concept was based on the cost of financing. Sure IBM is worth whatever it's trading at. However, let's say that I can earn 7 percent on my money, and you can earn 9 percent on your money. Given the assumption of our having different rates of return on our money, I should be able to buy IBM and sell it to you at a future date for some agreed price, and we would both be better off. For example, I might buy IBM at $100 and agree to sell it to you for $108 one year from now. I would make more than my 7 percent assumed alternative rate of return, and you would lock in ownership of IBM at less than your assumed opportunity cost of 9 percent annualized. The transaction would be mutually beneficial.

Wouldn't arbitrage drive that opportunity away?

Arbitrage will only eliminate opportunities where we both have the same costs of funds. If, however, your cost of funds is significantly higher or lower, then there will be an opportunity. In a more general sense, the markets might be priced very efficiently if everyone had the same costs of funds, received the same dividend, and had the same transaction costs. If, however, one set of investors is treated very differently, and persistently treated differently, then it should be possible to set up a transaction that offers a consistent profit opportunity.

Give me a specific example.

Instead of IBM, say we're talking about an Italian computer company. Assume that because of tax withholding, U.S. investors receive only 70 cents on the dollar in dividends, whereas Italian investors receive the full dollar. If this is the case, a consistent arbitrage becomes available, wherein a U.S. investor could sell the stock to an Italian investor, establish a hedge, and after the dividend has been paid, buy it back at terms that would be beneficial to both parties.

It almost sounds as if you are performing a service. If I understand you correctly, you find buyers and sellers who have different costs or returns, due to a distortion, such as differences in tax treatment. You then devise a transaction based on this difference in which each party ends up better off, and you lock in a profit for performing the transaction.

Exactly. The key word you used was *service*. That's one of the key reasons why the results we have delivered are so different from those of traditional investment managers, who buy and sell and then hope for the best.

How could you ever lose in that type of transaction?

Very easily. It is very important that there is a real economic trade in which the Italian investor actually buys the shares and is the holder of those shares at the time of the dividend payment. If that's the case, then there are real transactions, with real exposure to economic gains and losses, and something can go wrong. For example, if there is an adverse price movement after the trade and before we can fully implement the hedge, then we could lose money.

The trading opportunity based on the option model you developed in college, however, was obviously different, since it only involved U.S. markets. What was the idea behind that strategy?

In my model, I was using two different interest rates. I found that assumption led to a consistent profit opportunity.

Why were you using two different interest rates?

I used the risk-free interest rate [T-bill rate] to generate theoretical option values, and I used a commercial interest rate to reflect the perspective of an option buyer who had a cost of borrowing funds that was greater than the risk-free rate. As a consequence of using two different rates, trading opportunities appeared.

What precisely was the anomaly you found?

The market was pricing options based on a theoretical model that assumed a risk-free rate. For most investors, however, the relevant interest rate was the cost of borrowing, which was higher. For example, the option-pricing model might assume a 7 percent interest rate while the investor might have an 8 percent cost of borrowing. This discrepancy implied a profit opportunity.

What was the trading strategy implied by this anomaly?

An option box spread.

[If you are one of the few readers who understands this, congratulations. If, however, you think an option box spread is a quilt design, a sexual position, or some other equally accurate conjecture, don't worry about it. Any explanation I might attempt would only serve to confuse you further. Take my word for it. For the purpose of what follows, it is sufficient to know that an option box spread is a trade that involves the simultaneous implementation of four separate option positions.]

Given the substantial transaction costs (commissions plus bid/ask differentials), is this trade applicable in the real world?

You're quite right. Normally, the interest rate differences are not sufficiently wide to offer any consistent opportunity once trading costs are taken into account. The key point, however, is that there are exceptions, and it is these exceptions that provide the profit opportunity. For example, a corporation that has a large capital loss would have to pay the full tax rate on interest income, but would not have any tax obligation if they earned the equivalent income in an option trade [because the capital gain on the option trade would be offset by their existing capital loss]. Assume their short-term interest rate is 8 percent and they can implement an option box spread at levels that imply the same 8 percent return. Although it is the same return, the corporation would be much better off because the return is a capital gain instead of interest income. To them, the return would look more like 11 percent.

Where do you get your income on the trade?

Initially, we made money either by implementing the transaction for the corporation and charging a commission, or by taking the other side of the trade. The difference in the tax treatment of different parties is what creates the profit opportunity. I would add that although the examples I have given you used illustrations in which the economic profits were enhanced by tax benefits, most of our trades are not tax-related.

What was your job at Bear Stearns?

I had no specific responsibilities; I was just told to figure out how to add value to the company. I started a couple of months before the 1987 stock crash. While all my friends are trading stocks and bonds, and the market is crashing and layoffs are going on, I'm sitting there without any specific responsibility and a mission to figure out how to make money in the Bear Stearns style.

And exactly what is that?

To commit very little capital, take on very little risk, and still make a significant return consistently. And if you can't do that, they don't want to put their money into the trade. They are a very smart firm.

Even though you were left to come up with your own ideas, you must have had an immediate superior.

Sure, Elliot Wolk.

Did you learn anything from him?

A great deal. One useful piece of advice he gave me, which summarized the philosophy of Bear Stearns was: Never make a bet you can't afford to lose. My extreme aversion to risk traces back to Bear Stearns. To this day, I am deeply appreciative of the opportunity they gave me and for what I learned at the firm.

Why did you leave Bear Stearns?

Kidder made me a great offer. It was really hard to leave. My initial intentions were to stay at Bear Stearns for my whole career.

Was this the proverbial deal you couldn't refuse?

Yes.

Did Bear Stearns try to counteroffer?

I met with Ace Greenberg, Bear Stearns's CEO at that time, over the course of two days, but his only real response was advice. He told me that the deal sounded too good to be true and that I should just continue to make my bet with Bear Stearns. It turns out that he was right. It's a shame, because I was really excited about going to Kidder Peabody. Not only did the firm have a great history, but the opportunities that existed with General Electric as the majority shareholder were truly remarkable. Unfortunately, some misunderstandings and miscommunication with management caused an uncomfortable situation. At that point, it was best for me to just leave.

I already know the situation you're talking about. It was amply reported in the press. I prefer to get the story directly from you, however, as opposed to secondhand. I also know that the resulting legal suits were resolved, and therefore there is no legal restriction to your talking about the case.

The only restriction is that I really love not to dwell on it *[he laughs]*. I am glad it is all over. Kidder was great for me in many ways and bad for me in many ways. Essentially, they offered me a great deal to come over, and then the deal changed. Then they said a number of things that were very insensitive and impolite. So I left them and won the arbitration on the contract dispute. A suit on race discrimination ended up being unsuccessful—good riddance.

[Based on public documents, this suit was not lost on the merits of the discrimination case, but rather because the New York Court of Appeals ruled that the standard registration form signed by Fletcher as a condition of employment compelled arbitration. Although the court ruled against Fletcher's petition because it felt such a decision was dictated by the letter of the law, the written opinion appeared to reflect a reluctant tone: "We stress that there is no disagreement among the members of this court about the general proposition that racial, gender, and all other forms of invidious discrimination are ugly realities that cannot be countenanced and that should be redressable through the widest possible range of remedies . . ."]

If you don't mind my asking, other than this particular episode, have you encountered prejudice elsewhere in the industry?

I have definitely experienced some things, but it is usually more subtle. I really prefer not to dwell on it.

I'm just curious whether prejudice is still a factor.

Frankly, whenever there's a difficult situation, race is always one of those easy cards to play. For example, if someone is envious. Usually, nothing is direct. Ultimately it's a very subtle issue, and you never know for sure. Someone acts in a certain way, and you think it is one thing, but eventually you find out that it's not. In the last eight years, I haven't seen anything . . . actually, I guess I have seen a number of things that are somewhat direct *[laughing]*. My view is that as long as I do the best I can for the people who put their trust in me—my investors, my employees, and the companies I invest in—then everything else will take care of itself.

When I read about the whole episode, I thought it was pretty gutsy of you to bring a legal suit instead of taking a settlement. I assume that you just wanted to fight back.

I didn't want to be adversarial, but they were sooo . . . . You got me talking about it; I didn't want to talk about it. *[He laughs long and hard.]* Kidder was great, GE was great, and I really wanted to be there for a long time. If they had said to me, "We're going to pay you half the amount we agreed to, and we'll work out the remainder," I probably could have lived with that. I wouldn't have minded those issues if they were prepared to let me be part of the team and really participate and contribute going forward. But far worse than the compensation issue was the treatment—the attitude that I didn't belong and some of the comments from senior management.

So it wasn't just one person.

No, it wasn't just one person.

But what's odd is that you did so well for them.

Sometimes, I think that makes it worse.

But that's what I don't understand. They hired you. It's not as if they suddenly discovered you are black. Oh well, I guess there is

no reason to expect prejudice to be logical. How did you go about starting your own firm when you left Kidder?

I went back to Ace Greenberg. Bear Stearns set me up with an office and gave me access to its very supportive clearance department, which provided financing and brokerage services for professional investors.

What did Bear Stearns get out of this deal?

I still had very friendly relationships with the people at Bear Stearns. To some extent, they just wanted to help me out. But it was also beneficial to them because they gained a customer. Based on their previous experience with me, I'm sure they assumed that I would generate significant brokerage business for them.

After I left Ace's office, I went downstairs to the computer store and bought myself a Macintosh, which I set up on my dining room table. I constructed the spreadsheets for a transaction opportunity I saw would be feasible over the next few days and then faxed the sheets to a Fortune 50 company for whom I had done similar deals that had worked out well. They liked the idea and gave me the go-ahead. The next day I opened the account at Bear Stearns and did the other necessary preparations for the trade. On the third day, I executed the transaction, and on the fourth day, I went to the bank to open an account for $100 so that I could receive the fee as a wire transfer. In effect, Fletcher Asset Management was funded for $100.

Could you elaborate on the strategies you're using today.

A common theme in all our strategies involves finding someone who is either advantaged or disadvantaged and then capitalizing on their advantage or minimizing their disadvantage. Arbitrage opportunities are very difficult to find without that type of an angle.

We are still pretty active in the dividend capture strategy we talked about earlier. Our primary current activity, however, involves finding good companies with a promising future that need more capital, but can't raise it by traditional means because of a transitory situation. Maybe it's because their earnings were down in the previous quarter and everyone is saying hands-off, or maybe it's because the whole sector is in trouble. For whatever reason, the company is temporarily disadvantaged. That is a great opportunity for us to step in. We like to approach a company like that and offer financial assistance for some concession.

For example, in a recent deal involving a European software company, we provided $75 million in exchange for company stock. However, instead of pricing the stock at the prevailing market price, which was then $9, the deal was that we could price the stock at a time of our choosing up to three years in the future, but with the purchase price capped at $16. If the price of the stock falls to $6, we will get $75 million worth of stock at $6 per share. If, however, the stock goes up to $20, we will get $75 million worth of stock at a price of $16 per share because that was the maximum we agreed to. In effect, if the stock goes down we're well protected, but if the stock goes up a lot, we have tremendous opportunity.

Are you then totally eliminating the risk?

The risk is reduced by a very significant amount, but not totally. There is still risk if the company goes bankrupt. This risk, however, is small because we are only selecting companies we consider to be relatively sound. In fact, a senior officer of one of the companies we previously invested in is now part of our own staff and helps us evaluate the financial prospects of any new investments. With this expertise in-house, it would be rare for us to choose a company that went bankrupt.

The logic of the transaction is pretty clear to me. As long as the company doesn't go bankrupt, if the stock goes down, stays about unchanged, or goes up moderately, you will at least break even, and if it goes up a lot, you can make a windfall gain. Although there is nothing wrong with that, doesn't it imply that the vast majority of times these transactions will end up being a wash and that significant profits will occur only sporadically? Why wouldn't you end up with an equity curve that is fairly flat most of the time, with only occasional upward spikes?

Two reasons. First, the money we invest in the company doesn't just lie idle; it generates annual income—8.5 percent using the example we just discussed—until we price the stock. Second, since the maximum price we will have to pay for the stock is capped—$16 in our example—we can sell out-of-the-money calls against this position, thereby guaranteeing an additional minimum revenue.

[By selling options that give buyers the right to buy the stock at a specified price above the current price, Fletcher gives up part of his windfall profit in the event the stock price rises sharply. But, in exchange, he collects premiums (that is, the cost of the options) that augment his income on the deal regardless of what happens to the stock price.]

But are there always traded options in the companies you are financing through these stock purchase agreements?

Well, it's not always possible to get a perfect hedge. But even when there are no options traded for the specific company, we can sometimes use private "over-the-counter" options. We can also use index options against a basket of companies in our transactions. The assumption is that if the stock index rises a lot, then the stocks of the companies we have invested in are likely to rise sharply as well. In fact, since we are buying stocks that have been under pressure and are more speculative in nature, if the market does well, these stocks may rise more than the average.

Taking into account the interest income and the option-selling income, it appears that you are virtually guaranteed to make at least a moderate profit on every transaction of this kind, and only lose in the disaster scenario.

Even in the disaster scenario, which again is unlikely because of the way we select our stocks, we can still sometimes protect ourselves by buying out-of-the-money puts, which at the strike prices implied by a bankruptcy are pretty cheap.

How long have you been employing this type of strategy?

For about seven years, and it has now grown to become our single most important market activity. The strategy actually evolved from the dividend capture strategy. [The strategy described previously in Fletcher's example of U.S. investors holding shares in an Italian computer company.] One variation of the dividend capture strategy is dividend reinvestment, wherein companies allow shareholders to reinvest their dividends in the stock at a discounted price. We have been very active in buying shares from parties who did not want to be bothered with reinvestment. We would therefore be the recipient of

$1 million of dividends and then elect to reinvest it, receiving $1.05 million of newly issued stock.

Why would a company give you more stock than the amount of the dividend?

Because the companies that provided this offer wanted to conserve their capital and were willing to grant shareholders a 5 percent discount as an incentive to reinvest their dividends in the stock.

Is it common for companies to offer this type of dividend reinvestment?

It is popular among companies with high dividends who don't want to cut their dividends but need to preserve capital. For example, it was particularly prevalent among the banks in the early 1990s when they were trying to increase their equity.

Eventually, some companies started to offer shareholders the option to purchase additional discounted shares in an amount equivalent to the dividend reinvestment. Then some companies began waiving limits, allowing investors to buy virtually any amount of stock at a discounted price.

In the early 1990s, many banks were actively pursuing this type of program, and we participated heavily. That experience led us to going to a major U.S. electronics company in 1992 in what proved to be our first private equity funding deal. At the time, this company couldn't raise capital through a stock offering because they'd had a bad quarter and the prevailing attitude was: "I don't want to buy newly issued stock from that company." That's probably the best time to buy newly issued stock. When do you want to buy it—after they've reported record earnings *[he laughs]*? But that's the way it works, and it was a perfect opportunity for us to step in and say here's the check.

We told the company that we would buy $15 million worth of stock from them over a period of time. We stressed that we wanted it to be a very friendly and supportive deal. Therefore, instead of buying stock at a discount, we proposed being compensated by an option to buy more stock in the future. In this way, our incentives were perfectly aligned with the interests of management and shareholders. As we discussed earlier, in this type of arrangement, our most significant profit opportunity arises when the company does very well, although because of our hedge, we should be consistently profitable.

We had a wonderful relationship with this company. In fact, their former CFO ended up joining us. He's the one at Fletcher Asset Management who explains who we are to the companies we approach and manages the negotiations and ensuing relationships.

There's no better salesman than a satisfied customer. How did you sell a major corporation on your financing transaction, since you had never done anything like that before?

That's a good question. When I first approached them, we were this tiny firm working out of rented space at Bear Stearns. Their initial reaction was: Who are you? Merrill Lynch couldn't get us a secondary offering, Lazard is our adviser, and you are calling out of the blue to tell us that you can do the deal."

I talked to a neighbor in my apartment building, Steve Rattner, who was a senior banker at Lazard. I told him that I was interested in doing a deal with a company that his firm was advising. I asked him to help me. He made a few phone calls, and the next thing I knew, I was on a flight to Chicago along with a banker from Lazard and our attorney to meet with the company. When the deal was all done, Steve said to me, "That was an extremely interesting transaction. Have you thought about taking on outside capital?"

Didn't the idea of raising outside capital to fund your transactions occur to you before this deal?

Sure, the idea had come up a number of times before. However, every time we considered it, we asked ourselves why we should take money from investors, and give up the bulk of the profits, when we can borrow money to do the deal, and keep 100 percent of the profits?

Exactly, so why did you start a fund open to outside investors?

The big change was realizing that a friend like Steve could get us in the door where such a great transaction could happen. Wouldn't it be nice to have other friends like that who had a vested interest in our success.

So the primary motivation wasn't necessarily raising extra capital, but rather getting investors who would be allies.

Yes, that was the point Steve made that caught my attention. Raising capital, however, did provide some additional benefits over borrowing by allowing us to do many more transactions, thereby reducing our portfolio risk through greater diversification.

Using the U.S. electronics company as an example, I assume that if Steve had not been there, the deal would never have happened.

Exactly. We have some incredibly insightful people as investors whom I can call for advice.

It almost sounds as if you have selected your own investors.

Essentially, we have. We have turned away a number of investors, particularly in the U.S. fund.

If someone comes to you and wants to invest a couple of million dollars, you won't automatically open the account?

Oh no, we have actually researched everyone who wanted to invest before they invested.

So you actually screen your investors.

Yes, investors are screened by either us or our marketing representatives.

And the reason?

If we were just looking to raise as much money as we could, sure, the more the merrier. At this point, we just want supportive investors. It is not worth the trouble having an investor who would be a distraction. Maybe in the future, with other pools of money, we may be less judgmental, but right now we want investors who will be friends and allies.

But, surely, not every investor is someone who will have useful contacts or be a source of advice.

If they are not, though, then they are usually either friends or family. For example, the head trader's mother, who is a retired librarian, is one of our investors, as is my own mother, who is a retired school principal. In fact, eight of our mothers and mothers-in-law are investors in the fund. By the way, our mothers are the most demanding investors.

In what way?

They have no qualms about demanding an explanation for anything, from the reason for a slow start to the year to the reason for a particularly good month.

What prevents competitors from coming in and doing private equity funding deals similar to the ones you did with the U.S. electronics company and the European software company?

They come in all the time. In each of the strategies we have discussed, competition has increased and will continue to do so. That's the nature of the market. Our advantage is that we were there first. What is unique about our firm is that we never imitate someone else's strategy. Another advantage we enjoy is that we try to construct our deals so that they are fair to both the company and us. As a result of our approach, over time we have been able to evolve from doing deals with companies worth several hundred million dollars to companies whose market size is measured in billions.

Even though you have an advantage, with this one core strategy providing most of your profits, what happens if the field becomes sufficiently crowded to reduce the profit margins meaningfully?

Well, we are always working on developing new strategies. Our thinking is: Let the competition move in, we'll be on to the next thing.

For example?

For example, right now we are deliberately using strategies that are uncorrelated with the stock market. There is tremendous demand, however, for an investment program correlated with the stock market that could consistently outperform the S&P 500. I would love to take on that challenge.

A lot of people have come up with the idea of S&P enhancement programs. Haven't any of these enhanced S&P funds been successful?

Even the ones that have come close to doing it haven't quite done it. These funds have attempted to beat the S&P 500 by 1 percent or a few percent, but they have not been consistent.

How do they try to do it?

At one extreme, PIMCO buys S&P futures for the stock exposure and tries to provide the additional 100 basis points return by managing a fixed income portfolio.

Sure, that would work if interest rates are stable or go down. But if interest rates rise, aren't they taking the risk of a loss on their bond portfolio?

Yes, they definitely are. In effect, all they are really doing is taking the active manager risk in the fixed income market as opposed to the equity market.

What other approaches have people used to try to consistently outperform the S&P 500 benchmark?

Some people attempt to beat the S&P 500 by trying to pick the best stocks in each sector. They will balance their sector investments to match the S&P 500, but within each sector they will weight certain stocks more heavily than others. For example, they might weight their portfolio in favor of GM versus Ford, or vice versa, depending on their analysis.

Have you thought of a way of consistently beating the S&P 500?

Oh, sure.

Then why haven't you started trading it as a model program?

We've been very busy. We will probably start it soon.

How did the idea of an S&P 500 enhancement program come to you?

I kept reading about the never-ending debate between those who felt active managers were better and those who felt you couldn't beat the index, implying passive managers were better. I thought it would be really exciting to be able to consistently beat the index.

I understand how the idea for the product occurred to you, but what I am asking is how did you get the idea of how to do it?

I have to be tight-lipped here because we haven't launched this program yet. I was able to talk about our other strategies because the competition has already figured out what we are doing and has begun to move in.

So you haven't initiated this S&P 500 enhancement program yet, but once you do, the competition will know what you're doing.

Then we can talk about it *[he laughs]*.

The strategies you describe sound so well hedged and your risk numbers are so low that I'm curious if you ever had a trade that went really bad, and if so, what went wrong?

One of the companies we invested in declared bankruptcy. Our protective strategies worked well, but they can only work up to a limit.

What is the whole story?

Don't make me relive it *[he laughs]*. This is our worst story by far.

The worst story is always more interesting than the best story.

Yes, I always focus on this episode whenever I talk to new investors. The company, which was a marketer of prepaid phone cards, needed financing. Although the deal was marginal, we decided to do it. Two weeks after the deal was completed, the company announced that all their financial statements were wrong and would be revised for the past two years. The stock dropped over 70 percent overnight. It happened so quickly that we didn't have time to get our hedges fully in place. Although the company still had a viable business and assets, they declared bankruptcy to facilitate the sale of virtually all of their assets to another company.

How did you extricate yourself from this situation?

Fortunately, part of our deal was secured, placing us first in line in the bankruptcy proceedings. We have already recovered a large chunk of our capital and have a claim pending for more. If our due diligence is done correctly, then the companies we invest in should have significant liquidation value, which was the case here—the acquiring company wrote a check for more than $100 million. Of course, although the assets are there, we don't know how much more money, if any, we will recover on our claim.

What did you learn from this whole experience?

The fact that the company negotiated aggressively for granting us less protection than is the case for our normal deals should have acted as a warning signal. The blindsiding that came from the financial restatement was really brutal, but I don't know how that could have been avoided.

You've grown from a one-man shop to a thirty-plus-person firm. What have you learned about the process of hiring people since you started your company?

One of the best things I learned since starting a business was how to hire the right people. I used to hire anyone who insisted they were right for the job. If we had an open slot and someone said, "No problem, I could do that job," I would hire that person because I knew that if *I* said that, I could do it. Through experience I learned that most people who try to aggressively talk their way into a position can't do the job.

What have you changed in your hiring practices?

The people who have worked out best are the people that I had done business with successfully for years before I recruited them to join us. Literally, I went after them; they didn't come after me. That's been the big difference.

Fletcher's initial success came from a brilliant insight: *Even if the markets are efficient*, if different investors are treated differently, it implies a profit opportunity. Every strategy he has employed, at its core, has been based on a discrepancy in the treatment of different parties. For example, the profit opportunities in his current primary strategy—private equity funding—are made possible by the fact that some companies have much greater difficulty attracting investment funds than other companies with equivalent long-term fundamentals. By identifying these temporarily out-of-favor companies, Fletcher can structure a financing deal that offers these firms funds at a lower cost than they can find elsewhere while at the same time providing him with a high-probability, low-risk profit opportunity.

The two other main themes to Fletcher's trading success are *innovation* and *risk control*. Although the specifics of Fletcher's approach are not directly applicable to ordinary investors, these two principles still represent worthy goals for all market participants.

Update on Alphonse "Buddy" Fletcher Jr.

During the bear market, Fletcher was successful in preserving capital, but not in maintaining his returns. Measured from the start of the bear market (April 2000) through September 2002, Fletcher's original fund managed only a minuscule 2 percent cumulative return. Still, this performance compares very favorably with the equity markets, which saw contemporaneous cumulative declines of 45 percent in the S&P 500 and 75 percent in the Nasdaq.

Since the start of the bear market a little over two years ago, your flagship fund is up only a few percentage points. That's a lot

better than the indices, but before the advent of the bear market, was your goal to merely preserve capital during a protracted decline in equity prices, or did you expect to still make a double-digit return annually?

The insurance provided by our hedges allows us to successfully preserve capital. It does not, however, generate quality investment opportunities. Although we are seeing many more opportunities to invest directly in companies, interestingly, the number of acceptable opportunities has declined, leaving us with returns well below the historic average for our aggressive funds. Our more çonservative income arbitrage fund, however, has continued to perform, with the annualized return averaging near 9 percent since the start of the bear market.

What have you learned during the past two-plus years of a bear market that you didn't know or fully appreciate before?

It's more a matter of reinforcement than learning. The market of the past two years has underlined the importance of our emphasis on liquidity and the virtue of patience. We can't control when acceptable opportunities will appear, but we can certainly try to preserve our capital until those opportunities arrive.

An essential element of your core strategy is providing financing to companies. The accuracy of the company books is therefore very critical to your approach. In this light, have you been hurt by any instances of accounting deceptions that now seem to be coming to light in an almost routine fashion?

An essential element of our strategies is to invest directly in companies, and fortunately we have not been hurt by these current accounting incidents. Long before this current rash of scandals, we concluded that not every company's financial statements are complete and accurate. This skeptical approach has helped us avoid some problems.

AHMET OKUMUS

From Istanbul to Wall Street Bull

When Ahmet Okumus was sixteen years old, he visited the trading floor of the recently opened Istanbul Stock Exchange and was mesmerized. He was fascinated by trading, which on the Istanbul exchange resembled speculating far more closely than investing. It wasn't long before his initial enthusiasm became an obsession, and he began cutting classes regularly to trade stocks on the exchange.

Okumus knew that he wanted to become a money manager and realized that the country that offered the greatest opportunity for achieving his goal was the United States. In 1989, he immigrated to the United States, ostensibly to attend college but with the firm conviction that this was just a stepping-stone to his true career objective. Using a $15,000 stake from his mother, Okumus began trading U.S. stocks in 1992. This original investment had mushroomed to over $6 million by early 2000, an average annual compounded return of 107% (gross returns). In 1997, he launched his first hedge fund, the Okumus Opportunity Fund.

I interviewed Okumus at his Manhattan office, a distinctly unimpressive space. Coming off the elevator, I was greeted by a receptionist who did not work for Okumus but who clearly was shared by all the tenants on the floor. Okumus's office was small, badly in need of a paint job, and outfitted with ugly furniture. The single window offered little visual relief, providing a claustrophobic view of the side of the adjacent building. The office had one redeeming feature: it was cheap—actually, free (a perk for commission business). Okumus is evidently proud of this. Talking about how he got great deals on everything from his office space to his accountant, he says, "It's my nature. I love to get good deals. I don't pay up." It is a comment that is equally fitting as a description of his trading philosophy.

At the time of my interview, Okumus shared his small office with his college buddy, Ted Coakley III, whom he brought in to do marketing and assorted administrative tasks. (A subsequent expansion in staff necessitated a move to larger quarters.) Coakley's faith in Okumus is based on personal experience. In college, he was Okumus's first investor, giving him $1,000 to invest (in two $500 installments)—an investment that grew to over $120,000 in seven years.

Prior to 1998, Okumus's worst year was a gain of 61 percent (gross return). In 1998, a year when the S&P rose by 28 percent, he finished the year with only a minuscule 5 percent gain. I began my mid-1999 interview by questioning him about his uncharacteristically lackluster performance in 1998.

★

What happened last year?

It all happened in December. At the start of the month, I was up 30 percent for the year. I thought the rise in Internet stocks was a mania. Valuations had risen to levels we had never seen before. For example, Schwab has been publicly traded for over ten years. At the time I went short, the ratios of the stock price to the valuation measures—sales per share, earnings per share, cash flow [earnings plus depreciation and amortization] per share, book value per share—were higher than they had ever been before. [As he talks about these events, the pain of the experience is still very evident in his voice.]

What levels were these ratios at?

As an example, the price/earnings ratio was at 54 to 1. In comparison, at prior price peaks in the stock, the ratio had been anywhere from 20 to 1, to 35 to 1.

The valuation measures were at record highs and getting higher all the time. What made you decide to go short at that particular juncture?

Insiders [company management] were selling heavily. In Schwab, insiders always sell, but in this instance, the insider sales were particularly high.

Out of curiosity, why are insiders always net sellers in Schwab?

Because the company issued a lot of options to management, which get exercised over time.

What happened after you went short?

The stock went up 34 percent in one week and was still going up when I finally covered my position.

What other Internet or Internet-related stocks did you short in December 1998?

Amazon.

How can you even evaluate a company like Amazon, which has no earnings and therefore an infinite price/earnings ratio?

You can't evaluate it in any conventional sense. However, I had an idea of what price it shouldn't be, and Amazon was at that level. When I went short, Amazon's capitalization [the share price multiplied by the number of shares outstanding] was $17 billion, which made it equivalent to the fourth largest retailer in the United States. This seemed absurd to me.

Also, book sales fall off sharply during the first quarter following the heavy Christmas season sales. I thought the prospect of lower sales in the next quarter would cause the stock to weaken. When I went short, Amazon was up ninefold during the prior year and fourfold during the previous two months.

At what price was Amazon trading when you went short?

I didn't actually go short. I sold out-of-the-money call options. [In this transaction, the option seller collects a premium in exchange for accepting the obligation to sell the stock at a specific price above the market price.*] Since the options I sold were way out-of-the-money, the market could still go up a lot, and I wouldn't lose. I thought I might be wrong and the stock could go up some more, but I didn't think the stock would go up *that* much.

*Readers unfamiliar with options may find it useful to consult the short primer on options in the appendix.

What was the strike price of the options you sold?* Where was the market at the time?

The stock was trading around 220, and I sold the 250 calls. The stock could go up another 30 points before I lost any money on the trade.

How much did you sell the options for?

I sold them for 1⅛, but there were only three days left until expiration. I figured the stock was not going to go up 15 percent in three days. The day after I went short, one of the prominent analysts for the stock revised his price projection, which had already been surpassed by the market, from $150 to $400. Overnight, the stock moved from 220 to 260, and one day later it nearly reached 300. The options I had sold for 1⅛ were selling for 48. [Options trade in 100-share units. Therefore, each option he had sold for $112 was now worth $4,800.]

How much did you lose on that trade?

The trade killed me. Amazon cost me 17 percent of my equity, and Schwab cost me another 12 percent.

Had you used this type of strategy before—selling out-of-the-money calls?

Sure, but these types of price moves were totally unprecedented. There are a lot of Internet stocks that are up twenty- or thirtyfold during the past year, but I'm not touching them. I'm just sticking to what I know best: fundamentals and value.

What lesson did you learn from this entire experience?

Not to short Internet stocks *[he laughs]*.

Any broader lessons?

Don't get involved when there is too much mania. Just stick to things that have some predictability. You can't forecast mania. If a stock that should be selling at 10 is trading at 100, who is to say it can't go to 500.

What was your emotional state during this entire experience?

The funny thing is that I was already upset at the start of December because the year was almost over, and I was up only 25 percent, which was my worst year ever. After I took the loss on Schwab and Amazon

*The strike price is the price at which the option buyers could buy the stock by exercising their options. Of course, they would exercise their options only if the market price was above the strike price at the time of the option expiration.

and was barely up for the year, I was devastated. I remember going to Bloomingdale's with my girlfriend and not being able to stay in the store because every time I saw a price sign, it reminded me of the stock market. After ten minutes, I just had to leave. For about a week after I got out of these trades, I couldn't look at the *Investor's Business Daily* section that showed how the market was doing to date.

Was this your worst emotional experience in the market?

Absolutely. It was by far the worst experience; I had never felt like that before.

But when I look at your track record, I see that December 1998, when you lost 16 percent, was only your second worst month and was far eclipsed by August 1998, when you lost a staggering 53 percent. How come August 1998, which seems so much worse on paper, doesn't register on your emotional barometer?

The reason my August 1998 decline was so large was that I was caught 200 percent long during the month's big stock market decline. Even though I was down much more during August, I was confident in the fundamentals of my stocks. They were just selling at ridiculously low valuations. The price/earnings ratio of my portfolio was only 5. Some of the stocks I was long were even selling below net cash—you never see that. I knew the stocks I held were absolute bargains and that they couldn't stay that low for long. I wasn't worried about their going down much further. In contrast, in December I lost money because I was short Internet stocks, and there was no way to know when they would stop going up.

So the difference between August and December was your confidence level: In August you felt completely confident, even though you lost much more, and in December you felt out of control.

Exactly.

Even though you recovered August's entire huge loss in only two months, do you consider it a mistake to have put yourself in a position of being 200 percent long during a bear market?

Yes. This led to one of the three changes I made to my trading rules at the start of 1999. The first, which we discussed before, was don't participate in mania. The second was never to have more than a 100 percent *net* position, either long or short. [In August 1998 Okumus had been 200 percent long and 0 percent short, or 200 percent *net* long.]

What was the third change in your trading rules?

I started using options for the specific purpose of reducing downside volatility.

Was this change a response to investor feedback? Were some of the investors who were impressed by your net returns scared off by the volatility in your returns, especially the 53 percent decline in August 1998?

Yes, the rule changes I made were definitely influenced by investor feedback. Investors told us that they didn't want month-to-month volatility. Consequently, I started focusing much more on month-to-month performance. Before, when I was managing money for only myself, my family, and a few clients, my sole goal was long-term capital appreciation. It was as if I were running a marathon and only concerned about my finish time; I didn't care about the individual split times. Now that I am managing much more money for investors who are concerned about the monthly numbers, it's as though I'm running a marathon, but everyone is paying attention to every hundred meters. As a result, even though my main goal is still long-term capital appreciation, I'm focusing a lot more on the monthly numbers because I want to grow the fund much larger.

How did you first get involved in the stock market?

I was always interested in finance and currencies. As a kid, I would read the sports page of the newspaper, just like my friends, but I also read the financial page. In 1986, they opened the Istanbul Stock Exchange. The newspapers didn't even have a stock market column until 1987. When they did start reporting stock prices, I noticed that the prices changed every day. It got my attention. I figured if you were smart, you could make money off of this because there had to be a reason why prices were changing.

At first, I just followed prices in the paper. Then I realized that the stock exchange was close to my school. One day, I skipped school to go down to the exchange and see how it worked.

Describe the Istanbul Stock Exchange.

It's completely modernized now, but at the time there was a bar across the middle of the room, which separated the spectators from the floor brokers. In the front of the room there were boards with bid and asked prices for each stock.

How many stocks were traded on the exchange at the time?

About thirty.

Was there one floor broker for each stock?

No, the floor brokers worked for different brokerage firms; they could all trade in any stock.

How did you interact with the broker if you wanted to buy or sell a stock?

You would yell, "Hey, come here."

How big was the exchange?

Oh, about ten times bigger than this office [translation: extremely small].

How long did you watch the market before you made your first trade?

I watched it for a few weeks. One of the stocks, a construction company, which I knew was constantly getting new contracts, went down almost every day. This didn't make any sense to me, so I decided to buy some shares. The broker warned me not to buy the stock, assuring me that it was headed lower. But I bought the stock anyway because I knew it was a good company. Within two weeks after I bought it, the stock doubled. That experience really got me hooked. I said to myself that logic works. I realized that stocks moved for a reason, and I was determined to find the reason.

At the time, there was no market research whatsoever. I started doing my own research. The Istanbul Stock Exchange published sheets that showed current and previous year revenues, earnings, debt, and a few other statistics. No one paid any attention to these numbers. Since there were no books or articles available on the stock market, I just tried to interpret the statistics logically.

For example, if a company made $20 profits for every $100 in sales, I assumed it was a good company; if it only made $2 profits on every $100, I figured it wasn't so hot. I looked at the shares outstanding and the amount of profits, and I calculated what I thought the stock should be selling at. In effect, I created the price/earnings ratio for myself. When I came to the United States to attend college, I discovered that the price/earnings ratio and the other statistics I was looking at were the basic data people used to analyze stocks.

Did you continue to be net profitable after your first winning trade?

I did pretty well. Within a year or so, the people at the brokerage firm I was using started listening to me for advice. During this time, the stock market in Turkey went down from 900 to 350 and then back to 900. During the big decline, I managed to more than hold my own, and then when the market went back up, I did very well.

How were you able to make even a small profit during the phase when the stock market was going down sharply?

The stock market in Turkey is very speculative. The exchange has a 10 percent daily price limit. [The maximum permissible daily price move (up or down) in each stock was limited to 10 percent. Typically, when a market reaches limit up, trading will virtually cease, as there will be many buyers, but few sellers. An analogous situation would apply when the market is limit down.] Daily price limits are very common. I had a rule that I would buy a stock if it went down the daily limit three days in a row and then sell it on the first short-term bounce.

In other words, you were taking advantage of speculative excesses. Do you still trade that way?

No, I trade on the fundamentals.

Say you select a stock because you like the fundamentals. How do you decide when to begin buying it? Do you still wait for a sharp sell-off before you buy it?

Not necessarily. I have an idea of the value of the stock in my head, and when the stock goes low enough relative to that price, I'll buy it. For example, say I believe a stock has a value of $35. In order to give myself a wide margin of safety, I might buy it if it goes down to $20.

Do you always wait for the stock to reach your price before you buy it?

Definitely. I am never in a rush. I wait patiently until the stock gets to my number.

Using that approach, I assume you miss a lot of stocks.

Certainly, but my main goal is to make money on every investment, not necessarily to catch every trade. I don't have to make a lot on each trade, as long as I make something. Since 1992, 90 percent of my trades have been winners.

What percent of the stocks you research and decide to buy actually come down to your price?

Not many, maybe 10 to 20 percent. I follow what the other value managers in the industry are doing, and I know why they buy the stocks they do. I'm much stricter on my entries than they are. They may be willing to buy a company at sixteen times earnings, whereas I'm not willing to pay more than twelve. "Buy low and sell high" is something a lot of people say but very few people do. I actually do it.

When did you come to the United States?

I came here in 1989 to attend college. The funny thing is that when I came to the United States, the Turkish stock market, which had gone from 900 to 350 and back to 900 while I was trading it, went from 900 to 4,000 in six months. I was very upset.

Did you come just to attend college, or did you have any thoughts of trying to stay permanently?

My intention from the very beginning was to become a fund manager in the United States. This is the biggest market, and in the United States the sky is the limit, whereas in Turkey, the opportunity is very limited.

Did you ever look at the United States stock market before you came here?

No, but from the first day I arrived in the United States, I started to focus on the U.S. stock market. I wanted to learn what made stocks move.

How did you start?

By reading as much as I could.

What books did you find most beneficial or influential?

I very much liked *Stock Market Logic* by Norman Fosback. For one thing, that book taught me to focus on insider trading [buying and selling by a company's senior management and board of directors], which has become an important element in my approach. I also found books on Warren Buffett's methodology very useful.

What aspect of Warren Buffett's methodology appealed to you?

The concept of determining a stock's value and then buying it at a discount to that number in order to allow for a margin of safety.

What other books did you find useful?

One Up on Wall Street by Peter Lynch gave me an appreciation of the importance of common sense in stock investing. Peter Lynch also pointed out that your odds in a stock are much better if there is significant insider buying.

How do you measure whether insider buying is significant?

I compare the amount of stock someone buys with his net worth and salary. For example, if the amount he buys is more than his annual salary, I consider that significant.

So you're looking at a breakdown of insider buying statistics, not just the total numbers.

I am very detailed. I don't think there is one other person who is more focused on insider activity than I am.

What else is important in interpreting insider trading activity?

You have to make sure that insider buying represents purchases of new shares, not the exercise of options.

Is insider buying an absolute prerequisite, or will you sometimes buy a stock you like that reaches your entry price target, even if there is no insider buying?

Most of the time I won't. I want to see the insiders putting their money in their own company. Of course, if management already owns a significant portion of the company, they don't have to buy more. For example, insiders already own about 65 percent of the shares in J. D. Edwards—a stock I currently like—so I don't need to see any additional buying. In contrast, in some companies, insiders only own about 1 percent of the firm. In companies with low insider ownership, management's primary motivation will be job security and higher bonuses, not a higher stock price.

Do you do your research by computer or manually?

Manually. I think that's the best way because you learn much more.

What is the universe of stocks that you are following?

Anything on the Big Board and Nasdaq.

How many stocks is that, roughly?

About ten thousand.

How can you possibly do research on ten thousand stocks manually?

I spend a hundred hours a week on research. I follow all the stocks that I have researched at one time or another during the past eleven years, which is a substantial number. I also pay close attention to stocks making new fifty-two-week lows. A good company that I've identified from previous research does not have to make a new low for me to get interested. If it is down a lot, even if it doesn't hit a new low, I'm on it.

How are you aware of all the stocks that have witnessed significant declines?

Besides looking at the list of new fifty-two-week lows, the *Daily Graphs* chart book contains about half the stocks I follow, and I review it weekly to see which stocks have declined a lot.

So you're always looking at stocks that have done poorly.

Always. I usually don't even consider buying a stock unless it's down 60 or 70 percent from its high. In the seven years I have traded U.S. stocks, I have never owned a stock that made a new high. I think that must be a pretty unusual statement.

Are you implying that when you flip through the charts, you only pay attention to stocks that have been moving down?

That's correct, with one exception: If the stock has been moving sideways and the earnings have been moving up, I might pay attention.

Then are all the stocks you buy at or near recent lows?

Not all. If it's a company that I know well and the fundamentals are very strong, I might go long, even if the stock is significantly above its low. For example, Microchip Technology is currently at $35, which is well below its high of $50, but also well above last year's low of $15. Even though it's well off its low, I'm still selling puts in the stock because their business is improving tremendously.

Selling puts represents a bullish position. The seller of a put receives a premium for the obligation to buy a stock at a price called the *strike price* during the life span of the option. This obligation is activated if the option is exercised by the buyer, which will happen if the stock price is below the strike price at the option expiration.

For example, assume that a stock is trading at $13 and that a put option on the stock with a $10 strike price is trading at $1. If the stock is trading above $10 when the option expires, the seller will have a $1 profit per share (a $100 profit per option contract, which represents 100 shares). If the stock is trading below $10 at the option expiration, the option will presumably be exercised, and the seller of the option will be required to buy the stock at $10, no matter how low the stock is trading.

Okumus, who typically sells puts with strike prices below the current market price (called out-of-the-money puts), will earn a profit equal to the option premium paid by the option buyer if the stock declines modestly, remains unchanged, or goes up. However, if the stock declines by a wide margin, he will be obligated to buy the stock at an above-market price (the strike price) at the time of the option expiration.

What motivates you to sell puts in a stock instead of just buying the stock?

Any stock that I sell a put on, I am happy if they put me the stock [exercise the put option, requiring Okumus to buy the stock at the strike price]. I don't sell a put on a stock unless I would be happy to own the stock at the strike price.

For example, I'm currently short some $10 puts on J. D. Edwards, which is trading near $13. I hope they put me the stock because I would love to own it at $10. If they do, I'll still have the premium, and if I buy the stock at $10, I know I will make money.

But most of the time when I sell puts, the market never declines enough for the option to be exercised. This, of course, is okay too because I still keep the premium as a profit.

In other words, selling put options is an alternative way for you to be buying stocks. If it doesn't go down to the strike price, you still earn the premium, and if does go down to the strike price, that's also fine because that's the price you would have bought the stock at anyway.

Exactly. By selling puts, I am getting paid by the market while I'm waiting for the stock to come down to my price. Also, for some stocks, it may only be possible to make money by selling puts as opposed to buying the stock.

For example, value stocks have been very much out of favor in recent years. There are stocks that are trading at only five to six times earnings. The earnings are growing, insiders are buying, and the stocks are just sitting there. At the same time, the S&P is going up like crazy. You can't make money by buying these stocks, but you can by selling the puts. If you sell put options, you don't have to be right about the stock going up; all you need in order to make money is for the stock not to go down by much.

Let's say that there is a stock trading at 35, and you decide you would like to be a buyer at 30. Why not always sell the 30 put and collect the premium, since if it went to 30, you would buy it anyway? This way, you would always make the premium as a profit, whether the stock went down to 30 or not.

Because you always have to consider your opportunity costs. If I sell puts, I need to put up margin against the position. Sometimes the premium I could collect for selling the put wouldn't justify tying up the money needed for the position. I could do better investing that money elsewhere.

Let's go back to when you arrived in the United States. You said earlier that you started researching the U.S. stock market when you first came here, which also approximately coincided with the beginning of college. How did you allocate your time between studying for college and studying the stock market?

On average I would say 35 percent school and 65 percent stock market, but the stock market percentage kept going up over time. By the beginning of my senior year, I was devoting 90 percent of my time to the stock market, and I quit school altogether.

Weren't you at all reluctant about quitting college a year before you were going to get your degree?

No, because I just couldn't wait to get started. Also, I was a finance major, and my teachers knew a lot less than I did about the stock market and investing.

What did they teach you in college about the stock market?

They teach you theories, and theories don't work most of the time.

For example?

The efficient market hypothesis [the concept that the market immediately discounts all known information], which in my opinion is ridiculous.

Why is it ridiculous?

Because different market participants will do research of varying quality. The market price will reflect the average assessment of all investors. If you can do research that most other people do not, you might be able to discover something that most of the rest of the market doesn't know and benefit from that knowledge. There are a lot of things that I know about my companies that most other investors don't. Therefore, my evaluation of these companies is not going to be the same as theirs. Why then should a stock always trade at the right price level?

When you buy a stock, do you know where you want to get out before you get in?

Certainly. I always have a target price at which I will get out, assuming the fundamentals haven't changed. If the fundamentals get stronger, however, I might raise my target.

What is this target based on? Is it some specified percent gain?

Yes, a percent gain.

What percent?

It depends how cheaply I buy the stock, but on average 20 to 25 percent.

What you are doing sounds like the exact opposite of Peter Lynch, who says you should go for a "ten-bagger" [buy stocks that you think can increase tenfold]; you're not even going for a double, or even close to it.

I never go for home runs. That's why I should do well in a bear market.

I assume that when you sell a stock, you look to buy it back when it dips.

Certainly, as long as the fundamentals don't change.

But don't you often find yourself taking a moderate profit on a stock, and then the stock never dips enough to give you a chance to repurchase it?

That happens a lot of time, but I don't worry about it. My main goal is not to lose money. If you can make money consistently, you will do just fine.

Most of your trading history has been with a small amount of money. Now that you have started a fund and are doing well, that amount will increase dramatically. How will trading much larger sums of money affect your approach?

It won't change anything. The stocks I buy are all well-known names with lots of liquidity. This is deliberate. When I first started, my attitude was that I had to think big. Therefore I made sure to adopt a style that could be used with much larger sums of money.

The period during which you have traded has coincided with one of the greatest bull markets in history. What happens to your approach if we go into a major bear market?

I hope we get a bear market. All the momentum players will get killed; all the Internet players will get killed; all the growth players will get killed; the value players, however, will do okay. The companies that I buy are already in bear markets. They are trading at five to six times earnings. They don't have room to go much lower. Remember, the stocks that I buy are already down 60 to 70 percent from their highs.

Okay, I could see why you would lose a lot less in a bear market than investors using other approaches. But if the S&P index comes off 20 or 30 percent, I would assume that your stocks would go down as well.

That's fine, I'll just hold. I know the value of my companies. I don't second-guess myself when I make an investment. A lot of other money managers have rules about getting out of their stocks if they go down by some specified amount, say 7 percent or 10 percent. They have to do that because they are not sure about what they are buying. I do tremendous research on any stock that I buy, and I know how much it is worth. In fact, if a stock I buy goes down 10 percent and the fundamentals haven't changed, I might well buy more.

But if you never use any stop-loss points, what happens if a company you buy goes bankrupt? How much of an impact would an event like that have on your portfolio?

It will never happen. I don't buy any companies that have even a remote chance of going bankrupt. I buy companies that have a good balance sheet, a high book value, consistent business track records, good management, and large insider buying ownership. These are not the type of companies that go bankrupt.

How do you know when you are wrong in a position?

If the fundamentals change and the stock no longer meets my criteria for holding it at the current price.

What if the price is going against you, but the fundamentals haven't changed?

Then I will just buy more.

How many different stock positions do you typically hold at one time?

About ten. Simple logic: My top ten ideas will always perform better than my top hundred.

What is the maximum amount of your portfolio that you would allocate to a single stock?

At this point, the maximum I would hold on any single stock is about 30 percent of the portfolio. It used to be as high as 70 percent.

That sounds like an extremely large maximum position on one stock. What happens if you are wrong on that trade?

I make sure that I know the fundamentals and that I am not wrong.

But there may be some reason for a stock going down that you don't know about.

No.

How can you say no for sure?

Because I know the companies I buy. For example, if I buy Viasoft at $7, a company that has $5 per share in cash and no debt, what is my downside—$2?

What is your approach on the short side?

I look for stocks that are trading at a huge multiple to earnings. However, after my experience with Internet stocks last year, I've added a rule that there has to be a catalyst. Now, regardless of how extremely overvalued a stock may be, I won't sell it until there has been a catalyst for change.

So another mistake you made in shorting Amazon and Schwab last year, besides selling into a mania, was selling without a catalyst.

Exactly. Even though those stocks may be overvalued, the direction of the fundamentals is still strong. Although Amazon is not making any money, they continue to grow their revenues and meet their sales targets. As long as this is the case, the market is not going to sell the stock off sharply.

It seems it would be very difficult for you to apply your methodology to the short side. On the long side, you are buying stocks that have already declined sharply and are trading at prices that represent strong value. In other words, you are buying at a point where your risk exposure is relatively low. In contrast, when you are shorting a stock, no matter how high you sell it at, there is always an open-ended risk, which is the exact opposite of your buying approach. How can you even approach the short side?

I make sure that the fundamentals are broken before I go short. Even if Schwab today were trading at a hundred times earning, I wouldn't short it as long as the trend in the fundamentals was still improving. I would wait for the fundamentals to start deteriorating.

But you might get another mania that drives the stock higher, even though the fundamentals are deteriorating.

Once the fundamentals get broken, market manias get broken as well. For example, there was a mania in Iomega a few years ago. Once the fundamentals started to break down, the mania ended.

But how do you deal with the problem of unlimited risk?

All my longs are long-term investments, but my shorts are usually short-term precisely because of the danger of unlimited risk.

How would you rate the quality of Wall Street research?

Not very good.

For what reason?

Most analysts don't have a logical reason why a stock should be at a given price. As long as the company does well, they don't care what the price is. Typically, if a stock reaches their target, they will just raise the target, even though the fundamentals haven't changed.

We have seen an incredible bull market during the 1990s. Is the magnitude of this advance justified by the fundamentals?

For two reasons I think we are witnessing the biggest financial mania ever in the stock market. First, the stock market price/earnings ratio is at a record high level. Second, the average profit margin of companies is at its highest level ever.

What do you mean by profit margin?

The amount of profit per sales. For example, if the profit margin is 20, it means the company is making $20 in profits for every $100 in sales.

Why then is a high profit margin a negative?

Because there is virtually no room for further improvement.

What do you read?

Everything, including financial newspapers and magazines, tons of company reports, and all sorts of trade journals. The trade periodicals I read depend on my existing and prospective positions. For example, last year I owned a company that was making products for urinary disorders, so I read *Urinary Times.*

What is the specific checklist you use before buying a stock?

The stock must meet the following criteria:

1. The company has a good track record in terms of growing their earnings per share, revenues per share, and cash flow per share.
2. The company has an attractive book value [the theoretical value of a share if all the company's assets were liquidated and its liabilities paid off] and a high return on equity.
3. The stock is down sharply, often trading near its recent low. But this weakness has to be due to a short-term reason while the long-term fundamentals still remain sound.
4. There is significant insider buying or ownership.

5. Sometimes a company having a new management team with a good track record of turning companies around may provide an additional reason to buy the stock.

What are the trading rules you live by?

- Do your research and be sure you know the companies that you are buying.
- Buy low.
- Be disciplined, and don't get emotionally involved.

What are your goals?

My goal is to be the best money manager in the industry. After the fund reaches its ten-year anniversary, I hope to have the best track record for the prior ten years, nine years, all the way down to five years. Anything shorter than five years could indicate someone who is just lucky or using a style that is temporarily in favor with the market.

Okumus has developed a trading style that assures he will miss 80 to 90 percent of the winning stocks he identifies and typically realize only a small portion of the advance in the stocks he does buy. He also brags that he has never owned a stock that has made a new high. These hardly sound like characteristics of a great trading approach. Yet these seeming flaws are actually essential elements of his success. Okumus has only one overriding goal: to select individual trades that will have a very high probability of gain and a very low level of risk. To achieve this goal he has to be willing to forgo many winners and leave lots of money on the table. This is fine with Okumus. His approach has resulted in over 90 percent profitable trades and a triple-digit average annual return.

Okumus's bread-and-butter trade is buying a stock with sound fundamentals at a bargain price. He looks for stocks with good growth in earnings, revenues, and cash flow, and significant insider buying or ownership. Strong fundamentals, however, are only half the picture. A stock must also be very attractively priced. Typically, the stocks Okumus buys have declined 60 percent or more off their highs and are trading at price/earnings ratios under 12. He also prefers to buy stocks with prices as close as possible to book value. Very few stocks meet Okumus's combination of fundamental and price criteria. The majority of the stocks that fulfill his fundamental requirements never decline to his buying price. Out of the universe of ten thousand stocks Okumus surveys, he holds only about ten in his portfolio at any given time.

One element of market success frequently cited by Market Wizards, both in this volume and its two predecessors, is the age-old trading adage: Cut your losses short. Yet Okumus's methodology seems to fly in the face of this conventional wisdom. Okumus does not believe in liquidating a stock position because it shows a loss. In fact, if a stock he buys moves lower, he may even buy more. How can Okumus be successful by doing the exact opposite of what so many other great traders advise?

There is no paradox. There are many roads to trading success, although none are particularly easy to find or to stay on. Cutting losses is important only because it is a means of risk control. While all successful traders incorporate risk control into their methodology, not all use cutting losses to achieve risk control. Okumus attains risk control by using an extremely restrictive stock selection process: He buys only financially sound companies that have already declined by well over 50 percent from their highs. He has extreme confidence that the stocks he buys have very low risk at the time he buys them. To achieve this degree of certainty, Okumus passes up many profitable trading opportunities. But because he is so rigorous in his stock selection, he is able to achieve risk control without employing the principle of cutting losses short.

One technique Okumus uses to enhance his performance is the sale of out-of-the-money puts on stocks he wishes to own. He sells puts at a strike price at which he would buy the stock anyway. In this way, he at least makes some profit if the stock fails to decline to his buying point and reduces his cost for the stock by the option premium received if it does reach his purchase price.

Okumus is very disciplined and patient. If there are very few stocks that meet his highly selective conditions, he will wait until such opportunities arise. For example, at the end of the second quarter in 1999, Okumus was only 13 percent invested because, as he stated at the time, "There are no bargains around. I'm not risking the money I'm investing until I find stocks that are very cheap."

Update on Ahmet Okumus

Okumus managed to keep rolling along during the first two calendar years of the bear market, with his flagship fund scoring impressive gains of 49 percent in 2000 and 31 percent in 2001. In 2002, however, Okumus hit a speed bump. Okumus's fund finished September at the low point of a drawdown and down over 40 for the year to date—the same percentage decline as the devastated Nasdaq index and a loss significantly larger than the 29 percent decline in the S&P 500. Even with this huge loss, Okumus remained miles ahead of the indexes in cumulative terms: since inception (August 1997), his fund was up 218 percent compared with declines of 14 percent in the S&P 500 and 26 percent in Nasdaq composite.

Okumus's large losses in 2002 stemmed from two causes. First, he turned bullish for reasons discussed in this follow-up and increased his net long exposure above 100 percent at a time when the equity markets continued to plummet. Second, his analysis indicated that the best bargains were in the technology sector, which is where Okumus concentrated his holdings, and this sector was particularly hard hit during the 2002 decline. At the time this follow-up interview was conducted (August 2002), Okumus was down 21 percent year-to-date—a loss that would nearly double by the end of the following month (the time of this writing).

Okumus buys stocks that he considers to be deeply undervalued. As long as the fundamentals don't change, he will hold these positions regardless of how much prices decline. This approach is both the reason why he experiences periodic large drawdowns as well as the reason why these declines have been followed by huge rebounds. Since its inception in 1997, Okumus's flagship fund has experienced three prior large drawdowns: two equal to 20 percent and one equal to a gargantuan 53 percent. In all three cases, the fund recovered to new highs within two months of the end of the drawdown. Will Okumus repeat with a quick, huge rebound for a fourth time? The answer should be known by the time this book is in print, but I wouldn't bet against him. [Late item: By the time these pages were being proofread one month later, Okumus had recovered the entire year's loss.]

I believe you recently have gone the most net long you have been in some time. Is that right?

That's right, we are the most net long we've been since the summer of 1998.

What is your motivation?

Cheap valuations and insider buying. In technology, we are seeing the largest amount of insider buying in thirteen years. For example, in Sun Microsystems, insiders were sellers for ten years. They stopped selling two quarters ago and bought some shares last quarter. Just yesterday, there was a news item that the chief technology officer bought one million shares!

Have you changed your methodology at all during the bear market?

No, it's exactly the same. We invest just like a businessman buying an asset. If we buy something that's worth $20 at $9, it could go to $6, but as long as we correctly assess the value, we should end up making money.

How much money are you managing now?

Over $500 million.

That's quite a dramatic increase since we did our original interview. At that time, your portfolio was very concentrated. Given the large growth in assets under management, I assume you can't be anywhere near as concentrated as you used to be.

We used to have about ten positions; now it's closer to twenty, including both longs and shorts. The bulk of our assets, however, are still in the top ten positions.

So you are still very concentrated.

As I said, we haven't changed anything.

Although the fundamentals of the companies you hold appear very sound—as you previously phrased it, you are buying $20 of value for $9—isn't there a possibility that the fundamentals you are basing your valuations on could be misleading because of

questionable, or even deceptive, accounting? And since you run a very concentrated portfolio, isn't there the risk that a single event of corporate misrepresentation could have a large negative impact on performance?

No, because we don't buy companies with debt. All of the companies that have been involved in recent scandals have been companies with a ton of debt. They create off balance sheet items or book expenses in the wrong places to hide their debt. Also, insider buying is typically a feature of most of our long-side holdings. How many insiders do you know who buy their company stock before committing a fraud?

You never buy companies with debt?

Never say never. But we buy companies with debt less than 10 percent of the time, and in those cases they have less than 30 percent debt to equity.

How many people do you have in the organization now?

Eighteen.

Do you remember how many people you had when I first interviewed you?

[He laughs long and hard.] I also remember what you said about my office: "cheap, ugly furniture." If I was an investor, I would love that!

Since our interview, you launched a market neutral fund. What was the motivation for adding this fund?

It was actually Sir John Templeton's idea. He was worried about the market. He thought it made sense to combine my stock selection skills with a market neutral approach. I thought it was a good idea as well, but I was hesitant because I didn't want to spend too much of my time coming up with short ideas; I was afraid it would interfere with my long side research. When I explained this to Templeton, he said, "Why don't you just make up the difference between your long and short positions by shorting stock indexes?" That made a lot of sense to me. It is a very simple idea, but very effective. It made it possible for me to start the market neutral fund without detracting from my ability to manage the net long funds.

At our original interview, you referred to the prior bull market as a "mania." With the Nasdaq down over 80 percent from its

peak at the July low and the S&P down about 50 percent at its corresponding low, do you think these prices sufficiently corrected for the prior excess, or do you believe the bear market will continue?

Who knows? All I know is that I own good leading companies at bargain prices.

MARK MINERVINI

Stock Around the Clock

Minervini comes off as a bit cocky, not because he thinks he's better than the markets—in fact, his respect for the markets and an appreciation of his own fallibility underlie his whole trading philosophy—but rather in the sense that he feels he is better than most of his peers. And, frankly, if he can even remotely continue to match his spectacular performance of the past five years in coming years, then this conceit may not be misplaced. I sensed that he took particular pleasure in the knowledge that as a self-taught dropout (from junior high school, no less!) he has run circles around most Ph.D.s trying to design systems to beat the market.

After dropping out of school, Minervini supported himself as a drummer. Trying to get Minervini to talk about his early experiences as a musician was a futile and frustrating effort. Despite my repeated entreaties that a discussion of a trader's background was essential in giving an interview some color and life, he seemed intent on not providing any details about his career as a drummer. I had the distinct impression that his responses were being guided by the hand of an unseen publicist. He either gave the most general of answers or somehow managed to divert the discussion back to the stock market. Sample question (asked with growing weariness): "Is there anything *at all with any specificity* that you can tell me about your experiences as a musician? Answer: "I was attracted to music because I liked the freedom, which is what attracted me to the stock market. . . ." Finally, after much prodding, he summarily acknowledged that he played for several bands, cut a record, appeared on an MTV video, worked as a studio musician, and owned his own studio. End of story.

Minervini became interested in the stock market in the early 1980s while still in his teens. His early dabbling soon grew into a full-time obsession. He sold his studio and used the proceeds to stake his trading. Initially, he lost everything—an experience he describes in the interview. He realized that his worst mistake had been depending on others for advice, so he embarked on an intensive program of self-education and research.

After nearly a decade of research and market experience, Minervini developed a well-defined trading methodology. In mid-1994, confident that his trading approach was sufficiently refined, and encouraged by his steadily improving performance, Minervini consolidated his various accounts into a single account that was to become his track record. (Previously, he maintained several accounts, partially to facilitate comparing different strategies.) In the five and a half years since initiating this account, Minervini's performance has been nothing short of astounding. His average annual compounded return during the period has been a towering 220 percent, including his 155 percent first place finish in the 1997 U.S. Investing Championship. Most traders and money managers would be delighted to have Minervini's worst year during this span—a 128 percent gain—as their best year. But return is only half the story. Amazingly, Minervini achieved his lofty gains while keeping his risk very low: He had only one down quarter—barely—a loss of a fraction of 1 percent.

Minervini launched his own hedge fund, the Quantech Fund, LP, in 2000. He is also president of the Quantech Research Group, an institutional research firm that provides stock selections based on Minervini's proprietary selection methodology. Minervini spends his days managing money and his nights running computer screens and scouring company fundamentals.

I interviewed Minervini in his midtown Manhattan office. The interview was conducted over the course of two afternoons. Minervini was clearly under the weather, acknowledging that he was running a temperature of 103 degrees. He chose not to cancel our meetings, however, because by his own admission, being interviewed in a *Market Wizard* book was one of his lifetime goals. He was not about to let a virus deter him from checking another item off his list of career objectives.

When I arrived, Minervini was in his office, looking at a stock chart on his computer screen and timing the entry of a trade. After hanging up the phone he commented to me:

"I hope I don't get a good fill."

Come again?

A good fill is a death blow. The average investor who puts in a buy order when the market is at 27 is thrilled if he gets a fill at 26¾. I would probably just turn around and get out of the position. Stocks that are ready to blast off are usually very difficult to buy without pushing the market higher. If I put in an order for ten thousand at 27 and the floor comes back to me and says, "We can only do three thousand at 27. The market is at 27¼. What do you want to do now?" it reinforces my belief that the timing of the trade is right.

What was the motivation for the stock you just bought?

The motivation is always the same. Although I may hold the position much longer, I am buying the stock because I think it will go up within hours or at most days.

Yes, but what gives you that conviction?

You mean besides seventeen years of experience? The starting point is a quantitative screen based on the characteristics of the stocks that witnessed the largest and most rapid price advances during the past century. A good book on this concept, which may be out of print, is *Superperformance Stocks* by Richard Love.

What are some of the common denominators of stocks that share this rapid price gain characteristic?

They tend to be less familiar names. More than 80 percent of the stocks are less than ten years old. Although many of these stocks are newer companies, I avoid low-priced stocks. Stocks that are low are usually low for a reason. Typically, the stocks I buy are $20 or higher, and I never buy stocks under $12. My basic philosophy is: Expose your portfolio to the best stocks the market has to offer and cut your losses very quickly when you're wrong. That one sentence essentially describes my strategy.

What are some of the other characteristics of the largest winning stocks?

One thing that would surprise most people is that these stocks typically trade at above-average price/earnings (P/E) ratios, *even before they become big winners*. Many investors limit their selections to stocks with low P/E ratios. Unfortunately, avoiding stocks just because the P/E seems "too high" will result in missing out on some of the best market moves.

A protracted discussion followed wherein I asked specifics about Minervini's trade selection process. His answers could be described most kindly as general, and perhaps more accurately as evasive. Assuming that the target market audience for this book is not insomniacs, I see little purpose in repeating any of this conversation here. Finally, sensing that I was finding his responses frustratingly ambiguous, he continued in a measured tone.

Look, none of this is a black box. You have all these people trying to come up with formulas to beat the market. The market is not a science. The science may help increase the probabilities, but to excel you need to master the art of trading.

People always want to know what's in my computer model. I think that is the least relevant issue to successful trading. Of course you need an edge, but there are a thousand ways to get an edge. Some people use strategies that are completely opposite mine, yet we can both be very profitable.

Developing your own strategy is what is important, not knowing my strategy, which I have designed to fit my personality. Understanding my trading philosophy, my principles, and my money management techniques, that may be valuable. Besides, I think most people overemphasize stock selection.

What do you mean?

I think people spend too much time trying to discover great entry strategies and not enough time on money management. Assume you took the top two hundred relative strength stocks [the two hundred stocks that outperformed the market average by the greatest amount during a specified number of past months] and placed the names on a dart board. Then each day, you threw three darts and bought the resulting stocks, and whenever any stock went down, say, 10 percent from your entry level, you sold it instantaneously. I would be willing to bet that you would make money because you are exposing yourself to a group of stocks that is likely to contain some big potential winners while at the same time you are cutting your losses.

You're not saying that if you took the entire list of stocks and threw darts, you would make money as long as you cut your losses at 10 percent. You're specifying that the list has to be preselected in some way—in your example, the stocks with the highest relative strength.

I was only using an extreme example to illustrate a point: Containing your losses is 90 percent of the battle, regardless of the strategy. In addition, if you put yourself in a position to buy stocks that have the potential to go up a lot, your odds will be better.

In other words, the odds will be better if you buy stronger stocks.

The odds will be better that you will buy stocks that go up a lot. Of course, the odds may also be better that you will buy stocks that go down a lot. But you don't have to worry about that—do you?—since you are cutting your losses.

Then I assume that, as a general principle, you believe in the idea of relative strength—buying stocks that have been going up more than the market averages.

Or down less. One way to use relative strength is to look for stocks that hold up well during a market correction and are the first to rebound after the market comes off a relative low; these stocks are the market leaders.

When you first started trading stocks, what method did you use to select your buys?

[He laughs heartily at the recollection.] I didn't have any method. I was buying low-priced stocks that were making new lows. I was also taking tips from brokers.

Tell me about that.

The worst experience was in the early 1980s when my broker talked me into buying a stock that was trading just under $20. The stock came off about 4 or 5 points, and I was really concerned. He told me not to worry. He assured me that the stock was a bargain and that the sell-off was a once-in-a-lifetime buying opportunity. He claimed that the company had developed an AIDS drug that was going to get FDA approval. He actually convinced me to buy more. The stock kept on sinking. Eventually I couldn't buy any more because I ran out of money. The end of the story is that the stock fell to under $1, and I lost all my money.

How much did you lose in that trade, and how much had you lost up till that point?

Altogether, I lost about $30,000 to $40,000, with about half the amount on that trade. Even worse, part of the loss was borrowed money.

Did that experience cause you to lose any of your zeal for the stock market?

No, but it was very upsetting and discouraging. I literally cried. What hurt the most was that I thought I had lost my chance because I had wiped out my trading stake. But no matter what happened, I never stopped believing that there were great trading opportunities available every day. It was just a matter of my figuring out how to identify them. My mistake had been surrendering the decision-making responsibility to someone else. I was convinced that if I did my own work, I would be successful.

What gave you that conviction? It certainly wasn't your trading results.

It's just my personality. I don't give up very easily. Perhaps the single most important factor was that I had a great passion for the game. I think almost anyone can be net profitable in the stock market given enough time and effort, but to be a great trader, you have to have a passion for it. You have to love trading. Michael Jordan didn't become a great basketball player because he wanted to do product endorsements. Van Gogh didn't become a great painter because he dreamed that one day his paintings would sell for $50 million.

Was your passion for the market related to the opportunity to make a lot of money?

Initially I might have been attracted to the stock market because of the money, but once I got involved, making money was not the issue.

What was the issue?

The issue was winning. The issue was being the best at something. My goal is to be the best trader in the world. If you're the best, you don't have to worry about money; it comes flying through the window.

What did you learn from your experience in losing all your money?

I realized that no one was going to do it for me; I had to do it for myself. My broker still got a commission, but I was sitting there broke. Incidentally, although I didn't realize it then, I now fully believe that losing all of your money is one of the best things that can happen to a beginning trader.

Why?

Because it teaches you respect for the market. It is much better to learn the lesson that you can lose everything when you don't have that much money than to learn the same lesson later on.

I guess that implies you are not an advocate of paper trading for beginners.

Absolutely. I think paper trading is the worst thing you can do. If you are a beginner, trade with an amount of money that is small enough so that you can afford to lose it, but large enough so that you will feel the pain if you do. Otherwise, you're fooling yourself. I have news for you: If you go from paper trading to real trading, you're going to make totally different decisions because you're not used to being subjected to the emotional pressure. Nothing is the same. It's like shadowboxing and then getting in the ring with a professional boxer. What do you think is going to happen? You're going to crawl up into a turtle position and get the crap beat out of you because you're not used to really getting hit. The most important thing to becoming a good trader is to trade.

How did you make the transition from failure to success?

My results were transformed when I understood that what counts isn't how often you're right, but how much you profit on your winning trades versus how much you lose on your losing trades. On average, I'm only profitable about 50 percent of the time, but I make much more when I'm right than I lose when I'm wrong.

I meant at the very beginning. How did you go from losing all your money following a broker's tip to developing your own successful methodology?

It was a slow, gradual process that took years of research and trading experience. I also read just about every book I could find on the markets and successful individuals. Out of the hundreds of books that I read, there were probably no more than ten that had a major influence on me. However, I don't think there is any such thing as a bad book. Even if you only get one sentence out of a book, it's still worthwhile. Sometimes, one sentence can even change your life.

Okay, tell me a sentence that changed your life.

"The fruits of your success will be in direct ratio to the honesty and sincerity of your own effort in keeping your own records, doing your own thinking, and reaching your own conclusions." In other words, take 100 percent responsibility for your results.

Which book is this quote taken from?

How to Trade in Stocks by Jesse Livermore.

What other lessons did you get out of that book?

There were many important messages. The basic message is not to have a rigid opinion; the market is never wrong. He also talked about the need for patience, not only in waiting for the right moment to enter a position, but also in riding a gain in a winning position. The message that really hit home with me was the importance of protecting your profits, not just your principal.

What changed for you after reading Livermore's book?

I was astonished at how relevant the book still was to today's market. It inspired me to go back and look at the stocks of the early 1900s and even earlier. I found that there is really nothing different in the markets. I was amazed at how many of Livermore's observations matched my own.

Such as?

The importance of money management.

Of course, Livermore himself didn't exactly excel in that department. [Livermore made and lost several fortunes. He ultimately committed suicide after wiping out one too many times.]

On a day-to-day basis Livermore did cut his losses. Unfortunately, from time to time he would let his urge to gamble get the better of him. That urge is what destroys many traders.

What else helped you become a successful trader?

Playing poker. I think that anyone who wants to be a trader should learn how to play poker.

Can you elaborate on that?

The first time I seriously watched a poker game in a casino I noticed that the average winning hand was over $50, but that it only cost you 50 cents to see the first three cards. I couldn't believe that for half a buck I could get a pretty good idea of my chances of winning a hundred times that amount. If I folded fifty times and won only once, I would still win twice as much as I lost. Those seemed like terrific odds to me. That's how I got started playing poker. My strategy was to play only super-high-probability hands.

Didn't everyone just fold once you played a hand?

No, and you know why?—because they were not disciplined, and they wanted to play. The key is to know when to do nothing. Most people, even if they have a winning strategy, will not follow it because they lack discipline. For example, everyone knows how to lose weight: you eat less fat and exercise. So why are most people overweight (assuming they don't have a medical problem)? Because they lack discipline.

I guess the analogy to the markets is that when you put on a trade, for a short while you get to see how it works out for limited risk. If it isn't working out, you take a small loss, and if it goes in your favor, you have the potential for a large gain.

That's right. I have a saying: "Being wrong is acceptable, but staying wrong is totally unacceptable." Being wrong isn't a choice, but staying wrong is. To play any game successfully, you have to have some skill, an edge, but beyond that it's money management. That's true whether you're playing poker or investing. In either case, the key is managing the downside. Good traders manage the downside; they don't worry about the upside.

You can't get beat if you have a great defense. I would always prefer to bet on a football team that has a great defense as opposed to one that has a great offense. If a trade doesn't work out quickly, I take a small loss, and I may have to take a small loss many times.

What if you get stopped out of a trade five times? Don't you find it difficult to get back in the sixth time?

Not if it meets my criteria. Again, poker provides a good analogy. Previous hands mean nothing. The current hand determines the probabilities. You have to make the correct decision based on that information. Whether you lost or won in previous hands is totally irrelevant. Therefore, I have no problem putting on the same trade many times.

Early on, when I got stopped out of a position, that was it. I wiped it out of my mind and started looking for another stock. I began to notice, however, that many times I would get stopped out of a stock, then look at it a few months later and see that it had doubled or even tripled. I would exclaim to myself, "God, I was in that stock!" I realized that I needed to develop a plan to get back on board after I was stopped out of a position.

I guess there is a psychological difficulty involved in reentering a position at a higher price after you've been stopped out.

Yes, and even worse, you might get stopped out again. If you are, can you get in a third time? I can do it as many times as necessary to get the trade right. Sometimes when a stock stops you out several times, it sets up as a much higher probability trade.

Can you give me a specific example?

Let's say I buy a stock because of a signal by my model and the market dips enough to stop me out. The stock then witnesses a huge reversal and closes near the high of the day. That price action may be an indication that there was a shakeout, which knocked out most of the weak hands, and the stock is ready to go up. Putting the long position back on at that point may well be a higher probability trade than the original trade.

In that type of situation, do you get in on the close or on the next opening?

It depends. I have specific setups that must be met before I enter the trade.

What do you mean by a setup?

The initial condition is based on the long-term price action. Then there are confirming fundamental conditions, which may be overridden in certain circumstances. Finally, determining the entry point is based strictly on the price action.

I assume the type of price action you're using for confirmation to enter a trade is much shorter term than the type of price action you initially use to screen for a potential buy candidate?

That's correct.

In other words, you might call your combination of entry conditions a price action sandwich.

That's exactly what it is—a price action sandwich.

One of Minervini's associates who had been sitting in as an observer during the interview chuckled at this last remark. Apparently he considered the analogy apt and had certainly never heard the methodology described this way.

Were there any other major pivotal points in your transition from failure to success?

After I had been trading for several years following my initial wipeout in the markets, I decided to do an analysis of all my trades. I was particularly interested in seeing what happened to stocks after I sold them. When I was stopped out of a stock, did it continue to go lower, or did it rebound? When I took profits on a stock, did it continue to go higher? I got tremendous information out of that study. My most important discovery was that I was holding on to my losing positions too long. After seeing the preliminary results, I checked what would have happened if I had capped all my losses at 10 percent. I was shocked by the results: that simple rule would have increased my profits by 70 percent!

Yes, but did you take into account the fact that by capping your losses, you were also knocking out some previous winners that initially went down more than 10 percent and then rebounded?

You're absolutely right, and that was the next thing I checked. I found that it didn't make too much of a difference. Capping my losses at 10 percent only knocked out a few of my winners. I noticed that the winning trades usually worked from the onset. I realized that it was not only totally unnecessary to go through the pain of holding on to positions with large open losses, but also actually detrimental to do so.

I also realized that by holding on to some of my losing positions for extended periods of time, I was tying up my capital. Therefore, the impact of the large losers went beyond the losses themselves, since holding on to these positions was keeping me from making profits elsewhere. If I took this impact into account, the benefit of capping my losses was astronomical.

Based on your earlier comments, you are obviously risking far less than the 10 percent maximum loss cap you used in this study. How do you decide where to place your stop-loss points?

Not every trade I put on is the same. I will use much wider stops on long-term trades than short-term trades. I will also use much wider stops when I think the market is in the early stages of a bull move than if I think the market is overdone and due for a correction. The essential principle is that the stop-loss point should be a function of the expected gain.

Do any other experiences stand out as important in your transformation into a highly successful trader?

I learned not to impose any artificial restrictions on my upside potential. At one point during the summer of 1995, I was up over 100 percent year to date, which achieved my original goal for the entire year. I was seriously considering booking the year. A friend of mine asked, "What makes you think you can't make 200 percent?" I thought about it for a day or two, and said to myself that he's right. I ended that year up 407 percent.

I know you use both fundamental and technical analysis. Do you weight one more than the other?

Roughly speaking, I would say my weighting is fifty-fifty. But there is an important distinction between the relative importance I assign to price action versus fundamentals. Although I would never bet on my fundamental ideas without some confirming price action, I might consider buying a stock with apparent negative fundamentals if its relative price performance is in the top 2 percent of the market.

Why is that?

Because the price action may be telling you that the stock is discounting a potential change in the fundamentals that is not yet evident. The combination of strong price action and weak current fundamentals often occurs in turnaround companies or companies with a new technology whose potential is not yet widely understood.

How many charts do you review each day?

I run preliminary computer screens on roughly ten thousand companies and narrow the list down to about eight hundred stocks. Each night, I review the charts for all these stocks. My first pass-through is very quick, and on average I'll spot about 30 to 40 stocks that look interesting. I then review these stocks more closely, scrutinizing the company's fundamentals, if I haven't already done so recently, and select several that might be considered for purchase the next day.

What length price charts do you look at?

Anything from ten years down to intraday, but I always look at a five-year, one-year, and intraday chart.

What kind of price patterns are you looking for when you put on a trade?

I don't use the conventional chart patterns. I don't find them particularly useful.

So what do you look for in a chart?

Many of the patterns that I have observed and found useful are more complex variations of conventional chart patterns. I have a list of patterns that I've named. These are patterns that repeat over and over. They have repeated since the 1800s, and they will repeat forever. When I look at charts and see these patterns, I don't know how anyone in the world could miss them. But, of course, they do, just as I did early in my career.

How many of these patterns are there?

About twenty.

Can you provide one as an example.

I'd rather not.

How did you discover these patterns?

I started with common chart patterns and found that they worked

great sometimes and didn't work at all at other times. I spent a lot of time focusing on *when* patterns worked.

I constantly try to figure out how the market can trick or frustrate the majority of investors. Then after the majority have been fooled I get in at what I call the "point of smooth sailing." A so-called failed signal can actually be the beginning of a more complex pattern that is far more reliable than the initial signal based on a conventional pattern.

For example.

For example, assume a stock breaks out of a trading range on high volume. It looks great. People buy it, and then the stock collapses. In this scenario, most people will view the original breakout as a failed technical signal. The original breakout, however, may be only the beginning of a more complex pattern that is far more reliable than the breakout itself.

Could you detail one of these patterns?

I don't want to do that. It's not that I think revealing them would make a difference. I could print a description of these patterns in *The Wall Street Journal,* and I think that 99 percent of the people who would read the article wouldn't use them or use them the way I do.

Then why not reveal them?

Because it's not what's important to trading successfully. What is important is controlling your losses and having a plan. Besides, for someone to be successful, they have to develop their own methodology. I developed my method for myself; it wouldn't necessarily be a good fit for anyone else.

Although I am convinced that Minervini believes this is true, I also think he doesn't want to divulge any of his original chart analysis because, on some level, he obviously must think that such a disclosure might adversely affect the efficacy of the patterns he uses, which is perfectly reasonable. My further efforts to get him to provide some specifics about his chart methodology proved futile. He didn't even want to reveal the names of his chart patterns on the record; he read a list of their names to me only after I had turned off my tape recorder.

I assume you use these price patterns as triggers to get you into a trade. Do you also use them to get out of a trade?

Yes.

The same patterns?

Yes and no. The same patterns are interpreted differently, depending on where they occur. For example, if a pattern occurs during a collapse as opposed to during a runaway bull market, it might have a precisely opposite interpretation. You can't blindly interpret a pattern without considering where it occurs within the larger price picture.

When you said earlier that you don't look at conventional chart patterns, do you mean to imply that you don't attach any significance to breakouts to new highs?

No, a stock going to a new high is typically a bullish event because the market has eliminated the supply of all previous buyers who had a loss and were waiting to get out at even. That's why stocks often run up very rapidly once they hit new high ground—at that point, there are only happy investors; all the miserable people are out.

But don't stocks often break out to new highs and then come right back into the prior range?

That usually doesn't happen if you buy breakouts to new highs after a correction to the first leg in a bull trend. In that case, stocks usually take off like a rocket after they break out to new highs. Less skilled traders wait to buy the stock on the pullback, which never comes.

When do you get breakouts that fail?

In the latter stages of a bull market after the stock has already run up dramatically. Chart patterns are only useful if you know when to apply them; otherwise, you might as well be throwing darts.

What advice would you have for a novice whose goal was to become a successful trader?

First and foremost, understand that you will always make mistakes. The only way to prevent mistakes from turning into disasters is to accept losses while they are small and then move on.

Concentrate on mastering one style that suits your personality, which is a lifetime process. Most people just cannot weather the learning curve. As soon as it gets difficult, and their approach isn't working up to their expectations, they begin to look for something else. As a result, they become slightly efficient in many areas without ever becoming very good in any single methodology. The reality is that it takes a very long time to develop a superior approach, and along the way, you are going to go through periods when you do poorly. Ironically, those are the periods that give you the most valuable information.

What else?

You need to have a plan for every contingency. When a pilot and copilot are flying a jetliner and something goes wrong with an engine, you can be sure that they don't have to figure out what to do on the spur of the moment; they have a contingency plan. The most important contingency plan is the one that will limit your loss if you are wrong. Beyond that, you need a plan to get back into the trade if you're stopped out. Otherwise, you'll often find yourself getting stopped out of a trade, and then watching the position go up 50 percent or 100 percent while you're on the sidelines.

Don't you then find yourself sometimes getting stopped out and reentering a trade multiple times?

Sure, but I don't have a problem with that. I would rather get stopped out of a trade five times in a row, taking a small loss each time, than take one large loss.

What are some other relevant contingency plans?

A plan for getting out of winning trades. There are two ways to liquidate a trade—into strength or into weakness—and you need a plan for both.

What other advice do you have for novice traders?

Many amateur investors get sloppy after gains because they fall into the trap of thinking of their winnings as the "market's money," and in no time, the market takes it back. It's your money as long as you protect it.

Also, you don't have to make all-or-nothing decisions. If a stock is up and you're unsure what to do, there's nothing wrong with taking profits on part of it.

What mistakes do people make in trading?

They let their egos get in the way. An investor may put in hours of careful research building a case for a company. He scours the company's financial reports, checks Value Line, and may even try the company's products. Then, soon after he buys the stock, his proud pick takes a price dive. He can't believe it! He makes excuses for the stock's decline. He calls his broker and searches the Internet, looking for any favorable opinions to justify his position. Meanwhile, he ignores the only opinion that counts: the verdict of the market. The stock keeps sliding, and his loss keeps mounting. Finally, he throws in the towel and feels completely demoralized—all because he didn't want to admit he had made a mistake in timing.

Another mistake many investors make is that they allow themselves to be influenced by what other people think. I made this mistake myself when I was still learning how to trade. I became friends with a broker and opened an account with him. We played this game called "bust the other guy's chops when his stock is down." When I had a losing stock position, I was embarrassed to call him to sell the stock because I knew he would ride me about it. If a stock I bought was down 5 or 10 percent, and I thought I should get out of it, I found myself hoping it would recover so I wouldn't have to call him to sell it while it was down. Before I knew it, the stock would be down 15 or 20 percent, and the more it fell, the harder it became for me to call. Eventually, I learned that you have to ignore what anybody else thinks.

Many people approach investing too casually. They treat investing as a hobby instead of like a business; hobbies cost money. They also don't take the time to do a post-trade analysis on their trades, eliminating the best teacher: their results. Most people prefer to forget about their failures instead of learning from them, which is a big mistake.

What are some misconceptions people have about trading?

They think it is a lot easier than it is. Sometimes people will ask me whether they can spend one weekend with me so I can show them how I do this stuff. Do you know what a tremendous insult this is? It's like my saying to a brain surgeon, "If you have a few extra days, I'd like you to teach me brain surgery."

The current market mania, particularly in the dot.com and other Internet stocks, has deceived many people into believing that trading is easy. Some guy buys Yahoo, makes four times as much as the best fund managers, and thinks he is a genius.

How important is gut feel to successful trading?

Normal human tendencies are traits that cause you to do poorly. Therefore, to be successful as a trader you need to condition abnormal responses. You hear many traders say that you have to do the opposite of your gut response—when you feel good about a position, you should sell, and when you feel terrible about it, you should buy more. In the beginning that's true, but as you condition yourself for abnormal responses, somewhere along the line you become skilled. Then your gut becomes right. When you feel good, you actually should go long, and when you fell bad, you should sell. That's the point when you know you have reached competency as a trader.

What differentiates you from the majority of traders who are a lot less successful?

Discipline. I don't think anyone is more disciplined than I am. When I put on a trade, I have a contingency plan for every possible outcome. I can't think of any circumstance that would be an exception. If there were, I would have a plan for that too.

What else?

I trade for a living. When you have to earn a living every day from trading, finding a way to be consistent becomes a necessity.

How do you know when you are wrong in a position?

The stock goes down. That's all you need to know.

How much vacation time do you take a year?

I don't take vacations during trading days. I haven't missed a day in the market in over ten years.

Even when you're sick?

Even when I'm sick. I've traded through pneumonia. I've traded with a temperature of 105 degrees.

What is your typical day like?

I get into work around 8 A.M. and work till about 7 P.M. Then I take a few hours to eat and exercise, and go back to work from ten at night until one in the morning. Then I do it all over again. Sunday I usually work from midday into the night. Saturday I rest and recharge.

No vacations, six-day workweeks, and fourteen-hour workdays. Don't you ever feel the need to take a break?

My desire to be the best trader is greater than my desire to take a break. I don't like to get out of the swing.

★

Sure, I would have liked it better if Minervini had been more forthcoming with the specifics of how he selects stocks and times his trades, but I have to agree with him that the most important advice he can give—and does provide—relates to his trading philosophy. The main points of this doctrine include:

- Rigorously control your losses.
- Develop a method that fits your own personality, and master that one style.
- Do your own research, act on your own ideas, and don't be influenced by anyone else's opinion.
- Have a contingency plan for every possible event, which includes how to get back into a trade if you are stopped out and when to take profits if the trade goes in your direction.
- Maintain absolute discipline to your plan—no exceptions!

Yes, I know, some of these points, such as discipline and loss control, have become clichés as trading advice. But this doesn't make these principles any less important. Why do you think they became clichés? The fact is that discipline and loss control are the two factors that were most frequently mentioned as keys to trading success by the traders I interviewed, both in this book and its two predecessors. The problem is that traders and investors have heard this advice so often that they often fail to hear it at all—and that would be a crucial mistake.

One exercise that Minervini did that proved extraordinarily helpful to him was to analyze his past trades. The insights of this analysis changed his trading style forever and helped him to make the transition from marginal performance to spectacular success. In his own case, Minervini found that by capping the maximum loss on his trades, he could dramatically increase his overall returns, even after allowing for winning trades that would have been eliminated by this rule. This discovery allowed him to make a lot more profit with much less aggravation. Other traders and investors may find that a similar comprehensive analysis of their past trades reveals patterns that point the way to improve their own performance.

Interestingly, the methodology that Minervini eventually developed was precisely the opposite of his instinctive approach as a novice, which was buying low-priced stocks that were making new lows. Success required not merely the adaptability to modify his initial approach, but also the flexibility to acknowledge that his original ideas were completely wrong. The lesson is that early failure does not preclude long-term success, as long as one is receptive to change.

★

Update on Mark Minervini

Minervini's 5½-year personal account track record at the time of the original interview (a 220 percent average annual compounded return) would have been difficult to maintain even under the best of circumstances. Minervini would be the first to admit that he is unlikely to generate outsized returns during a major bear market. Given his methodology, which is focused on early identification of potential superior performing companies, Minervini's trading reflects a definite long-side bias. When he is bearish on the market, he tends to spend a lot of time at or near the sidelines, protecting capital and waiting for a more opportune investment environment—a stance that, as he discusses in this update, has been less than popular with some of his investors. Not surprisingly, Minervini's fund, which was launched in January 2000, three months before the market top, has spent significant portions of the subsequent 2¾ years in or near cash. The track record reflects this predominant capital preservation mode: Since the start of the bear market (April 2000) Minervini is up only a modest 3 percent (compared with contemporaneous cumulative declines of 45 percent in the S&P 500 and 75 percent in the Nasdaq).

At the time of our last interview, you were just beginning to manage other people's money through a fund. What has that experience been like?

I found there were conflicts between my style of investing and institutional investors' concepts about investing.

What kind of conflicts?

My style of investing is to make large bets in concentrated positions and manage risk by using tight stops and closely monitoring the fundamentals of the companies in the portfolio. I have complete confidence in being aggressive when I feel it is warranted and staying out of the market for as long as I feel necessary when the investment environment is unfavorable. There were conflicts on both scores: Institutional investors don't want you to be highly concentrated, and they don't like the idea of being fully in cash.

If the market goes up during the month, and you're in cash, they'll say, "My other funds are up. My stocks are up. The Dow is up. What are you doing in cash?" If the market goes down a lot in a month and you were in cash, they'll want to know why you didn't have short positions on.

I'm not going to put on short positions for the sake of being short. I'm looking for a specific setup in a stock or the market in order to go short. If that setup doesn't occur, I won't go short. That doesn't mean the market won't go down. The type of sell signal I look for tends to occur when a market is rolling over from a top, not after it has been in a long slide, as is currently the case. You have to stay in your own area of confidence. For example, one of Warren Buffett's best friend's is Bill Gates. Yet Warren Buffett has never bought a single share of Microsoft because he considers the stock to be outside his area of confidence.

Also, my philosophy has always been to stay out of the market as much as possible. The less time I am in the market, the less risk I am taking. If dictated by market conditions, I'd rather make X percent having significant market exposure in only three months of the year than make the same amount while being in the market all the time.

Certain investors won't have the confidence level in my approach that I have and will very quickly question my strategy if I am in cash when the market is moving. If investors don't feel you are managing money the way they believe it should be managed, they'll redeem their investment. It's really quite ironic because they are hiring you for your advice. It's like going to a doctor and telling him how to treat you. But that is what happens in the investment world.

You were doing so well trading your own account, with no one to answer to. What was your motivation to get into managed money?

It was the challenge of moving beyond just trading my own money. I have always admired people such as Steve Cohen of SAC and Lee Ainslee of Maverick who have built organizations that employ many traders and manage large sums of money.

The net exposure in your Quantech fund is strongly skewed to the long side. How have you managed to be net profitable being net long in a steadily declining market?

An important part of success in the markets is knowing when to stay out of the game. Part of your strategy may be when not to apply your strategy. The Quantech fund has been in cash or nearly so for significant periods during its 2½-year life span, which has almost entirely coincided with the bear market. On rare occasions, the fund may even be modestly net short. For example, I was short the Dow index on September 11, by coincidence, of course.

Why were you short then?

It's amazing how the market seems to discount future events. I was short the Dow, and I was getting ready to go long defense stocks when the World Trade Center was hit. The only reason I didn't go long the defense stocks was because I was so bearish on the stock market. Imagine if I had been both short the Dow and long defense stocks; I think I would have had a visit from the FBI. The defense stocks were rallying, and the market was rolling over before the attack on the World Trade Center. I don't mean to suggest that the market was discounting the terrorist attack, but it is incredible that those two trades—short the stock market and long defense stocks—were the exact trades showing up most strongly in my technical work before September 11.

When we first did the interview you had never experienced a multiyear bear market. Have you learned any new trading lessons from the bear market of the past two years?

My strategy has not changed one iota. If anything, the bear market has only reinforced my conviction about staying out when the conditions for a trade are not there. In the long run, companies that generate cash flow and earnings, grow rapidly, and have new products or services are going to be rewarded. Of course I wait until the market action demonstrates that it recognizes those positive fundamentals because ultimately perception is all that matters.

Are you saying that your methodology has remained completely unchanged?

Yes. I will, however, revise my models to incorporate new information. For example, every year, I analyze all the stocks that were the best performers in the preceding year to refine the fundamental and technical profile I use to identify the stocks that are likely to be the biggest winners in the future.

Any thoughts about the recent accounting scandals?

Even though the U.S. accounting system may be the best one in the world, the very first word in the term GAAP (generally accepted accounting principles) tells you something is wrong. There shouldn't be any generalities in math. There should be specific ways to report. Those specifics may need to be tailored by sector—a retail company might have different guidelines than an insurance company—but within sectors, companies shouldn't have much latitude in deciding how to report their numbers. How can a company as complex as General Electric, which probably has hundreds of divisions and revenues that rival the GDP of many countries, come within one penny of their earnings estimates every quarter? Most companies are operating fully within the law. It's not that they're breaking the law; they're just taking advantage of it. Hopefully, recent events will lead to some improvements.

What's your very long-term market view?

Although the current price plunge will probably lead to a sharp rally on the first significant bullish surprise, I don't believe we are likely to see the re-emergence of a sustained uptrend like the one in the

1990s. One of the factors that contributed to the bull market of the 1990s was the psychological and economic boost provided by the fall of communism at the end of the 1980s. Now I see the threat of going back into a Cold War type situation, but with terrorism replacing communism.

What advice would you have for investors at this juncture?

The same advice I have always had. You need to realize that, ultimately, a stock is virtually 100 percent perception, and therefore prices can go anywhere. Most of the Internet companies were worth nothing, but they reached these incredible prices on perception. Think of the wealth that was made and lost in these stocks purely as a function of perception.

STEVE LESCARBEAU

The Ultimate Trading System

Steve Lescarbeau's systems are the next best thing to a daily subscription to tomorrow's *Wall Street Journal*. Lescarbeau invests in mutual funds. His goal is to hold them while they are going up and to be in a money market fund while they are going down. He times these asset transfers with such precision that he more than triples the average annual returns of the funds he invests in while sidestepping the bulk of their periodic downturns.

During the five years he has traded, Lescarbeau has realized an average annual compounded return of over 70 percent. As impressive as this may be, what is truly remarkable about his track record is that this high return has been achieved with extraordinary risk control: His worst equity decline from a month-end peak to a subsequent month-end low was a minuscule 3 percent. His consistency is also astounding: He has been profitable in 91 percent of all months, and his annual return has exceeded 50 percent every year.

For reasons he explains in the interview, Steve Lescarbeau is almost paranoid about revealing any details about his trading systems. He is also not interested in raising any money to manage. Why then did Lescarbeau even agree to do this interview? First, I assured Lescarbeau that he would see this chapter and have the opportunity to approve it before it was printed. Second—and this is just my guess—by his own account, Lescarbeau's initial research direction was inspired by the Gil Blake interview in my book *The New Market Wizards*. Perhaps agreeing to this interview was a courtesy granted for having provided this indirect aid to his own career.

Lescarbeau doesn't let up. Even though he has created some incredibly effective trading systems, he continues his research to find even better systems. His drive is not restricted merely to the markets; when he was in sales, he was consistently the top salesman in his company. Lescarbeau even approaches his leisure activities with intensity. He doesn't merely go for a bicycle ride; he goes for a hundred-mile bicycle ride—at least he did until he blew out his knee by doing excessive repetitions, at too high a setting, on a weight-training machine.

Lescarbeau works alone at his home in a small rural town outside of Albany, New York. The interview was started and completed in Lescarbeau's home office, a corner room with dark wood paneling, floor-to-ceiling bookcases, and windows overlooking his lawn. The middle portion of the interview was conducted over a buffet lunch at a local Italian restaurant, at which we were the only diners (due to the lateness of the hour for lunch, not the quality of the food).

How did you first get interested in the stock market?

I got involved in the financial services industry in 1983, working for a mutual fund company. To be perfectly candid, I switched into this field because I thought it was the place I could make the most amount of money as a sales kind of guy. I had a degree in chemistry from Boston University, which helped, but no training whatsoever on the financial side.

How do you go from chemistry to the sale of financial investments?

As a plug to BU, my degree in chemistry has been extremely helpful. I think that a physical science degree is as good as if not better than a financial degree because it trains you to be analytical. If there is anything I am really good at, it's being a researcher. I'm not a particularly good trader. When I got out of school, I was sick and tired of studying, and I just wanted to make money. I got a job in sales using my chemistry background.

You didn't try to get a job directly in chemistry?

No, chemists don't make any money, but salesmen do.

Didn't you figure that out in college?

Yes, when I was a senior *[he laughs]*.

What were you selling?

Filtration systems to the pharmaceutical and electronic industries. It was very high-tech stuff. I was very good at selling. I was number one in sales for three years in a row.

How did you develop the talent for sales?

I'm just a willful person.

How did you go from selling filtration systems to selling financial investments?

When I won the salesman-of-the-year award, one of the prizes was a trip to La Costa, California. I remember driving down the Monterey Peninsula, seeing all these phenomenal houses, and thinking that I would never make the kind of money to be able to afford a similar house if I stayed with my firm. That's when I decided to leave and do something where I could make more money. I looked into two fields—medical delivery and financial services—because the incomes were unlimited for a salesperson. In 1983, I took a job as a regional sales manager at a mutual fund company.

Did you have any experience in financial markets?

None whatsoever. In fact, when I won the salesman-of-the-year award at my previous job, they also gave me a hundred shares of stock. I didn't even know what it was. I guess you can't be much more ignorant of the market than that.

How did the new job work out?

I loved the job and did very well over the next few years. However, because of limitations that the company placed on me, I realized that if I wanted to take the next step, I would have to do something different.

I decided to become a stockbroker. I was interviewed and hired by Shearson Lehman Brothers. While I was there, I met Tim Holk, who was in managed futures—an area I knew absolutely nothing about. Tim had raised some retail money for Commodities Corporation. [At the time, Commodities Corporation had a group of in-house traders who managed the firm's proprietary funds as well as outside investor funds. Two of the traders I interviewed in *Market Wizards*—Michael Marcus and Bruce Kovner—achieved their early success at Commodities Corporation.] One day, I went down with Tim to meet with some traders at Commodities Corporation. After that meeting, I told Tim, "Screw the retail money; let's go after institutional money."

I cold-called Eastman Kodak. That initial call ultimately led to their opening a $50 million account—the largest investment ever in managed futures. They eventually upped their investment to $250 million.

What did you know about managed futures?

Nothing, but I did know enough to realize that it was a waste of time to call individuals and that it made a lot more sense to call institutions.

Then how did you sell Kodak on the product?

I told them, "Here is an investment that has no correlation with the stock market and has been compounding at about 30 percent per year." The Kodak account started me toward financial independence.

After the Kodak sale you must have thought: "This is really easy!"

I expected the money to pour in.

Were you successful at opening other accounts?

We tried to open other institutional accounts, but nothing happened. We basically had one account. No other institutions stepped up the plate.

So, on your first sales call, you landed a $50 million account, and then you never made another sale again.

It's hard to believe, but it's the honest-to-God truth. The Kodak account was my only source of income.

Still, given the size of the account, you had to be doing pretty well.

We were making a lot of money off the account, but the problem was that it was a typical managed futures account—up-and-down, up-and-down—it was sickening to watch. The traders would make money, and then they would give it all back. I was concerned about losing the account because of all the volatility. So I started looking around for something else to do.

Sometime around 1993, I became interested in a stock market

newsletter written by a guy in Texas. He put out recommendations on mutual sector funds and had a good track record. I called him up and suggested that we do a fund. He agreed, and the fund was launched in September 1993. He was the trader, and I raised the money.

Had he traded before this fund was formed?

No, he was just a newsletter writer. This was his first experience with trading real money.

Hadn't the idea of trading occurred to him before?

I think he was somewhat conservative. He had a good position at IBM, which he was reluctant to give up. He had been writing the newsletter on the side. I convinced him to leave IBM. In the first ten months I raised approximately $10 million. After the first year, he was up about 9 percent with a lot of volatility. I realized that this was not for me—the equity swings were just too volatile relative to the mediocre returns being realized.

By late 1994, I had become completely disenchanted. At the same time, I had begun doing my own research on mutual fund timing and thought I could do better. The trading manager and I agreed to split up. He kept the individual managed accounts, and I took over management of the partnership account.

You said you began doing research. Had you developed a trading method by the time you took over as the fund manager?

No, I didn't have enough confidence in my research. I knew I wasn't quite there yet.

Then what was your plan for trading the fund?

I didn't have any great plan. I just knew that what we were doing wasn't working. I had enough confidence in my abilities to believe that I could come up with something better.

So your trading method was still a work in progress at the time you took over the trading responsibilities.

Yes.

Did you consider delaying the split with your partner until you had developed your own trading strategy?

No, I knew I would come up with something. There was absolutely no doubt in my mind. I had never failed to succeed at anything that I put my mind to, and this was no different.

Still, you had never traded successfully.

The characteristics of being a good trader or investor are very similar to the traits needed for success in general. I think it would be very difficult to find someone who was not successful at what he was currently doing, put him in a trading position, and make him successful. I don't think that is going to happen. The same qualities that make you a successful person in whatever you're doing are going to make you successful in trading. You have to be very decisive, extremely disciplined, relatively smart, and above all, totally independent. I have those traits. Therefore, when I decided to become a money manager, it didn't require a leap of faith to believe that I would be successful.

Since you hadn't fully developed an alternative trading method when you began trading the fund, how did you make your trading decisions?

It was a joke. I didn't know what I was doing. I did what everyone else does. I looked at a chart, and if it looked strong, I bought it.

How long did this go on?

For most of the first quarter of 1995. I was lucky to finish the quarter up a few percent. By March 1995, I had systematized my approach and felt confident that I had come up with something that would work. I implemented an embryonic version of what I do now.

That implies that you have changed your system very substantially since you first started. Were these changes a consequence of ongoing research, or were they triggered by your trading experiences?

I had several important events in my track record that caused me to change significantly from what I had started out doing. I had a very good first year. I finished 1995 with a 58 percent gain and no losing months from the time I adopted my systematic approach.

In January 1996, however, I found myself down about 5 percent by midmonth. That may not sound like much to most people, but to me it was a huge amount. Because of that drawdown, I spent an enormous amount of time doing research on the computer and ended up making very significant changes to my methodology.

Everything went along well until late 1996, when my trading results went relatively flat. For the fourth quarter of 1996 and the first quarter of 1997 combined, I was up only a little over 1 percent. This was definitely not what I was looking for. I realized that I had to make some changes. During that period, I was on the computer all day, almost every day. In March 1997, I implemented some very significant changes to my systems. Since then, the performance has been quite good.

Although my systems have been unchanged since then, over time I realized that I could combine my systems with my experience. Now my systems tell me what to do, but there is also judgment involved. This judgment doesn't necessarily make me more money, but it does reduce my equity swings. I usually err on the side of caution if I lack conviction on a trade.

Can you give me an example of how you use judgment?

There is never any judgment whether to buy or sell; the only judgment is how much to buy or sell. The problem with system trading is that it doesn't tell you how to trade your portfolio; it just gives you buy and sell signals. I trade several different systems, each based primarily on one indicator. I might have a system that has been performing extremely well give me a buy signal, but I may decide to take a smaller-than-normal position because other systems are giving me contradictory indications.

What is another example of judgment causing you to deviate from the strict signals of your system?

Let's say the market has been trending up for a while, my systems are long, and I'm making a lot of money. Although everything may look great, I get uncomfortable when my equity line starts going above its long-term uptrend. I am likely to cut back my position size, anticipating that the equity line will come back to the long-term trend. Judgment like that saves me money rather than makes me money.

Judgment is also important in deciding which systems I use. Interestingly, the systems I used a few years ago are not doing particularly well anymore. Somehow I've been successful in changing so that I'm usually trading the best systems. I can't tell you how I've managed to do it. I guess it must be intuition.

If you stop trading a system because it shows some deterioration, do you sometimes go back to using it several years later?

No, because I replace inferior systems with superior systems. There is a reason why I replace trading systems, and the reason is that I have a better idea. I still keep an eye on old trading systems, but I won't use them.

Doesn't it sometimes happen that a discarded system begins performing better than a system you are currently using?

It probably will happen at some point, but it hasn't happened yet.

Do you trade individual stocks?

No, although it is very likely that my systems would also work on stocks. In fact, that's my next research project.

So, what is your trading vehicle?

Mutual funds, but I'm not a market timer. Let's discriminate between a market timer and what I consider myself—a market reactor. A market timer says, "The market is too risky here. I think the Dow is going down to 8,000 during the next three months." They have a view about what is going to happen. They prognosticate the market. I do not attempt to prognosticate the market. I react to what happens in the market.

Your actions, however, will be the same as a market timer. You will switch back and forth between a mutual fund and cash, based on the timing signals of your systems. Isn't that the same thing as a market timer?

The actions may be the same as a market timer, but the thinking is completely different. I make no predictions. I have absolutely no idea what is going to happen *[he laughs]*.

Why are you laughing?

I'm laughing about the people who do make predictions about the stock market. They don't know. Nobody knows. I don't think anybody has any idea what is going to happen in the stock market.

Does your own performance depend on the mutual funds you choose to trade?

Only to a very limited extent.

Do you trade mutual funds that represent the broader market?

I have tested my systems on marketwide funds, and they work well. But I usually prefer to go after a smaller area of the market. I'm looking for funds that would have a bit more zing on the upside, and the

S&P is not zing. Therefore, I'm much more likely to trade something like a technology fund than a broadly diversified fund.

I don't expect you to reveal the systems you are currently using. However, are there systems that you developed in the past and that worked for a while, but are worthless to you now? At least that would provide an illustration of what a system idea that worked for a while looks like.

I can give you an example of something that might not be too distant from what I used to do by describing my perception of Gil Blake's system. [Blake was a trader interviewed in *The New Market Wizards*.] Gil's approach was to follow different sectors, and if on a given day, a sector had both above-average volatility and above-average return, it would be considered a buy signal for that sector fund, or a "green light," to use his terminology. Then he would hold the long position in that fund until his sell condition was met, which might have been a down day, or the passage of a specific number of days following the buy signal, or some other liquidation condition.

That system provides a good example of the kind of thinking that I do. There is no reason why you couldn't implement that type of system today. Although it wouldn't do remotely as well as what I am using now, it would probably still work to some degree.

Did you have that type of idea before you read the Gil Blake chapter?

No. Reading the Gil Blake chapter was a key turning point for me. Although what I do now has nothing to do with what Gil was doing then, it at least helped me get to the point where I could start doing research on the computer.

Did you ever talk to Gil Blake?

Yes, I called him when I first started managing money and said, "My name is Steve Lescarbeau, and I just wanted to tell you that you're the reason I'm in this business." He groaned, "Oh God."

Yes, I could imagine how many times he had heard that line. If you had not read his chapter, would you have ended up in this business?

I don't know; it was that important.

Does your original trading system—the one inspired by Gil Blake's interview—still work?

It works, but it has degraded a lot.

Do you think this might be a temporary phase and that in the future it might start working very well again?

I doubt it.

Can you see yourself ever using it again?

No.

If you don't expect to ever use it again, and it's not related to what you are doing now, is there any reason why you couldn't talk about it more specifically?

Well, you never know *[he lets out a long laugh]*.

Are you still in the process of trying to improve what you are doing?

Absolutely. I'm trying to, but I don't know if I'll be able to. It's hard to improve on 60 percent a year,* but I'll be happy to maintain it. I'm constantly concerned that it is going to go away. In fact, I know it will. If you come back a year from now, I'll probably be doing something different. I'm sure what I'm doing now won't work as well as it has up until this point.

You are implying that systems have a life span.

There is absolutely no doubt about it. There is no way anyone could convince me otherwise. Systems definitely have a life span.

Why do you think that is?

I think it's because eventually enough people figure it out. When too many people jump on the bandwagon, the market takes it away. That's why I would be very skeptical about anyone being able to buy a trading system that worked—that is, a system that made money with an acceptable level of risk.

If you develop a system that you have thoroughly tested and truly believe works, don't tell anyone about it. Use it, because it's going to go away at some point in time. Understand that it won't last forever, and work on coming up with something different for when that happens.

*As of March 2000, Lescarbeau's average annual compounded return had risen to 70 percent.

I'm always concerned about people figuring out what I do, because I know if that happens, it's going to stop working. For example, the "January effect" is gone. [The January effect is the tendency for small capitalization stocks to outperform large capitalization stocks during January—a pattern that until 1993 had repeated in over 90 percent of all years since the mid-1920s. Then the pattern failed six years in a row. Lescarbeau is implying, quite plausibly, that the January effect's increasing publicity triggered its own demise.]

If too many people are using the same system, what mechanism in the marketplace causes the system to self-destruct?

I can't answer that question. It could just be a matter of too many people on the same side of the trade at the same time. Everything I have experienced tells me that systems have a life span, and not a terribly long life span.

That speaks to the death of systems; what about the birth of systems? Will systems start working at some point in time, say 1994, and then stop working a few years later? Or if you tested the systems you are currently using over the past twenty or thirty years, would you find that they worked over the entire time span, but it's just a matter of your not finding them until more recently?

Usually when I discover a system, it's been working all along. Having said that, though, I find that the systems that have done the best in the most recent past also tend to do the best in the immediate future. Therefore I tend to lean on the systems that have done the best very recently.

You say that systems have a limited life span, but by your own admission, the systems you are using have worked for over twenty years. Why couldn't they work for another twenty years?

I understand where you are going with that question, but I don't agree with the conclusion. I don't buy it because there is just a lot more money pouring into the markets. The best example is the commodity markets. When we sold the managed futures account to Kodak, the traders managing the account had systems with great track records;

these systems had been averaging 40 percent for fifteen years. They said there was no way that these systems would stop working. Well, they did. They stopped working because too many people started using similar systems.

Another classic example is O'Shaughnessy. His book *What Works on Wall Street* was terrific; it was well written and well researched. The performance of his funds, however, has been less than stellar.

What do you consider "less than stellar"?

[At this point, Lescarbeau looks up the performance of O'Shaughnessy's funds on his computer screen. He checks two of the funds and finds that they are up 43 percent and 46 percent. Although this doesn't sound too disastrous, during the same time period (late 1996 to mid-1999), the S&P 500 was up 89 percent. So, these funds made only about half as much as the S&P 500, which is representative of the benchmark they were designed to beat.] Great book. He tested his strategies all the way back to the early 1950s, but they don't work.

So, even though his strategies worked for over forty years at the time the book was published, they have stopped working in recent years.

You know what? Had he not published his book, they might well have continued to work. He should have just managed money and not published his book; of course, if he hadn't published the book, he probably wouldn't have raised any money.

Your premise is that his strategies stopped working because too many people were following the same ideas.

Exactly. The most important message I can give anyone who reads your book is that if you have a great idea, don't talk about it.

Some people I have interviewed say, "I could publish my system in the *Wall Street Journal* and it wouldn't make a difference." I take it that you don't agree.

I've read statements like that, and I couldn't disagree more.

You feel that if you described your system in *The Wall Street Journal*, it would stop working.

It would be over. Tomorrow *[he laughs]*!

At one point, you had investors, but you no longer do. What happened?

I had investors from 1995 through 1997. I did very well for them—I was up 58 percent in 1995, 50 percent in 1996, and 60 percent in 1997. By the end of 1997, I was managing about $35 million. It became very difficult to use my style of investment, which involves switching money in and out of mutual funds, because mutual funds don't like it if you trade more than four times a year.

But you trade more than four times a year now.

I trade a lot less money, and I have it spread out over more than twenty mutual funds.

So you stopped managing money for logistical reasons?

That and because investors can be such a pain.

What could your investors possibly have complained about? You made over 50 percent every year with hardly any losing months.

You can't even imagine the stuff they complained about. They complained that I didn't make enough money if I wasn't up at least 4 percent for the month. They complained that I made too much money because they had to pay taxes on the profits.

I can't believe it; you actually had someone complain that you made too much money!

I told him that I could lose money; then he wouldn't have to pay any taxes. I asked him if he would prefer that.

Some investors didn't trust me. Because the results were so good, they thought I was making up the numbers and had absconded with their money. They would call my accountant every month to ask if the money was really in the account.

If the market was up a lot on the day, they would call up and ask, "Are we in the market?" That would drive me crazy. If the market was down a lot, they would call up and ask, "Are we out of the market?" Of course, they always expected me to be on the right side of the market.

How much of your decision to get out of money management was due to the headaches given to you by mutual funds and how much was due to the headaches given to you by your investors?

Split equally! *[He laughs loudly.]* I think I used the headache I was getting from the funds as the excuse to give investors their money back. I did feel badly for those investors who had been with me from the beginning and had never opened their mouths.

Didn't the friends who were your original investors and hadn't bothered you try to talk you into not returning their money?

They did, but my problem was how to differentiate between this friend and that friend? Where do I draw the line? Therefore, I had to do it across the board.

Did you lose any friendships as a result?

No, although they still ask me to reconsider whenever we get together for a poker game.

It is interesting that so many of the traders I have interviewed are poker players.

I love playing poker.

I assume the stakes you are playing at are not terribly meaningful relative to the amount of money you are trading. You could stay in every hand, and it wouldn't make any difference to you.

It's pretty hard to get concerned about losing $200 when you've just lost $100,000, but I never let my income level interfere with the way I play. I play to win. If a hand is not a good bet, I get out.

Do you ever break your trading rules?

Only on the side of caution. I might take partial profits on a position, or not go fully long on a buy signal, but I will never hold after a sell signal.

Were you that disciplined from the very beginning?

Yes, because prior to that, I did all my screwing up in futures. I made every possible mistake you could make. I don't even have to go over them because they are all classic mistakes.

How long did you trade futures?

[He searches his memory for a while, as if trying to retrieve an experience from the distant reaches of his mind.] For about three years.

Were you a net loser?

Oh, big-time! I made money investing with other futures managers, but trading for my own account, I turned a $125,000 account into $50,000. I did everything wrong.

Were there any particularly painful trades during that period?

Too numerous to count.

What stands out?

I developed a currency trading system. I bought this computer software program that allowed you to optimize trading systems [to fine-tune the indicator values in a system so as to maximize the performance results for the tested price data]. Like any stupid trader, I optimized it completely. [He adjusted the system indicator values so that they best fit the past price data.] Of course, the results looked spectacular. [Because by optimizing, he was using hindsight to define and test the system. The problem is that the results will be very misleading when applied to unseen price data—namely, future price data.] I knew better, but I didn't think it applied to me.

In a span of two weeks, I lost about 50 percent of the money in my trading account. I started veering from the system, and every time I did, it was the absolute wrong time to do it. It was a nightmare. I realized I wasn't cut out to trade futures.

This sounds like the only thing you ever did where you failed. With everything else you kept at it until you succeeded. Why did you give up here?

Because I realized futures were a losing game. The commissions and slippage [the difference between the screen price and the actual trade execution price] placed the odds too much against you. If you have only a 50 percent chance of being right when you buy or sell, and you pay commissions and incur slippage costs, you have to lose over the long run.

But that 50 percent assumption presupposes that you don't have any edge in the market. Couldn't you have found patterns that had some reliability and gave you an edge similar to what you did in the stock market?

I couldn't do it. I couldn't find any patterns that worked.

Are you able to take any vacations?

Yes, as long as I have access to my computer. I own a vacation home on a lake in New Hampshire.

What if you wanted to go away and hike in the Swiss Alps, or for that matter even take a full-day hike in the White Mountains?

For five years, I have been available at 3:45 P.M. every day without exception. I have never taken a day off. The problem with taking a day off is that it will probably be the day you shouldn't have taken off.

What happened when you had your knee surgery? [Lescarbeau and I had compared notes on personal sports injuries on our drive back from the restaurant.]

I had outpatient surgery with general anesthesia. I returned home at around 11 A.M., very groggy, and went straight to bed. My wife was supposed to wake me at 3:30, but out of compassion, she decided to let me sleep. At 3:45, I woke up with a start. I was in the bedroom, which is on the other side of the house. I jumped out of bed and with excruciating pain hobbled down to my office. I looked at the screen, and based on what I saw, I sold half my portfolio.

An hour later, I returned to the office and looked at the screen again. I realized that I had totally screwed up. I couldn't figure out why I had sold anything. I had completely misread the information. As it turned out, the next day the market tanked. It was utter luck.

What percent of the time are you in the market?

About 50 to 55 percent of the time.

Do you use leverage?

Selectively. On average, I'm less than fully invested, even counting only those days when I am in the market. Occasionally, if conditions are right, I use leverage. But I have never been leveraged more that 140 percent of my capital—that's the limit of my comfort level. I have never lost money on a trade that I was leveraged on.

Do you ever go net short?

Ninety percent of my success is due to not doing things that are stupid. I don't sell winners; I don't hold losers; I don't get emotionally involved. I do things where the odds are in my favor. Shorting stocks is dumb because the odds are stacked against you. The stock market has been rising by over 10 percent a year for many decades. Why would you want to go against that trend?

Any advice for novice traders?

Don't confuse activity with accomplishment. I think one mistake novice traders make is that they begin trading before they have any real idea what they are doing. They are active, but they are not accomplishing anything. I hardly spend any time trading. Over 99 percent of my time is spent on the computer, doing research.

★

Although Lescarbeau refused to reveal any details about his own trading systems, he provides some important insights into the traits of a successful trader. One characteristic that I have repeatedly noticed in winning traders—and that is probably true of winners in any field—is that they are extremely confident. Perhaps no other trader I have interviewed has exemplified this quality better than Lescarbeau. He exudes confidence. Consider, for example, his description of the certainty that he would succeed as a money manager before he had even developed a methodology. (Lescarbeau's decision to assume trading responsibility before he had developed a trading method is not being held up as model of laudable behavior—on the contrary, for most people it would represent a reckless course of action—but only as an illustration of his sense of confidence.)

An honest assessment of your own confidence level may be the best indicator of your potential for success. If you are confident that you will succeed in the markets—not to be confused with *wanting* to be confident—then the odds are good that you will. If you are uncertain, then tread very gingerly with your risk capital. Confidence cannot be manufactured or wished into existence. Either you have it or you don't. Can't confidence be acquired? Sure, sometimes hard work—another trait of winning traders—can lead to proficiency, which can lead to confidence. But even then, until you are truly confident, proceed with great caution in the markets.

Another trait I have noticed among the Market Wizards is that they approach trading and sometimes other endeavors with an intensity bordering on obsession. Lescarbeau is a perfect example. He never misses a day—even surgery didn't prevent him from checking the market. Whenever the performance of his systems failed to meet his extraordinarily high standards, even though this meant nothing worse than a break-even quarter or two, he worked incessantly to develop better systems. Even his recreational activities—for example, bicycling and weight training—reflect an obsessive streak.

Is there any single trait that is shared by *all* great traders? Yes, discipline. Lescarbeau's unfailing sense of discipline is clear in all his actions. He has never decided to hold a position once he gets a sell signal. If his system tells him to liquidate, he's out—no questions, no second-guessing, no qualifications. He never thinks "I'll just give it one more day" or "I'll get out if it goes down another 2 points." For Lescarbeau, discipline also demands being there every day to check the system signals and enter the orders. Every day means every day; no minivacations, no days off—not even after surgery. The essence of discipline is that there are no exceptions.

Many people are attracted to the markets because they think it is an easy way to make a lot of money. Ironically, hard work is one of the key common denominators I have noted among the traders I have interviewed. Even though Lescarbeau has already developed trading systems that are incredible—his trading system results are by far the best I have ever seen and beyond anything I even thought possible—he continues his research without abatement. He doesn't relax even though what he is using is working and has been working for years, but instead he plows ahead daily, as if what he is using will cease to work tomorrow.

Risk control means longevity. Some traders achieve high returns for many years, but with large equity retracements as a by-product of their methodology. Although these traders can attain great track records, they often skate near the edge—and in doing so, they are always in danger of falling. A trader like Lescarbeau, who keeps his losses very low, has a much higher probability of long-term success.

★

Update on Steve Lescarbeau

Although Lescarbeau has fared quite well during the bear market—his family partnership was up 39 percent from April 2000 through September 2002—more than half the gains were realized before September 2000, and as indicated in the following update, Lescarbeau has lost confidence in the efficacy of his systems.

What happened in February 2001? [Lescarbeau's account was down 5 percent that month—a single-month decline that exceeded his previous worst peak-to-valley equity drawdown.]

The problem actually began in November 2000 when I lost over 3 percent, which at the time was the worst month I ever had. Although December approximately recovered the entire November loss and the system was profitable again in January, the November loss was an early warning sign that something was potentially wrong. Then came the February loss, and I knew I was dealing with something I had never seen before. It was a period when what I had been doing for many years simply didn't work.

How much time do you need to decide that a system is not working?

Well, there is no easy answer to that question. The system I was using at the time had worked for several years in real time and for decades in backtesting. So, maybe I was bit too slow in reacting.

When did you switch systems?

I basically stayed out of the market during April 2001. I really didn't know what I was going to do because I hadn't come up with anything. I just knew I couldn't continue to use the same system anymore because it had stopped working. By May, I had developed a modified system that was workable, but not one I felt really good about. By summer I came up with the system I am using now.

What would have happened if you had continued to use your previous system after March 2001?

It would have been a disaster. I would have been down 25 to 30 percent.

I know you have switched to what you consider improved systems several times in the past. Would some of these older systems have worked better?

They would have done even worse!

How is your current system different from the one you stopped using after March 2001?

Essentially, the system I use now makes it much more difficult to get a buy signal and much easier to get a liquidation signal. So I am making far fewer trades, and when I am in the market, it takes a smaller adverse price move to get me out. For example, I have not had a buy signal in nearly four months. With my old trading system, I would have been trading through this decline and getting killed.

If, on balance, your system tends to keep you out of the market during periods of declining prices, it seems like you should be able to significantly improve your results by going short during those times instead of going into cash. Why don't you use your liquidation signals as short signals?

The truth is that I have never been able to develop a system that could make money consistently—and consistently is the key word—on the short side.

Why couldn't you simply reverse to short on a liquidation signal instead of going neutral?

If I could go short the funds I buy, that would be great, but of course that's impossible. If I want to go short, I have to either buy a short stock index fund or directly go short stock indexes. The trouble is that my systems work tremendously better on the types of mutual funds I buy—aggressive growth funds—than on stock indexes, for which their performance is only mediocre.

After our original interview, you decided to accept investor money again. Then in the second quarter of 2001, you once again told investors that you were returning their money. What was the reason for this decision?

Because I had done so poorly, and I had completely lost confidence that the system I was using would continue to make any money. Moreover, not only did I lose confidence in my system, but I had no idea what I was going to do to fix it. It was just the low point in my career.

Although the system I subsequently developed kept me from losing money, in truth, my trading approach hasn't worked since the fall of 2000. For the past six months, I've hardly traded at all. I believe the drastic deterioration of the types of systems I use is a direct consequence of the Internet-related surge in hype and speculative activity, which has made the market much more random. There has been a marked decrease in market follow-through. Trends that used to last a week, last two days; trends that used to last two days, last three hours. I'm not bullish on my approach until we wipe out the excess, which I think will take years. Virtually all primary bull markets have been followed by bear markets and then a long period of malaise. This one will be no different.

I take it then that you don't anticipate any significant recovery in the stock market for the foreseeable future, despite the sharp price slide we've seen.

If you study the long-term history of stock prices you repeatedly see that it takes a very long time for markets to recover after major tops. As Schiller points out in his book *Irrational Exuberance,* after each of the three major peaks in the twentieth century—1901, 1929, and 1966—the stock market took roughly twenty years or so to get back to even [in inflation-adjusted terms]. Since the 2000 peak occurred at even significantly higher valuation levels than any previous market top, including 1929, it wouldn't be surprising if it took another twenty years to get back to that level [in inflation-adjusted terms]. The implication is that the market bottom probably won't come for another few years, and if it's like all other previous major bottoms, it won't occur until we are at extreme low levels.

How far down could you see the market going?

For me the magic number is five: somewhere around 500 in the S&P 500, somewhere around 5,000 in the Dow, somewhere around 500 in the Nasdaq 100, and sometime in about five years [2007].

That sounds almost mystical.

Well that's just my guess. Of course, I won't let this projection interrupt my trading. The next time I get a buy signal, I will buy.

What do you think is the biggest misconception people currently have about the market?

The biggest misunderstanding that the average investor has is the inability to comprehend the concept of years. People who know I trade the markets are constantly asking me where I think the bottom is going to be. "Are we almost there yet?" they ask. When I tell them I think the bottom is at least several years away, they look at me like I have three heads.

MICHAEL MASTERS

Swimming Through the Markets

Five years ago, Masters was an unemployed stockbroker; today, he is one of the largest stock traders in the country. Masters, an Atlanta-based fund manager, got his start in the business as a broker, but he never liked it. After five years and growing frustration, he virtually forced his own firing. With no other qualifications than desire and confidence, Masters decided to start his own fund. He raised his start-up capital by selling ten 1-percent shares in his new company at $7,000 per share (an astoundingly fortuitous investment for his initial backers).

In 1995, he launched the Marlin fund, a name that reflects his love of sportsfishing. During the five years he has managed the hedge fund, Masters has achieved the extremely rare combination of lofty returns and low risk: an average annual compounded return of 86 percent, with only three losing months—the worst a relatively minuscule 3 percent decline. As of April 2000, assets under management had grown past the half-billion-dollar mark, reflecting the combined influence of huge returns and a steady influx of new investors. Total assets would have been even larger, but Masters had decided to close his fund to new investment, reflecting his concern that excessive asset growth could impede performance.

Although its plus-one-half-billion-dollar asset base places Masters Capital Management among the larger hedge funds, the figure drastically understates the firm's trading activity. Because of Masters's extremely high turnover of positions—far more rapid than the industry average—the firm's level of transactions rivals that of the country's largest hedge funds and mutual funds.

During trading hours Masters's concentration on the market is intense and all-inclusive. To avoid any interruptions or distractions, he locks himself in the trading room with the company's trader, Tom Peil. The firm's research analysts know the computer lock combination and can gain entry if they have sufficiently urgent market information. With rare exception, Masters will not accept any phone calls during market hours. "He is so completely absorbed watching the market," says Peil, "that when an important call does come in, I can yell at him repeatedly to pick up the phone, and he won't hear me until I scream something ludicrous like 'purple dragons!'"

Masters is affectionately known as "the big sloppy" by his staff, a nickname that reflects both his size (six foot five) and the copious amounts of food he eats at his desk, leaving a wake of leftovers and dirty paper plates. One of Masters's idiosyncrasies is that he is so used to using a keyboard to navigate the computer screen—a habit that dates back to the premouse days when DOS reigned supreme—that he still refuses to use a mouse except when it is absolutely necessary. "Mike's keyboard clattering is a constant throughout the day," says Peil. "We joke that when Mike's time comes, they will have to bury him with his keyboard."

Although he quips about Masters's quirks, Peil's admiration for him comes through very strongly. Peil, a veteran of brokerage firm trading desks, was enjoying his retirement, trading his own account, when he met Masters. He was so struck with Masters's character and talent that he came out of retirement to join the firm as a trader. When I asked Peil what he found so impressive about Masters, he cited three factors, two of which were synonymous with honesty: "First, his integrity; second, his morality; and third, his determination to succeed."

Masters is an openly religious man. During our conversations, he referred to the importance of his belief in God to his life in general, and his trading in particular. "Believing in a higher power gives me the strength to deal with the losses that are an inevitable part of this business. For example, I lost millions of dollars today, which would have been difficult to handle otherwise." Although Masters didn't mention it himself, I learned that he tithes his income. He also works at a Christian mission regularly.

Since I was arriving in Atlanta in the evening and had to catch a connecting flight the next morning, Masters and I decided to conduct the interview over dinner. Masters suggested a favorite restaurant of his: Bacchanalia. The food was superb, and if you are ever in Atlanta, I can heartily recommend it, with one caveat: cabdrivers apparently can't find the place. My cab from the airport got lost, and for all I know the first two cabs the restaurant called to pick me up are still circling Atlanta.

How did you first get interested in the stock market?

My dad traded for a living back in the 1970s. When I was about eleven or twelve, I became curious about what he did and asked him a lot of questions. He gave me a book to read, *When to Sell Stocks* by Justin Mammis. Note that the title of the book wasn't *When to Buy Stocks*, but *When to Sell Stocks*. My dad's focus was mainly on short selling.

How did your dad do in the markets?

He did well enough to support a family for five or six years.

What happened after that?

He went back to school to earn an M.B.A. and then established a consulting business.

Did you learn anything about the markets from your dad?

Definitely. He taught me the importance of taking profits, which I have incorporated into our strategy.

Taking profits in what sense?

The idea that a profit isn't real until it is realized.

The other big influence for me were my uncles, Uncle Louie and Uncle Larry, who both traded stocks. When I was little, we would have family gatherings. Uncle Louie would be seated on one side, Uncle Larry on the other, and my dad across the table, and they would all be talking about the stock market. I was the only son, and I thought that's what men did. When I got into the business, Uncle Louie and Uncle Larry were accounts of mine, and I learned a lot from them.

What did they teach you?

The importance of discipline. If you have a loss, get out.

Did you go to college with the intention of becoming a money manager?

No, I went to college with the intention of becoming a doctor. Actually, I went to the University of Tennessee because I had a swimming scholarship. That experience helped a lot. There is no way I could be doing what I am today without that background.

How so?

Getting used to the pain. We did some crazy sets in training. We would swim as much as twenty thousand or twenty-five thousand meters a day. The coach would come over and say, "Okay, we're going to do a hundred 200s" [a hundred repeats of 200-yard intervals], and your heart would sink. You just knew it was going to hurt.

How far did you get in your swimming career?

I was a collegiate all-American in the sprint freestyle.

What does all-American imply?

It means that you are in the top eight in the NCAA championships.

Did you try out for the Olympics?

I went to the Olympic trials, but I didn't make it. I came down with the mumps the summer before the trials, and I didn't have enough time to get back into peak condition. I would, however, have ranked high enough the year before to have made the team.

Did you try out at the next Olympic trials?

Swimming is not a real profitable sport. I would have been twenty-six by the time of the next trials. I could have hung around, but I had been swimming a long time, and I'd had enough of it.

Do you still swim?

I swim a little bit, but not as much as I should. I just don't have the time.

How did you make the transition from being premed to being a trader?

When I got through organic chemistry, I realized that I didn't have any passion for going to medical school.

Why did you want to become a doctor in the first place?

When I was ten years old, I had a really bad accident and ended up in the hospital for many weeks. As a kid, I was impressed by watching the doctors in the hospital, and I thought it would be a good occupation. I liked the idea that the job combined both science and helping people.

What kind of accident?

I ran into a plate glass window. We had sliding doors out to our pool. One day I was running back into the house, and I thought I had left the doors open, but they were closed. I ran right into the glass and it shattered, cutting me all over. The cut in my leg went all the way through to my femur and severed my tendons. I don't know if you noticed, but I still have a limp. I had to relearn how to walk. Actually, that is how I first became involved in swimming; it was part of the therapy.

Your mom must have kept the windows very clean.

Yes she did. But after the accident she always made sure to have tape across the glass doors.

What changed your mind about becoming a doctor? There had to be more to it than not liking organic chemistry.

After two or three years in college, I realized that I really didn't have any desire to become a doctor; I was only on that track because of a goal I had as a ten-year-old. I took some finance courses, which I really enjoyed, including an investment course that was tremendous, and I switched my major.

What did you learn in that investment course?

The typical valuation theories—the Graham & Dodd–type stuff [a classic investment text].

Do you use that type of analysis in your own trading?

I don't use it much, but it's a good background to have. I think it's very useful just so that you can measure other investors' perceptions of what is important.

What part of the academic background might still find its way into your current approach?

Portfolio theory. The conventional theory is that you should diversify your portfolio so that you can remove the *unsystematic*, or company specific, risk. That way, if a company blows up, you don't get hurt by it. But that also means that you end up tracking the index. If your goal is to outperform the index, using that type of strategy makes it very difficult to succeed. We stand portfolio theory on its head. We actually try to *take* unsystematic risk by being in stocks when the unsystematic risk is high relative to the systematic risk (that is, at times when the stock's price movement will be more influenced by company-specific events as opposed to directional movements of the stock market as a whole).

What did you do after you graduated college?

I decided to go to business school, which allows you to put off the decision of doing anything for another couple of years. I applied to Emory, which is a local school, and I didn't bother applying anywhere else. I was told by the admission officer that they'd love to have me, but I didn't have the work experience, which I found out was one of the entry requirements at Emory at the time. The only work experience I had was mowing lawns and summer jobs at a steel mill, which didn't exactly qualify.

I decided to get work experience by applying for a job in the brokerage industry. There was a fellow who lived near me who worked at a brokerage firm and thought I was industrious because he had seen me mowing lawns in the neighborhood. Also, he had played college football, and he liked the idea that I had been a college athlete as well. He told me that he would give me a shot as a broker, even though I didn't have the typical profile.

What is the typical profile?

Sales experience.

Did they have a training course?

Yes, two weeks on how to sell.

What happened after the training course?

I was given a list of people to cold-call.

Was that difficult to do?

It was real difficult to do. I also did cold-call visits with one of the other trainees. We knocked on doors in the neighborhood, trying to get people to open accounts. One time we went into a grocery store, and it turned out that the owner's brother-in-law had lost all his money in the stock market. The grocery owner chased us out of his store, swinging a big loaf of bread at us, and yelling, "I don't want to talk to you brokers. Get out of here!" *[He laughs lengthily at the recollection.]*

I guess you were lucky it wasn't a hardware store. What percent of your cold calls were you able to convert into accounts?

About 1 percent. After I had been in the business for a while, I figured out that I wanted to be on the managing side, not the selling side. The company, however, wanted you to sell financial products. If you were a broker who wanted to manage money, they looked at you as if you had two heads.

Were you successful as a broker?

I was able to survive, which I guess is somewhat successful. One of the problems I had with my company was that I thought their commission structure was too high. So I just changed it.

Did you have approval to do that?

I didn't.

You just unilaterally lowered commissions?

Yes, because the commissions were just too high to trade.

So you realized even then that paying full commissions would make trading a losing game?

Absolutely. If the clients are not going to win, they are not going to stay with you.

How did your company react to your lowering commissions?

They were upset when they found out about it.

By how much did you reduce commissions?

About 90 percent. Of course, now you have discount brokerage, but it was different then.

What did you know at the time that was right, and what did you know that was wrong?

I learned that if I thought ahead about events, I usually made money, but if I waited until events happened, I would lose. For example, I remember situations where a company reported positive earnings, but the stock sold off because the news had already been discounted. That was a good lesson for me.

When did you make the transition from a broker to a fund manager?

I reached a point where the trading in my own account was becoming reliably profitable, and I felt I was ready to go out on my own. But the actual move was a forced issue.

Forced issue in what sense?

I was fired. I had a number of discretionary accounts that were below the firm's minimum. The office manager said, "You can't trade these accounts below the company minimum."

I said, "Yes I can."

He said, "No you can't. You're out of here!"

It was something that I psychologically really wanted to happen. I guess I just needed a good kick in the ass to make the transition. I wasn't comfortable being a broker anymore.

Why is that?

Because anytime you're trying to make money for both the firm and the client, there is a built-in conflict. I wanted to manage money on a performance basis because I thought it was far cleaner. I had some ethical problems with the brokerage business.

Such as?

There are subtle pressures for you to push stocks the firm is underwriting and to sell mutual funds with whom the firm has a relationship, even though they may be lower-rated funds.

What if you try to sell other mutual funds?

You may get a lower commission on the sale, and in some cases you may not get any commission at all.

What happened after you got fired?

I spoke to my dad about what I should do, and he suggested that I should try going out on my own. Although I liked the idea of having my income based on my performance, I was concerned about whether anyone would be interested in having me manage their money when my only experience was being a broker.

What made you believe that you could be a successful money manager?

Except for my dad and my wife, Suzanne, everyone said that you couldn't trade successfully and advised me against trying to do it. Your books [*Market Wizards* and *The New Market Wizards*] were actually very helpful because they showed me that it was possible. Just knowing that was very important. I realized that if somebody could make money trading, so could I. Also, the fact that I had competed successfully at the highest levels of swimming gave me confidence that I could excel in this business as well.

But what was that confidence based on? Were you getting trading results anything like those you are getting now?

For years, I had done only slightly better than breakeven in my own account. But my trading results were just beginning to improve significantly when I was fired.

What changed?

I started focusing on catalysts. One thing that helped me tremendously was writing the software for my trading ideas. My father wrote a lot of software for his food service consulting business, and he advised me, "If you really want to know something, you should write software for it."

What did you put in your model?

All types of inputs, but I found that the catalysts outweighed everything else. As a result, the model ended up focusing almost completely on the catalysts.

What exactly do you mean by *catalysts*?

A catalyst is an event or an upcoming event that has the potential to trigger a stock price move by changing the market's perception about a company.

Isn't a catalyst by definition a one-time event? How do you model one-time events?

Most catalysts are repetitive events—earnings are reported four times a year; retail companies report same-store sales monthly; airline companies report load factors monthly, and so on.

How do you use an event such as an earnings report to make trading decisions?

There have been lots of academic studies to show that stocks with positive earnings surprises tend to outperform the market, but the margin of improvement is relatively moderate. Frequently, you may find that when you buy a stock after a positive earnings surprise, you are buying it near a price peak because the earnings surprise was already discounted.

How could it be discounted if it was a "surprise"?

We are talking about two different things. An "earnings surprise" is defined by academics and Wall Street as a number that is above or below the consensus estimate by some minimum margin. Whether an earnings surprise is discounted or not, however, depends on the price trend before the report's release. For example, if a stock goes up 10 points in a flat market during the week prior to the earnings report, and earnings are reported as only a nickel better than the consensus, it may be a "surprise" in terms of the academic definition, but it's probably already discounted.

Don't any of the academic studies consider the stock price trend before a number's release?

No, they only look at whether a number beats the consensus expectations. Although this is still useful information, by considering other factors, such as the price trend in the stock before the release of the earnings report and the magnitude of the difference between reported earnings and expected earnings, you can significantly increase the probabilities of a successful trade.

For example, if I crossed a street without looking, I could decrease my chances of getting hit by a car by crossing at 2 A.M. instead of midday. That would be analogous to the information these academic studies use—it is worthwhile, but there is lots of room for improvement. What if I listened when I crossed the street? That would reduce the odds of my getting hit by a car even more. What if I not only listened, but looked one way? My survival odds would increase further. What If I looked both ways? I would increase my chances even more. That's what we're doing in our analysis. We are trying to increase the probabilities of a trade being successful as much as possible.

Therefore, as an example, I assume that if a stock moved down before a positive earnings surprise, it increases the probabilities of a bullish market response.

Absolutely. If a stock goes down before a report because of negative expectations and then there is a positive earnings surprise, there will be shorts who have to cover, new investors who want to buy, and a completely undiscounted event. In this type of situation you can get a tremendous response in the stock.

But won't the stock gap up sharply after earnings are reported and eliminate the profit opportunity?

The stock price will go up, but usually it will not fully discount the change. That is one of the problems with the *efficient market hypothesis*. The market doesn't discount all information instantaneously.

What happens when you put on a position before a report because you anticipate a better-than-expected figure and the actual number is worse than expected or vice versa?

We just get out, usually right away. We make lots of trades, and I make mistakes all the time. Every day I come in and get humbled *[he laughs]*.

The whole Street focuses on events that provide catalysts; what gives you the edge?

Our whole focus is looking for catalysts. It's not just part of our strategy; it is our strategy.

How do you decide when to get out of a position?

One thing that has been tremendously helpful is the use of time stops. For every trade I put on, I have a time window within which the trade should work. If something doesn't happen within the time stop, the market is probably not going to discount that event.

What is your balance between longs and shorts?

Our net position averages about 40 percent net long and has ranged between 90 percent net long and 10 percent net short. A typical breakdown would be 50 percent long and 10 percent short, with the remainder in cash.

That's a pretty large portion to keep in cash.

We have a dual mission: to make money for our investors and to preserve capital. Keeping about 40 percent in cash acts as a performance stabilizer.

How are you able to trounce the index returns while keeping such a large portion of your capital in cash?

We look at our business like a grocery store. You can get leverage in two ways: by taking on larger positions or by turnover. Just like a grocery store, we're constantly getting inventory in and moving it out the door. If we have a piece of meat that's going bad, we mark it down to get rid of it.

Typically, how long might you hold a position?

On average, about two to four weeks.

What percent of your trades are profitable?

Just over 70 percent.

Do you use technical analysis?

We use technical analysis not because we think it means something, but because other people think it means something. We are always looking for market participants to take us out of a trade, and in that sense, knowing the technical points at which people are likely to be buying or selling is helpful.

Do you use the Internet as an information source?

The main thing I use on the Internet is TheStreet.com. I like Jim Cramer's running market commentary. This Web page is one of the best Internet resources available to the ordinary investor. One thing I would caution investors about, however, is paying attention to chat rooms, where the information can be very tainted because people have an agenda.

Are there trades that have provided valuable lessons?

Hundreds. When you order business cards, you get a huge stack of them. I hardly ever hand out any business cards because I am not in marketing. Instead, I use the back of my business cards to jot down trade lessons. For any trade that I find instructive regarding market behavior, I'll write down the stock symbol and a brief summary of what I think I learned from the trade. That's how I developed and continue to build my trading model.

I believe that writing down your trading philosophy is a tremendously valuable exercise for any investor. Writing down your trading ideas helps clarify your thought process. I can remember spending many weekends at the library writing down my investment philosophy: what catalysts I was looking for; how I expected them to affect a stock; and how I would interpret different price responses. I must have accumulated over five hundred pages of trading philosophy. Frankly, it was a lot of drudge work, and I could only do it for so long in one sitting. But the process was invaluable in developing my trading approach.

What other advice do you have for investors?

One of the benefits of having been a retail broker is that I got to see a lot of people's mistakes. Based on this experience, the most important advice I can offer investors is: Have a plan. Know why you are buying a stock, and know what you are looking for on the trade. If you just take a step back and think about what you are doing, you can avoid a lot of mistakes.

Masters's approach can be summarized as a four-step process:

1. *Learn from experience*. For any trade that is instructive (winner or loser), write down what you learned about the market from that trade. It doesn't make any difference whether you keep a trader's diary or use the back of business cards, as Masters does; the important thing is that you methodically record market lessons as they occur.
2. *Develop a trading philosophy*. Compile your experience-based trading lessons into a coherent trading philosophy. Two points should be made here. First, by definition, this step will be unachievable by beginners because it will take the experience of many trades to develop a meaningful trading philosophy. Second, this step is a dynamic process; as a trader gathers more experience and knowledge, the existing philosophy should be revised accordingly.
3. *Define high-probability trades*. Use your trading philosophy to develop a methodology for identifying high-probability trades. The idea is to look for trades that exhibit several of the characteristics you have identified as having some predictive value. Even if each condition provides only a marginal edge, the combination of several such conditions can provide a trade with a significant edge.
4. *Have a plan*. Know how you will get into a trade, and know how you will get out of the trade. Many investors make the mistake of only focusing on the former of these two requirements. Masters

not only has a specific method for selecting and entering trades, but he also has a plan for liquidating trades. He will exit a trade whenever one of the following three conditions are met: (a) his profit objective for the trade is realized; (b) the expected catalyst fails to develop or the stock fails to respond as anticipated; (c) the stock fails to respond within a predefined length of time (the "time stop" is triggered).

★

Update on Michael Masters

Masters managed to maintain his profitability during the first two calendar years of the bear market, albeit at more moderate levels, but three-quarters of the way through 2002, he seemed in danger of experiencing his first losing year. Since the start of 2000 through September 2002, he was up 13 percent. While this return may not sound all that impressive and is far below his previous pace, it is worth noting that during the corresponding period, the S&P 500 was down 45 percent and the Nasdaq plummeted 71 percent.

What is your view of the current market?

It has all the earmarks of a classic bear market. The Nasdaq during the past couple of years looks very similar to the Dow from late 1929 through 1932.

Why are you comparing the 1929 Dow to the current Nasdaq as opposed to the current Dow or even the S&P 500?

Just because they look very similar on the charts.

What are the implications of that comparison?

The implications are simply that the percentage price declines could end up being very similar. During 1929–1932, the Dow declined nearly 90 percent. At the recent lows [July 2002], the Nasdaq had fallen nearly 82 percent from its March 2000 peak. Of course, another near 8 percent decline measured relative to the peak would imply another 40 percent plus decline measured relative to the recent low. I don't necessarily believe we need to match the 1929–1932 bear market since current economic conditions are obviously far better than they were in the Great Depression. But then again, in terms of the average annual price rise, the 1990s bull market was more extreme than the 1920s bull market.

What are your long-term expectations for the market?

I think the indexes will maintain a broad trading range, much like we experienced in the late 1970s. We will probably see bullish phases where the market rallies by 30 percent or more, but these will likely be followed by one- to two-year bear markets.

From an investor's perspective, it almost sounds like you are anticipating an average annual return near the dividend yield for the next five to ten years.

I think that's probably a reasonable estimate. I don't think you'll get much more than that.

Well, that's a fairly bearish outlook. It certainly implies significant underperformance relative to the market's long-term average of near 10 percent per year. What makes you so negative?

It's primarily a reversion to the mean argument.

In other words, the excess on the upside was so extreme that we are probably facing a long-term period of underperformance.

Yes, that's my assumption. Although I believe Fed efforts to avoid deflation—a stance made more likely by the experience of Japan in the 1990s—will lead to earnings growth, this improvement will come at the expense of higher inflation and reduced multiples. The net result should be close to a wash for long-term equity prices. Commodities, however, will probably do very well over the long run because the Fed has no choice but to inflate.

Of course, if you are right, it implies that bonds, which are at long-term highs, will trend lower over the long run. The irony is that many people who have been burned in the stock market and are seeking "safety" in the bond market will probably compound the damage by losing money in bonds.*

*Although bonds pay a steady return, many less sophisticated investors do not sufficiently appreciate the fact that price declines in bonds due to higher interest rates can outweigh interest income, resulting in negative total returns. With interest rates at long-term lows, the danger of negative total returns in bonds is significant, particularly if Masters is correct in his expectations for increased inflation over the long term.

Yes, if you're placing money in bonds as a long-term investment, you are essentially betting that we will repeat the Japanese experience—that is, that the Fed won't be successful in avoiding deflation—which is not a bet I would make.

How is trading in the bear market different from trading in the bull market?

The symmetry between the euphoric bull market of 1999 and this year's unrelenting bear market is quite amazing. In 1999, a company announcement that it was expanding its business to the Internet would be sufficient to propel its stock price $20 higher overnight. This year, a *Wall Street Journal* story about a company's accounting is enough to trigger a near instantaneous $20 decline in the stock price. So you are seeing the same type of crazy price moves, except they are on the downside instead of the upside. The fear in 2002 is just as intense as the greed in 1999. The analogy is that long positions are now subject to the same type of sudden large irrational adverse price moves as short positions were in the 1999 bull market. However, just as in 1999, I believe the current situation will be temporary.

What advice would you have for investors at this juncture?

I think the only way you will make money in the U.S. stock market over the next ten years is by adopting a contrarian approach. Whenever there is panic in the air, as there was in July 2002, you have to be a willing buyer, even though you may not want to be. Then if a year later, prices have rebounded and optimism appears to be returning to the market, you will have to get out. In other words, if you can do the opposite of what people around you are doing, you should be able to make good returns.

The contrarian approach went out of style in the 1990s because people just wanted what was hot. But if you go back to the 1960s and 1970s, the only way to make money was to be a buyer near the lower part of the trading range and a seller near the upper part of the range. I believe we are facing a similar situation over the next five to ten years, or longer.

JOHN BENDER

Questioning the Obvious

If John Bender is right about options*—and, given his performance, there is good reason to believe he is—then virtually everyone else is wrong. Bender asserts that the option pricing theory developed by Nobel Prize–winning economists, which underlies virtually all option pricing models used by traders worldwide, is fundamentally flawed. This contention is not just a theoretical argument; Bender's entire methodology is based on betting against the price implications of conventional option models. Bender places trades that will profit if his model's estimates of price probabilities are more accurate than those implied by prevailing option prices, which more closely reflect standard option pricing models.

Bender has maintained a surprisingly low profile, in view of the large sums of money he is managing and his excellent performance. His fund did not show up in any of the industry databases I checked. As was the case for the majority of interview subjects in this book and its two predecessors, I found Bender through networking with industry contacts.

Bender graduated with high honors from the University of Pennsylvania in 1988, receiving a degree in biophysics. During his summers as an undergraduate, Bender held several scientific jobs, including positions at Livermore Labs and the Marine Biological Laboratories at Woods Hole. Although he liked science, he was disenchanted because the career scientists he observed were forced to spend much of their time seeking

*It is recommended that readers unfamiliar with options first review the brief primer on options in the appendix before reading this chapter.

grants instead of doing research. At the same time, he became intrigued with the markets and saw that they provided a challenging application for his analytical skills.

Bender began trading his own account after graduation, but he had only a few thousand dollars of risk capital. After a year, he was able to raise $80,000 in financial backing. He traded this account from August 1989 through March 1995, averaging a compounded annual return of 187 percent during this period, with only three losing quarters, the worst being an 11 percent decline.

After taking a sabbatical, Bender launched his fund in August 1996, with returns over the subsequent three and a half years averaging 33 percent. Although still quite respectable, you might wonder what caused this steep decline in returns relative to the performance in his personal account in prior years. The answer is very simple: leverage. For the fund, Bender reduced his leverage by a factor of approximately 4 to 1 (which because of the effect of monthly compounding reduced the annual return by a greater amount), placing a strong emphasis on risk control. To date, the fund's worst decline from an equity peak to a subsequent low has been only 6 percent. In addition to managing hundreds of millions in his own fund, Bender also manages an undisclosed allocation from the Quantum fund, for which he trades currency options.

It is quite common for Market Wizards to use a portion of their substantial trading profits to support favorite charities or causes. I found one of Bender's uses for his winnings particularly noteworthy for its originality, long-lasting impact, and hands-on directness in mitigating a problem before the opportunity for action disappears: He is buying up thousands of acres of the Costa Rican rain forest to protect this area from destruction by developers.

A day before leaving for New York City to conduct interviews for this book, I learned that Bender was scheduled to be in the city at the same time. Since he lives in Virginia, which is not near any of the other traders I planned to interview, it seemed convenient to arrange a meeting on our mutually coincident visit to New York. The only problem was that my schedule was already booked solid. We decided to meet for a late dinner. To simplify the logistics, Bender booked a room at my hotel.

We met in our hotel lobby before leaving for dinner. It was an extremely warm summer evening. Bender was wearing a suit and tie, while I had considered substituting Dockers for jeans a sufficient concession to being dressed for dinner. Bender, who had made the reservations, expressed concern whether I would be allowed into the restaurant dressed as I was and suggested calling to make sure. I assured him that I usually did not encounter any problems because of my casual dress. He seemed almost disappointed when this proved to be the case. As the evening progressed, I became aware that Bender was clearly uncomfortable in his suit and tie, which was obviously atypical dress for him as well, and somewhat envious of the fact that I had gotten away going casual. His large frame seemed to strain in his more formal clothes.

The interview was conducted over a wonderful multicourse meal in a sushi restaurant. We left nearly four hours later, just short of midnight, when we suddenly realized that we were the last remaining diners and that the staff was milling about impatiently, waiting for us to depart. We took a brief break upon returning to the hotel, I to visit my orphaned wife, who had accompanied me to the city, and Bender to check on trades on the Tokyo Stock Exchange in which his firm is a heavy participant. When we met again in the hotel lobby fifteen minutes later, Bender was wearing shorts, a sloppy T-shirt, and a look of relief at having been freed from his suit and tie. The interview finished at three-thirty in the morning as the second of my three-hour tapes rolled to an end.

What was your career goal in college?

My plan was to be a research physicist.

What area of physics were you interested in?

I majored in biophysics. One of the projects I spent a lot of time on was trying to develop a method for displaying three-dimensional information using a light microscope. When you look at very small structures inside of a cell, you essentially have two choices: you can look at them with an electron microscope or you can look at them with a light microscope. If you use an electron microscope, you have

the advantage that it magnifies objects very well. The problem is that you don't have any idea whether the cell you see bears any resemblance to what it looked like when it was alive because in order for the image to show up, you first have to infuse the cell with heavy metals. I don't know about you, but I'm sure that if someone shot me and placed me in a vat of molten lead, I wouldn't come out looking anything like what I look like. The method of observation changed the object being observed. People would write papers saying that they had found a new structure in a cell, but then it would turn out to be merely an artifact of metal crystals precipitating inside the cell.

Everyone recognized the problem with using electron microscopes. Therefore the preferable approach was to try to use light microscopes. The main problem with light microscopes, however, is that when you use the extremely high magnification needed to look at very small objects, the depth of field approaches zero. You can see one flat slice in focus and everything else is out of focus, which makes it very difficult to view three-dimensional objects. If you try to view more than one layer, all you get is mud because the out-of-focus information wins out. To circumvent this obstacle, we had to come up with programs that would filter out the out-of-focus information. It's a very interesting mathematical problem.

Why did you gravitate away from physics?

Physics was a lot of fun as a student. Everyone wants you to provide research help. You get a chance to work on stuff you find interesting, write research papers, and show everyone how smart you are. When you are no longer a student, however, you have to support yourself in the eyes of the institution, which means writing endless grant proposals and churning out papers for the main reason of getting tenure. You end up spending 90 percent of your time *not* doing physics. I would be busy working on physics all day while the other people in the lab would be tearing their hair out writing grant proposals. I realized that wasn't for me.

When did you first get interested in the market?

When I was growing up, I spent all my time thinking about math and physics. I was a bit of a twisted kid. I started looking at the options market as early as high school because I thought it was a fun way to apply the mathematics I was learning.

When did you start trading?

In my senior year of college. The thing that I liked about trading was that the only limitation you had was yourself.

What did you trade?

Stocks and stock options on the Philadelphia Stock Exchange.

How did you end up trading on the floor?

I had a friend who was a market maker. I went down to the floor with him a few times and decided it was a perfect job for me. I had always been interested in the markets and mathematics, and option trading combined the two perfectly.

How did you get the money to trade when you first started out on the floor of the exchange?

I was able to raise $80,000 from a few backers who were professional gamblers. Because I was a serious Go and backgammon player, I had met some of the world's best backgammon and poker players. One of my investors had just won the World Series of poker and another investor was one of the most successful backgammon players in world.

What did they get for backing you?

Initially, 50 percent of my profits. I eventually bought them out. There are a lot of similarities between gambling and trading, although gambling is a bad term.

Because?

Because it implies that your results depend on luck. The people that I'm talking about look at poker or backgammon as a business, not a game of chance. There are a few things that are essential to success in both trading as well as playing gambling games as a business. First, you have to understand edge and maximize your edge. Second, you have to be able to deal with losing. For example, a world-ranked backgammon player could lose $100,000 to a total pigeon because of bad luck. If that happens, he can't lose his head. He has to stay calm and continue to do what he is supposed to be doing. Third, you have to understand gambler's ruin—not playing too big for your bankroll.

It might seem that if you have an edge, the way to maximize the edge is to trade as big as you can. But that's not the case, because of risk. As a professional gambler or as a trader, you are constantly walking the line between maximizing edge and minimizing your risk of tapping out.

How do you decide what is the right balance?

There is no single right answer to that question. It depends on the individual person's risk tolerance. Let's say you saved up enough money to live out your life in relative comfort but without the ability to make extravagant expenditures. I come along and offer to give you ten-to-one odds on the flip of a coin. The only catch is that you have to bet your entire net worth. That bet has a tremendous edge, but it is probably a bet that you wouldn't want to make, because the value of what you can gain, even though it is a much larger sum of money, is much less than the value of what you could lose. If, however, you are just out of college with $10,000 in savings and your whole earnings career ahead of you, you would probably want to take the same bet. As a fund manager, the correct answer as to how to maximize your edge will depend not only on your own risk characteristics, but also on your perception of the risk profiles of your investors.

How long did you trade on the floor of the Philadelphia stock exchange?

Just over five years.

How did you do?

By the time I left, I had turned my initial $80,000 stake into over $7 million after paying back my investors.

If you were doing so well, why did you leave the floor?

As I made more money, it became increasingly difficult to invest it trading only two or three stocks; it made sense to go off the floor in order to be able to diversify.

How have you been able to make such consistent gains trading options?

To make money in options, you don't need to know what the price of the stock is going to be; all you need to know is the probability distribution [the probabilities of a stock being at different price levels at the time of the option expiration].*

If the Almighty came to me and said, "I won't tell you where IBM is going to be one month from now, but you've been a pretty good boy, so I will give you the probability distribution," I could do the math—and it's not very complicated math—and tell you exactly what every option that expires on that date is worth. The problem is that the Almighty is not giving me or anyone else the probability distribution for the price of IBM a month from now.

The standard approach, which is based on the Black-Scholes formula, assumes that the probability distribution will conform to a normal curve [the familiar bell-shaped curve frequently used to depict probabilities, such as the probability distribution of IQ scores among the population]. The critical statement is that it "assumes a normal probability distribution." Who ran out and told these guys that was the correct probability distribution? Where did they get this idea?

[The Black-Scholes formula (or one of its variations) is the widely used equation for deriving an option's theoretical value. An implicit assump-

*A probability distribution is simply a curve that shows the probabilities of some event occurring—in this case, the probabilities of a given stock being at any price on the option expiration date. The x-axis (horizontal line) shows the price of the stock. The y-axis (vertical line) shows the relative probability of the stock being at different prices. The higher the curve at any price interval, the greater the probability that the stock price will be in that range when the option expires. The area under the curve in any price interval corresponds to the probability of the stock being in that range on the option expiration date. For example, if 20 percent of the area under the curve lies between 50 and 60, it implies that there is a 20 percent chance of the stock being between 50 and 60 on the option expiration date. As another example, if 80 percent of the area under the curve corresponds to prices under 60, the 60 call option, which gives the holder the right to buy the stock at 60, would have an 80 percent chance of expiring worthless.

The shape of the probability distribution curve, which is a snapshot of the probabilities of prices being at different levels on the option expiration date, will determine the option's value. The true shape of this curve is unknown, of course, and can only be estimated. The assumptions made regarding the shape of this curve will be critical in determining the value of an option. Two traders making different assumptions about the shape of the probability distribution will come to two different conclusions regarding an option's true value. A trader who is able to come up with a more accurate estimate of the probability distribution would have a strong edge over other traders.

tion in the formula is that the probabilities of prices being at different levels at the time of the option expiration can be described by a normal curve*—the highest probabilities being for prices that are close to the current level and the probabilities for any price decreasing the further above or below the market it is.]

A normal distribution would be appropriate if stock price movements were analogous to what is commonly called "the drunkard's walk." If you have a drunkard in a narrow corridor, and all he can do is lurch forward or backward, in order for his movements to be considered a random walk, the following criteria would have to be met:

1. He has to be equally likely to lurch forward as backward.
2. He has to lurch forward by exactly the same distance he lurches backward.
3. He has to lurch once every constant time interval.

Those are pretty strict requirements. Not many variables meet these conditions. Stock prices, I would argue, don't even come close [substituting daily price changes for the drunkard's steps].

I don't mean to suggest that Black and Scholes made stupid assumptions; they made the only legitimate assumptions possible, not being traders themselves. In fact, they won the Nobel Prize for it. Although, to be honest, that always seemed a bit strange to me because all they used was high school mathematics. All my trading operates on the premise that the most important part is the part that Black-Scholes left out—the assumption of the probability distribution.

Why do you say with such assurance that stock prices don't even come close to a random walk?

As one example, whether you believe in it or not, there is such a thing as technical analysis, which tries to define support and resistance levels and trends. Regardless of whether technical analysis has any validity, enough people believe in it to impact the market. For example, if people expect a stock to find support at 65, lo and behold, they're willing to buy it at 66. That is not a random walk statement.

*See note starting on page 237.

I'll give you another example. Assume people get excited about tech stocks for whatever reason and start buying them. Which funds are going to have the best performance next quarter when mom-and-pop public decide where to invest their money?—the tech funds. Which funds are going to have the best inflows during the next quarter?—the tech funds. What stocks are they going to buy?—not airlines, they're tech funds. So the tech funds will go up even more. Therefore they're going to have better performance and get the next allocation, and so on. You have all the ingredients for a trend. Again, this is not price behavior that is consistent with a random walk assumption.

You've seen this pattern increasingly in the recent run-up in the U.S. stock market. The rampant uptrend has been fueled by constant inflows into the same funds that are buying the same stocks, driving these stocks to values that are ridiculous by any historical valuation. You have stocks that have reproduction values of $20 million—someone's Web page system—trading at $1 billion or more. Are they really worth that? I don't want to be the one to say no—after all, they are trading there—but I think ultimately you're going to see the same thing you saw with RCA during the TV boom: a run-up to stratospheric levels and then a crash.

If these companies do their job right and the Internet is what it's supposed to be, with every company having access to every customer, they're going to be cutting one another's margins to the point where very few companies will make much money. If you pick up an issue of *The New Yorker*, you can find twenty ads for booksellers on the Internet. It's a classic example of an industry with perfect competition. There will be some exceptions because there are brand names and some people will do their job better than others, but can the structure support the valuations that are currently out there for the industry? I doubt it.

Why are we seeing valuations for stocks that are so far above their historical levels? Has something changed fundamentally?

Because of the repetitive cycle of price strength bringing in new buying, which causes more price strength. An important factor that has amplified the rally in the Internet stocks is the limited supply of shares in these companies. Most Internet stocks float only about 20 percent or less of their shares.

Another major development during the past five to ten years has been a substantial upward shift in the amount of money insurance companies and pension funds allocate to stock investments. As hedge fund managers, we think we are huge if we are trading one billion dollars. That is nothing compared with insurance companies and pension funds that have assets of trillions of dollars.

If I understand you correctly, your basic premise is that stock price movements are not random and therefore the assumption that prices are normally distributed, which everyone uses to determine option values, cannot be the accurate mathematical representation of the true market. Does that imply that you've come up with an alternative mathematical option pricing model?

Not in the sense that you are probably thinking. It's not a matter of coming up with a one-size-fits-all model that is better than the standard Black-Scholes model. The key point is that the correct probability distribution is different for every market and every time period. The probability distribution has to be estimated on a case-by-case basis.

If your response to Bender's last comment, which challenges the core premises assumed by option market participants, could best be summarized as "Huh?," and assuming that you really care, then you should probably reread the explanation of probability distribution (footnote, page 228). In essence, Bender is saying that not only are conventional option pricing models wrong because they make the unwarranted assumption that prices are normally distributed, but the very idea that any *single* model could be used to estimate option prices for different markets (or stocks) is inherently wrong. Instead, it is necessary to use a different model for every market (or stock).

How do you estimate the probability distribution?

By looking at everything from the fundamentals to technical factors to who is doing what in the market. Each stock has its own probability distribution that depends on a host of factors: Who has what position? Where did the major buyers accumulate their positions? Where are their stop-loss points? What price levels are likely to be technically significant?

Can you get that type of information reliably?

I get that information off the floors in the case of stocks and stock options and from the banks in the case of currencies.

How do you turn information like who is doing what into an alternative option pricing model?

The best example I can think of involves the gold market rather than stocks. Back in 1993, after a thirteen-year slide, gold rebounded above the psychologically critical $400 level. A lot of the commodity trading advisors [money managers in the futures markets, called CTAs for short], who are mostly trend followers, jumped in on long side of gold, assuming that the long-term downtrend had been reversed. Most of these people use models that will stop out or reverse their long positions if prices go down by a certain amount. Because of the large number of CTAs in this trade and their stop-loss style of trading, I felt that a price decline could trigger a domino-effect selling wave. I knew from following these traders in the past that their stops were largely a function of market volatility. My perception was that if the market went back down to about the $390 level, their stops would start to get triggered, beginning a chain reaction.

I didn't want to sell the market at $405, which is where it was at the time, because there was still support at $400. I did, however, feel reasonably sure that there was almost no chance the market would trade down to $385 without setting off a huge calamity. Why? Because if the market traded to $385, you could be sure that the stops would have started to be triggered. And once the process was under way, it wasn't going to stop at $385. Therefore, you could afford to put on an option position that lost money if gold slowly traded down to $385–$390 and just sat there because it wasn't going to happen. Based on these expectations, I implemented a strategy that would lose if gold declined moderately and stayed there, but would make a lot of money if gold went down huge, and a little bit of money if gold prices held steady or went higher. As it turned out, Russia announced they were going to sell gold, and the market traded down gradually to $390 and then went almost immediately to $350 as each stop order kicked off the next stop order.

The Black-Scholes model doesn't make these types of distinctions. If gold is trading at $405, it assumes that the probability that it will be trading at $360 a month from now is tremendously smaller than the probability that it will be trading at $385. What I'm saying is that under the right circumstances, it might actually be more likely that gold will be trading at $360 than at $385. If my expectations, which assume nonrandom price behavior, are correct, it will imply profit opportunities because the market is pricing options on the assumption that price movements will be random.

Could you give me a stock market example?

I'll give you a stock index example. Last year [1998], it was my belief that stocks were trading on money inflows rather than their own intrinsic fundamentals. IBM wasn't going up because the analysts were looking at IBM and saying, "Here's the future earning stream and we predict the price should rise to this level." IBM was going up because people were dumping money into the market, and managers were buying IBM and other stocks because they had to invest the money somewhere.

A market that is driven by inflows can have small corrections, but it has to then immediately recover to new highs to keep generating new money inflows. Otherwise, money inflows are likely to dry up, and the market will fall apart. Therefore, this type of market is likely to either trend higher or break sharply. There is a much smaller-than-normal chance that the market will go down 5 or 6 percent and stay there. Based on this assumption, last year I implemented an option strategy that would make a lot of money if the market went down big, make a little bit if the market went up small, and lose a small amount if the market went down small and stayed there. The market kept up its relentless move upward for the first half the year, and I made a small amount of money. Then the market had a correction and didn't recover right away; the next stop was down 20 percent. I made an enormous amount of money on that move.

Each of your examples has been very market specific. If I said to you that you could come up with any alternative model you wished instead of Black-Scholes, but you had to apply it to all markets, could you do any better than Black-Scholes?

No, given that restriction, the assumption that prices are random is as good as any other assumption. However, just because Black and Scholes used a one-size-fits-all approach doesn't mean it's correct.

Don't other firms such as Susquehanna [a company whose principal was interviewed in *The New Market Wizards*] also trade on models based on perceived mispricings implied by the standard Black-Scholes model?

When I was on the floor of the Philadelphia Stock Exchange, I was typically trading on the other side of firms such as Susquehanna. They thought they had something special because they were using a pricing model that modified the Black-Scholes model. Basically, their modifications were trivial.

I call what they were doing TV set–type adjustments. Let's say I have an old-fashioned TV with an aerial. I turn it on, and the picture is not quite right. I know it's supposed to be Mickey Mouse, but one ear is fuzzy and he is a funny color green. What do I do? Do I sit down and calculate where my aerial should be relative to the location of the broadcast antenna? No, I don't do that. What I do is walk up to the TV, whack it a couple of times, and twist the aerial. What am I doing? I'm operating totally on feedback. I have never thought once about what is really going on. All I do is twist the aerial until the picture looks like what I think it should—until I see Mickey Mouse in all of his glory.

The market-making firms would make minor adjustments to the Black-Scholes model—the same way I twisted the aerial to get Mickey Mouse's skin color to be beige instead of green—until their model showed the same prices that were being traded on the floor. Then they would say, "Wow, we solved it; here is the model!" They would use this model to print out option price sheets and send in a bunch of kids, whom we called "sheet monkeys," to stand on the floor and make markets. But did they ever stop to think about what the right model would be instead of Black-Scholes?" No. They merely twisted the aerial on the TV set until the picture matched the picture on the floor.

This approach may be okay if you are a market maker and all you are trying to do is profit from the price spread between the bid and the offer rather than make statements about which options are fundamentally overpriced or underpriced. As a trader, however, I'm trying to put on positions that identify when the market is mispriced. I can't use a model like that. I need to figure out fundamentally what the real prices should be, not to re-create the prices on the floor.

Even though you manage a quarter of a billion dollars you seem to keep an incredibly low profile. In fact, I've never seen your name in print. Is this deliberate?

As a policy, I don't do interviews with the media.

Why is that?

My feeling is that it is very difficult for a money manager to give an honest interview. Why would I want to be interviewed and tell the world all my best investment ideas? Let's say I am a fund manager and I have just identified XYZ as being the best buy around. Why should I go on TV and announce that to the world? If I really believe that is true, shouldn't I be buying the stock? And if I am buying it, why would I want any competition?

Well, you may already be in the position.

Exactly. The only time anyone touts a position is when they have it on and want to get out. When you turn on some financial TV program and see someone tell you to buy a stock, there's a good chance he's telling you to buy what he wants to sell. I've seen fund managers recommend the stock on TV and then seen their sell orders on the floor the same day.

There is an alternative scenario. You could be bullish on XYZ and have just bought your entire position. If that is the case, it would be beneficial for you to have other people buying the stock, even if you have no intention of selling it.

Isn't that also self-serving and unethical?

No, I would argue that if I own XYZ and want to get out of it, and then I go on TV to tout the stock—that is unethical. But if I have just bought XYZ and own all I want, and I am a long-term

investor who doesn't intend to get out of the stock for another six to eight months, I don't see anything wrong with recommending the stock.

Maybe not in that case. But being on the floor, I've seen all sorts of conflicts between trade recommendations and a firm's own trading activity.

Such as?

I'll give you an example that is a matter of public record and involves over-the-counter stocks—those total dens of thievery. It became recognized that some companies recommended stocks to their clients and then sold the same stocks themselves all day long. Not only were these firms the largest sellers of a stock on the day after they recommended it, but they were also the largest buyers of the stock during the preceding week. Here is how they explained it—I'm paraphrasing, but I am not making any of this up: "These over-the-counter stocks have very little liquidity. If we just recommend the stock, our clients won't be able to buy it because the market will run away. Therefore we have a to buy a few million shares of the stock before we recommend it, so that when we do, we have supply to sell our customers." The SEC, which looked into this practice, accepted their argument, and they continue to do this. It's perfectly legal.

If you took the cynical attitude that all Wall Street recommendations are made to get the firm's large clients or the firm itself out of positions, you would make money. I had a friend who made money using exactly that strategy. In my own trading, when I am estimating the price probability distribution for a stock, and a number of Wall Street firms put out buy recommendations on that stock, it grossly changes the probability distribution—the chances of that stock dropping sharply become much larger.

Why is that?

If a bunch of brokerage firms recommend AOL, after two or three weeks, we figure that everyone who wanted to buy the stock has already bought it. That's the same reason why most fund managers underperform the S&P: They buy the trendy stocks and the stocks where all the good news is. The fact is that they may be buying a good company, but they're getting it at a bad price. Conversely, when a stock gets hit by really bad news, and every analyst downgrades the stock, it's probably a good buy. It may be a bad company, but you are getting a good price—not necessarily right away, but after a few weeks when all the selling on the news has taken place. It's not the current opinion on the stock that matters, but rather the potential change in the opinion.

It doesn't sound like you have a very high regard for Wall Street analysts.

If you tune in CNBC and see a stock that has announced horrendous earnings and is down 40 percent, the next morning, you'll see every analyst on the Street dropping the stock from their recommended list. Where were they the day before? Even though the news is already out and the stock is down 40 percent in after-hours trading, they get credit for recommending liquidation of the stock on the previous day's close because the market hasn't officially opened yet. When you look at their track record, it appears that they recommended liquidating the stock at $50, even though at the time, the stock was trading at $30 in the off-the-floor market before the official exchange opening. Conversely, if a stock announces good news, and the stock is trading sharply higher before the official exchange opening, analysts can recommend a buy and get credit for issuing the recommendation on the previous close.

★

Bender provides some very important insights for option traders, and we'll get to those in a moment. But the most important message of this chapter is: Don't accept anything; question everything. This principle is equally relevant to all traders, and I suspect to all professions. The breakthroughs are made by those that question what is obviously "true." As but one example, before Einstein, the idea that time was a constant seemed so apparent that the alternative was not even considered. By questioning the obvious and realizing that the accepted view had to be wrong (that is, time was variable and dependent on relative velocity), Einstein made the greatest strides in the history of science.

One of the basic tenets of option theory is that the probabilities of different prices on a future date can be described by a normal curve.* Many traders have tweaked this model in various ways. For example, many option market participants have realized that rare events (very large price increases and decreases, such as the October 19, 1987, stock market crash) were far more common in reality than predicted by a normal curve and have adjusted the curve accordingly. (They made the tails of the curve fatter.) Bender, however, has gone much further. He has questioned the very premise of using a normal curve as the starting point for describing prices. He has also questioned the convention of using a single model to describe the price behavior—and by implication option prices—of different markets and stocks. By ditching the concept that price movements behave in the random fashion implicitly assumed by a normal distribution and by dropping the assumption of a universal model, Bender was able to derive much more accurate option pricing models.

Ideally, options should be used to express trades where the trader's expectations differ from the theoretical assumptions of standard option pricing models. For example, if you believe that a given stock has a chance that is much greater than normal of witnessing a large, rapid price rise before the option expiration date, then purchasing out-of-the-money call options might be a much better trade (in terms of return versus risk) than buying the stock. (Out-of-the-money call options are relatively cheap because they will only have value at expiration if the stock price rises sharply.)

As another example, let's say there is an upcoming event for a stock that has an equal chance of being bullish or bearish. But if it is bullish, you expect that a large price rise will be more likely than a moderate price rise. Standard option pricing models, of course, assume that a moderate price rise is always more likely than a large

*To be precise, the representation is a lognormal curve, which is a normal curve of the log values of stock prices. In a lognormal curve, an increase by a factor x is considered as likely as a decrease by a factor $1/x$. For example, if $x = 1.25$, a price increase by a factor of 1.25 (25 percent) is considered as likely as a price decrease by a factor of 1/1.25, or 0.80 (20 percent). The lognormal curve is a better fit than the normal curve because prices can rise by any amount, but can decline only by 100 percent. If applied to prices instead of the log of prices, the symmetry of a normal curve could only be achieved by allowing for negative prices (an impossible event), which in fact is what some early option theoreticians did.

price rise. Insofar as your assumptions are correct and not already discounted by prevailing option prices, it would be possible to construct an option trade that would stack the odds in your favor. As one example, you might sell at-the-money call options and use the premium collected to buy a much larger number of cheaper out-of-the-money call options. This strategy will break even if prices decline, lose moderately if prices rise a little, and win big if prices rise a lot.

The key to using options effectively is to sketch out your expectations of the probabilities of a stock moving to different price levels. If these expectations differ from the neutral price assumptions that underlie a normal distribution curve and standard option pricing models, it implies that there are option strategies that offer a particularly favorable bet—assuming, of course, that your expectations tend to be more accurate than random guesses.

★

Update on John Bender

Bender closed his fund in late 2000, a consequence of a brain aneurysm he suffered earlier in the year. While the stock markets plunged in 2000 (declines of 10 percent in the S&P 500 and 39 percent in Nasdaq), his fund registered an astonishing 269 percent return.

Since closing his fund, Bender has devoted his energies to preserving the Costa Rican rain forest. Bender has used his market winnings to establish a reserve in which he has accumulated ownership of over 5,000 acres. Bender is thrilled that there are already indications of a marked recovery in animal numbers on the reserve. Speaking of poachers, he explains, "Since our land is patrolled and there is land fifty miles away that isn't, they go there." Next, he is planning to reintroduce near-extinct wildlife species into the preserve. Bender's desire to expand the reserve is a primary reason he is considering resuming his trading career, albeit at a much less frenzied pace.

I don't want to ask questions that are too personal, but I don't know how to avoid the subject. Just tell me if you feel uncomfortable talking about it. Did the aneurysm occur while you were trading?

Ironically, it occurred while I was on a long weekend vacation in Costa Rica. At the time, I thought that was kind of weird. I subsequently found out that it is more common for aneurysms to occur when there is a break from high stress than during a period of stress. For example, it is much more common for aneurysms to occur on a weekend than during a weekday.

I know your fund closed a little over a half year after you suffered your aneurysm. Did you recover quickly enough to have any involvement with the fund before it closed, or did your staff just gradually liquidate the positions?

Actually, I was back to watching the markets and supervising the portfolio in terms of risk management within about a month. I wasn't that active in trading, though, because I had speech problems. I couldn't pick up the phone and place an order because it would have been impossible for someone to understand me, and even if I could be understood, I was embarrassed by my speech. I could, however, relay important information to my wife, Ann, who could then relay the message to the appropriate people.

Given the seriousness of your medical condition, why did you return to such stressful activity so quickly?

The fund held huge positions. I felt an obligation to my investors to watch those positions so that they could be closed down in an orderly fashion. As it turned out, during the period before the fund closed—the second and third quarters of 2000—a lot of the events I had anticipated would happen in the markets occurred, and the fund made a huge amount of money.

Was the aneurysm the reason you gave up trading?

It was certainly a wake-up call that my lifestyle had degraded to a point where something had to change. I realized that trading twenty hours a day and sleeping two hours during weekdays was not a sustainable schedule. I also had a friend who was a trader and had just suffered a heart attack at forty-one. Another very important influence was my growing involvement in preserving the Costa Rican rain forest. I felt I wanted to devote my life to the preserve. All of these factors contributed to my decision to quit trading.

Did you view this as a permanent exit or did you expect to return to trading at some future point?

If you asked me at the time, I would have said I probably wouldn't come back. But that would have been my best guess; I didn't know for sure.

Have you begun trading again?

No, but I did start watching the market seriously several weeks ago. If I do resume trading, it will be on a limited basis, trading only in the U.S. time zone, not the twenty-hour days I was doing before.

We've seen a dramatic slide in stock prices since our original interview. Any thoughts about this situation?

I don't want to come off sounding too high and mighty, but this is what I thought would happen when we did our interview.

Namely?

Namely what Warren Buffett has been saying all along: The widespread adoption of a new technology doesn't mean that anyone is going to make a profit. As he points out, most airline companies failed, even though the airplane was a wonderful invention, which lots of people use. Similarly, most car manufacturers also failed, even though almost everyone uses cars. During the late stages of the bull market, you had all these people running around saying that the Internet was going to change the world, and therefore you had to invest. Well, yes the Internet will change the world, but that doesn't mean it's a good investment.

There was also the distortion of the positive feedback loop—higher Internet stock prices influenced more buying of Internet stocks, causing still higher prices and so on. This can only go on for so long before a negative feedback develops. Consider what happened with IPOs during the latter stages of the bull market. Companies with $10 million of computer equipment and an idea that had no barrier to entry were selling at capitalizations of $4 billion. The day when somebody pays billions for a company that takes millions to set up is the day you are going to see twenty smart people start twenty more companies that look exactly the same. And that is precisely what happened.

It's obvious that the combination of wildly inflated stock prices and the absence of barriers to entry had striking bearish implications for Internet companies. But why would the Internet be bearish for other companies?

Because the Internet lowers the barriers to entry into a huge range of different businesses. Unless there is intellectual property involved, your competition is endless. Anyone can now put up a web site for minimal cost and sell the same products as established companies with lots of infrastructure. They don't need a marketing department; they can use the Internet. They don't need a distribution center; they can use UPS. The Internet also makes it easier for consumers to do searches and buy on price comparisons. Unless you are producing an item that involves intellectual property, I would argue that eventually you are going to see your profits go to zero.

Are you still bearish now with stock prices having already declined very sharply from their 2000 highs? What is your long-term view for the market at this juncture?

Have we reached a correct valuation for stocks compared with other bear market lows? No, but I don't think this bear market will end in the usual way with stock prices falling to extreme low valuation levels as is typical at market bottoms. There is just too much money available for investment for that to happen. It's a demographic argument. We are at the threshold of a time period when the baby boomers will be at their peak earning years. At the same time, their expenses will be declining, as more of their mortgages are paid off and their kids get out of college or leave the household. This combination of trends will create a huge pool of money that needs to be invested somewhere. A lot of people right now are willing to let their money sit in cash because they're scared. But cash investments are paying almost nothing. It won't take much to sway people to start putting money back into stocks because the alternative implies almost no return.

DAVID SHAW

The Quantitative Edge

In offices situated on the upper floors of a midtown Manhattan skyscraper, Shaw has assembled scores of the country's most brilliant mathematicians, physicists, and computer scientists with one purpose in mind: to combine their quantitative skills to consistently extract profits from the world's financial markets. Employing a myriad of interrelated, complex mathematical models, the firm, D. E. Shaw, trades thousands of stocks in more than ten countries, as well as financial instruments linked to these stock markets (warrants, options, and convertible bonds). The company seeks to profit strictly from pricing discrepancies among different securities, rigorously avoiding risks associated with directional moves in the stock market or other financial markets (currencies and interest rates).

Shaw's secretiveness regarding his firm's trading strategies is legendary. Employees sign nondisclosure agreements, and even within the firm, knowledge about the trading methodology is on a need-to-know basis. Thus, in my interview, I knew better than to even attempt to ask Shaw explicit questions about his company's trading approach. Still, I tried what I thought were some less sensitive questions:

- What strategies were once used by the firm but have been discarded because they no longer work?
- What fields of math would one have to know to develop the same strategies his firm uses?
- What market anomalies that once provided trading opportunities have so obviously ceased to exist that all his competitors would be aware of the fact?

Even these circumspect questions were met with a polite refusal to answer. Although he did not use these exact words, the gist of Shaw's responses to these various queries could be succinctly stated as: "I prefer not to answer on the grounds that it might provide some remote hint that my competitors could find useful."

Shaw's flagship trading program has been consistently profitable since it was launched in 1989. During its eleven-year life span, the program has generated a 22 percent average annual compounded return net of all fees while keeping risks under tight control. During this entire period, the program's worst decline from an equity peak to a month-end low was a relatively moderate 11 percent—and even this loss was fully recovered in just over four months.

How has D. E. Shaw managed to extract consistent profits from the market for over a decade in both bullish as well as bearish periods? Clearly, Shaw is not talking—or at least not about the specifics of his company's trading strategies. Nevertheless, based on what Shaw does acknowledge and reading between the lines, it may be possible to sketch a very rough description of his company's trading methodology. The following explanation, which admittedly incorporates a good deal of guesswork, is intended to provide the reader with a flavor of Shaw's trading approach.

We begin our overview with *classic arbitrage*. Although Shaw doesn't use classic arbitrage, it provides a conceptual starting point. Classic arbitrage refers to the risk-free trade of simultaneously buying and selling the same security (or commodity) at different prices, therein locking in a risk-free profit. An example of classic arbitrage would be buying gold in New York at $290 an ounce and simultaneously selling the same quantity in London at $291. In our age of computerization and near instantaneous communication, classic arbitrage opportunities are virtually nonexistent.

Statistical arbitrage expands the classic arbitrage concept of simultaneously buying and selling *identical* financial instruments for a *locked-in* profit to encompass buying and selling *closely related* financial instruments for a *probable* profit. In statistical arbitrage, each individual trade is no longer a sure thing, but the odds imply an edge. The trader engaged in statistical arbitrage will lose on a significant percentage of trades but will be profitable over the long run, assuming trade probabilities and transaction costs have been accurately estimated. An appropriate analogy would be roulette (viewed from the casino's perspective): The casino's odds of winning on any particular spin of the wheel are only modestly better than fifty-fifty, but its edge and the laws of probability will assure that it wins over the long run.

There are many different types of statistical arbitrage. We will focus on one example: pairs trading. In addition to providing an easy-to grasp illustration, pairs trading has the advantage of reportedly being one of the prime strategies used by the Morgan Stanley trading group, for which Shaw worked before he left to form his own firm.

Pairs trading involves a two-step process. First, past data are used to define pairs of stocks that tend to move together. Second, each of these pairs is monitored for performance divergences. Whenever there is a statistically meaningful performance divergence between two stocks in a defined pair, the stronger of the pair is sold and the weaker is bought. The basic assumption is that the performance of these closely related stocks will tend to converge. Insofar as this theory is correct, a pairs trading approach will provide an edge and profitability over the long run, even though there is a substantial chance that any individual trade will lose money.

An excellent description of pairs trading and the testing of a specific strategy was contained in a 1999 research paper written by a group of Yale School of Management professors.* Using data for 1963–97, they found that the specific pairs trading strategy they tested yielded statistically significant profits with relatively low volatility. In fact, for the twenty-five-year period as a whole, the pairs trading strategy had a higher return and much lower risk (volatility) than the S&P 500. The pairs trading strategy, however, showed signs of major deterioration in more recent years, with near-zero returns during the last four years of the survey period (1994–97). A reasonable hypothesis is that the increased use of pairs-based strategies by various trading firms (possibly including Shaw's) drove down the profit opportunity of this tactic until it was virtually eliminated.

What does Shaw's trading approach have to do with pairs trading? Similar to pairs trading, Shaw's strategies are probably also based on a

*Evan G. Gatev, William N. Goetzmann, and K. Geert Rouwenhort. *Pairs Trading: Performance of a Relative Value Arbitrage Rule*. National Bureau of Economic Research Working Paper No. 7032; March 1999.

structure of identifying securities that are underpriced relative to other securities. However, that is where the similarity ends. A partial list of the elements of complexity that differentiate Shaw's trading methodology from a simple statistical arbitrage strategy, such as pairs trading, include some, and possibly all, of the following:

- Trading signals are based on over twenty different predictive techniques, rather than a single method.
- Each of these methodologies is probably far more sophisticated than pairs trading. Even if performance divergence between correlated securities is the core of one of these strategies, as it is for pairs trading, the mathematical structure would more likely be one that simultaneously analyzes the interrelationship of large numbers of securities, rather than one that analyzes two stocks at a time.
- Strategies incorporate global equity markets, not just U.S. stocks.
- Strategies incorporate equity related instruments—warrants, options, and convertible bonds—in addition to stocks.
- In order to balance the portfolio so that it is relatively unaffected by the trend of the general market, position sizes are probably adjusted to account for factors such as the varying volatility of different securities and the correlations among stocks in the portfolio.
- The portfolio is balanced not only to remove the influence of price moves in the broad stock market, but also to mitigate the influence of currency price swings and interest rate moves.
- Entry and exit strategies are employed to minimize transaction costs.
- All of these strategies and models are monitored simultaneously in real time. A change in any single element can impact any or all of the other elements. As but one example, a signal by one predictive technique to buy a set of securities and sell another set of securities requires the entire portfolio to be rebalanced.
- The trading model is dynamic—that is, it changes over time to adjust for changing market conditions, which dictate dropping or revising some predictive techniques and introducing new ones.

I have no idea—and for that matter will never know—how close the foregoing description is to reality. I think, however, that it is probably valid as far as providing a sense of the type of trading done at D. E. Shaw.

Shaw's entrepreneurial bent emerged at an early age. When he was twelve, he raised a hundred dollars from his friends to make a horror movie. Since he grew up in the L.A. area, he was able to get other kids' parents to provide free help with tasks such as special effects and editing. The idea was to show the movie to other kids in the neighborhood for a 50-cent admission charge. But the plan went awry when the processing lab lost one of the rolls of film. When he was in high school, he formed a company that manufactured and sold psychedelic ties. He bought three sewing machines and hired high school students to manufacture the ties. The venture failed because he hadn't given much thought to distribution, and going from store to store proved to be an inefficient way to market the ties.

His first serious business venture, however, was a success. While he was at graduate school at Stanford, he took two years off to start a computer company that developed compilers [computer code that translates programs written in user languages into machine language instructions]. Although this venture was very profitable, Shaw's graduate school adviser convinced him that it was not realistic for him to earn his Ph.D. part-time while running a company. Shaw sold the company and completed his Ph.D. work at Stanford. He never considered the alternative of staying with his entrepreneurial success and abandoning his immediate goal of getting a Ph.D. "Finishing graduate school was extremely important to me at the time," he says. "To be taken seriously in the computer research community, you pretty much had to be a faculty member at a top university or a Ph.D.-level scientist at a leading research lab."

Shaw's doctoral dissertation, "Knowledge Based Retrieval on a Relational Database Machine," provided the theoretical basis for building massively parallel computers. One of the pivotal theorems in Shaw's dissertation proved that, for an important class of problems, the theoretical advantage of a multiple processor computer over a single processor computer would increase in proportion to the magnitude of the problem. The implications of this theorem for computer architecture were momentous: It demonstrated the inevitability of parallel processor design vis-à-vis single processor design as the approach for achieving major advances in supercomputer technology.

Shaw has had enough accomplishments to fulfill at least a half dozen extraordinarily successful careers. In addition to the core trading business, Shaw's firm has also incubated and spun off a number of other companies. Perhaps the best-known of these is Juno Online Services, the world's second-largest provider of dial-up Internet services (after America Online). Juno was launched as a public company in May 1999 and is traded on Nasdaq (symbol: JWEB). D. E. Shaw also developed DESoFT, a financial technology company, which was sold to Merrill Lynch, an acquisition that was pivotal to the brokerage firm's rollout of an on-line trading service. FarSight, an on-line brokerage firm, and D. E. Shaw Financial Products, a market-making operation, were other businesses developed at D. E. Shaw and subsequently sold.

In addition to spawning a slew of successful companies, D. E. Shaw also has provided venture capital funding to Schrödinger Inc. (for which Shaw is the chairman of the board of directors) and Molecular Simulations Inc., two firms that are leaders in the development of computational chemistry software. These investments reflect Shaw's strong belief that the design of new drugs, as well as new materials, will move increasingly from the laboratory to the computer. Shaw predicts that developments in computer hardware and software will make possible a dramatic acceleration in the timetable for developing new drugs, and he wants to play a role in turning this vision into reality.

By this time, you may be wondering how this man finds time to sleep. Well, the paradox deepens, because in addition to all these ventures, Shaw has somehow found time to pursue his political interests by serving on President Clinton's Committee of Advisors on Science and Technology and chairing the Panel on Educational Technology.

The reception area at D. E. Shaw—a sparsely furnished, thirty-one-foot cubic space, with diverse rectangular shapes cut out of the walls and backlit by tinted sunlight reflected off of hidden color surfaces—looks very much like a giant exhibit at a modern art museum. This bold, spartan, and futuristic architectural design is, no doubt, intended to project the firm's technological identity.

The interview was conducted in David Shaw's office, a spacious, high-ceilinged room with two adjacent walls of windows opening to an expansive view to the south and west of midtown Manhattan. Shaw must be fond of cacti, which lined the windowsills and included a tree-size plant in the corner of the room. A large, irregular-polygon-shaped, brushed aluminum table, which served as a desk on one end and a conference area on the other, dominated the center of the room. We sat directly across from each other at the conference end.

You began your career designing supercomputers. Can you tell me about that experience?

From the time I was in college, I was fascinated by the question of what human thought was—what made it different from a computer. When I was a graduate student at Stanford, I started thinking about whether you could design a machine that was more like the brain, which has huge numbers of very slow processors—the neurons—working in parallel instead of a single very fast processor.

Were there any other people working to develop parallel supercomputers at that time?

Although there were already a substantial number of outstanding researchers working on parallel computation before I got started, most of them were looking at ways to connect, say, eight or sixteen processors. I was intrigued with the idea of how you could build a parallel computer with millions of processors, each next to a small chunk of memory. There was a trade-off, however. Although there were a lot more processors, they had to be much smaller and cheaper. Still, for certain types of problems, theoretically, you could get speeds that were a thousand times faster than the fastest supercomputer. To be fair, there were a few other researchers who were interested in these sorts of "fine-grained" parallel machines at the time—for example, certain scientists working in the field of computer vision—but it was definitely not the dominant theme within the field.

You said that you were trying to design a computer that worked more like the brain. Could you elaborate?

At the time, one of the main constraints on computer speed was a limitation often referred to as the "von Neumann bottleneck." The traditional von Neumann machine, named after John von Neumann, has a single central processing unit (CPU) connected to a single memory unit. Originally, the two were well matched in speed and size. Over time, however, as processors became faster and memories got larger, the connection between the two—the time it takes for the CPU to get things out of memory, perform the computations, and place the results back into memory—became more and more of a bottleneck.

This type of bottleneck does not exist in the brain because memory storage goes on in millions of different units that are connected to each other through an enormous number of synapses. Although we understand it imperfectly, we do know that whatever computation is going on occurs in close proximity to the memory. In essence, the thinking and the remembering seem to be much more extensively intermingled than is the case in a traditional von Neumann machine. The basic idea that drove my research was that if you could build a computer that had a separate processor for each tiny chunk of memory, you might be able to get around the von Neumann bottleneck.

I assume that the necessary technology did not yet exist at that time.

It was just beginning to exist. I completed my Ph.D. in 1980. By the time I joined the faculty at Columbia University, it was possible to put multiple processors, but very small and simple ones, on a single chip. Our research project was the first one to build a chip containing a number of real, multibit computers. At the time, we were able to place eight 8-bit processors on a single chip. Nowadays, you could probably put 512 or 1,024 similar processors on a chip.

Cray was already building supercomputers at the time. How did your work differ from his?

Seymour Cray was probably the greatest single-processor supercomputer designer who ever lived. He was famous for pushing the technological envelope. With each new machine he built, he would use new types of semiconductors, cooling apparatus, and wiring schemes that had never been used before in an actual computer. He was also a first-rate computer architect, but a substantial part of his edge came from a combination of extraordinary engineering skills and sheer technological audacity. He had a lot more expertise in high-speed *technology*, whereas my own focus was more on the *architecture*—designing a fundamentally different *type* of computer.

You mentioned earlier that your involvement in computer design had its origins in your fascination with human thought. Do you believe it's theoretically possible for computers to eventually think?

From a theoretical perspective, I see no intrinsic reason why they couldn't.

So Hal in *2001* is not pure science fiction.

It's hard to know for sure, but I personally see no compelling reason to believe that this couldn't happen at some point. But even if it does prove feasible to build truly intelligent machines, I strongly suspect that this won't happen for a very long time.

But you believe it's theoretically possible in the sense that a computer could have a sense of self?

It's not entirely clear to me what it would mean for a computer to have a sense of self, or for that matter, exactly what we mean when we say that about a human being. But I don't see any intrinsic reason why cognition should be possible only in hydrocarbon-based systems like ourselves. There's certainly a lot we don't *understand* about how humans think, but at some level, we can be viewed as a very interesting collection of highly organized, interacting molecules. I haven't yet seen any compelling evidence to suggest that the product of human evolution represents the only possible way these molecules can be organized in order to produce a phenomenon like thought.

Did you ever get to the point of applying your theoretical concepts to building an actual working model of a supercomputer?

Yes, at least on a small scale. After I finished my Ph.D., I was appointed to the faculty of the department of computer science at Columbia University. I was fortunate enough to receive a multimillion-dollar research contract from ARPA [the Advanced Research Projects Agency of the U.S. Department of Defense, which is best known for building the ARPAnet, the precursor of the Internet]. This funding allowed me to organize a team of thirty-five people to design customized integrated circuits and build a working prototype of this sort of massively parallel machine. It was a fairly small version, but it did allow us to test out our ideas and collect the data we needed to calculate the theoretically achievable speed of a full-scale supercomputer based on the same architectural principles.

Was any thought given to who would have ownership rights if your efforts to build a supercomputer were successful?

Not initially. Once we built a successful prototype, though, it became clear that it would take another $10 to $20 million to build a full-scale supercomputer, which was more than the government was realistically likely to provide in the form of basic research funding. At that point, we did start looking around for venture capital to form a company. Our motivation was not just to make money, but also to take our project to the next step from a scientific viewpoint.

At the time, had anyone else manufactured a supercomputer using parallel processor architecture?

A number of people had built multiprocessor machines incorporating a relatively small number of processors, but at the time we launched our research project, nobody had yet built a massively parallel supercomputer of the type we were proposing.

Were you able to raise any funding?

No, at least not after a couple months of trying, after which point my career took an unexpected turn. If it hadn't, I don't know for sure whether we would have ultimately found someone willing to risk a few tens of millions of dollars on what was admittedly a fairly risky business plan. But based on the early reactions we got from the venture capital community, I suspect we probably wouldn't have. What happened, though, was that after word got out that I was exploring options in the private sector, I received a call from an executive search firm about the possibility of heading up a really interesting group at Morgan Stanley. At that point, I'd become fairly pessimistic about our prospects for raising all the money we'd need to start a serious supercomputer company. So when Morgan Stanley made what seemed to me to be a truly extraordinary offer, I made the leap to Wall Street.

Up to that point, had you given any thought to a career in the financial markets?

None whatsoever.

I had read that your stepfather was a financial economist who first introduced you to the efficient market hypothesis.* Did that bias you as to the feasibility of developing strategies that could beat the market? Also, given your own lengthy track record, does your stepfather still believe in the efficient market hypothesis?

Although it's true that my stepfather was the first one to expose me to the idea that most, if not all, publicly available information about a given company is already reflected in its current market price, I'm not sure that he ever believed it was *impossible* to beat the market. The things I learned from him probably led me to be more skeptical than most people about the existence of a "free lunch" in the stock market, but he never claimed that the absence of evidence *refuting* the efficient market hypothesis proved that the markets are, in fact, efficient.

Actually, there is really no way to prove that is the case. All you can ever demonstrate is that the specific patterns being tested do not exist. You can never prove that there aren't any patterns that could beat the market.

That's exactly right. All that being said, I grew up with the idea that, if not impossible, it was certainly extremely difficult to beat the market. And even now, I find it remarkable how efficient the markets actually are. It would be nice if all you had to do in order to earn abnormally large returns was to identify some sort of standard pattern in the historical prices of a given stock. But most of the claims that are made by so-called technical analysts, involving constructs like support and resistance levels and head-and-shoulders patterns, have absolutely no grounding in methodologically sound empirical research.

But isn't it possible that many of these patterns can't be rigor-

*There are three variations of this theory: (1) *weak form*—past prices cannot be used to predict future prices; (2) *semistrong form*—the current price reflects *all publicly known* information; (3) *strong form*—the current price reflects *all* information, whether publicly known or not.

ously tested because they can't be defined objectively? For example, you might define a head-and-shoulders pattern one way while I might define it quite differently. In fact, for many patterns, theoretically, there could be an infinite number of possible definitions.

Yes, that's an excellent point. But the inability to precisely explicate the hypothesis being tested is one of the signposts of a pseudoscience. Even for those patterns where it's been possible to come up with a reasonable consensus definition for the sorts of patterns traditionally described by people who refer to themselves as technical analysts, researchers have generally not found these patterns to have any predictive value. The interesting thing is that even some of the most highly respected Wall Street firms employ at least a few of these "prescientific" technical analysts, despite the fact that there's little evidence they're doing anything more useful than astrology.

But wait a minute. I've interviewed quite a number of traders who are purely technically oriented and have achieved return-to-risk results that were well beyond the realm of chance.

I think it depends on your definition of technical analysis. Historically, most of the people who have used that term have been members of the largely unscientific head-and-shoulders-support-and-resistance camp. These days, the people who do serious, scholarly work in the field generally refer to themselves as quantitative analysts, and some of them have indeed discovered real anomalies in the marketplace. The problem, of course, is that as soon as these anomalies are published, they tend to disappear because people exploit them. Andrew Lo at MIT is one of the foremost academic experts in the field. He is responsible for identifying some of these historical inefficiencies and publishing the results. If you talk to him about it, he will probably tell you two things: first, that they tend to go away over time; second, that he suspects that the elimination of these market anomalies can be attributed at least in part to firms like ours.

What is an example of a market anomaly that existed but now no longer works because it was publicized?

We don't like to divulge that type of information. In our business, it's as important to know what *doesn't* work as what does. For that reason, once we've gone to the considerable expense that's often involved in determining that an anomaly described in the open literature no longer exists, the last thing we want to do is to enable one of our competitors to take advantage of this information for free by drawing attention to the fact that the published results no longer hold and the approach in question thus represents a dead end.

Are the people who publish studies of market inefficiencies in the financial and economic journals strictly academics or are some of them involved in trading the markets?

Some of the researchers who actually trade the markets publish certain aspects of their work, especially in periodicals like the *Journal of Portfolio Management*, but overall, there's a tendency for academics to be more open about their results than practitioners.

Why would anyone who trades the markets publish something that works?

That's a very good question. For various reasons, the vast majority of the high-quality work that appears in the open literature can't be used in practice to actually beat the market. Conversely, the vast majority of the research that really does work will probably never be published. But there are a few successful quantitative traders who from time to time publish useful information, even when it may not be in their own self-interest to do so. My favorite example is Ed Thorpe, who was a real pioneer in the field. He was doing this stuff well before almost anyone else. Ed has been remarkably open about some of the money-making strategies he's discovered over the years, both within and outside of the field of finance. After he figured out how to beat the casinos at blackjack, he published *Beat the Dealer*. Then when he figured out how to beat the market, he published *Beat the Market*, which explained with his usual professorial clarity exactly how to take advantage of certain demonstrable market inefficiencies that existed at the time. Of course, the publication of his book helped to eliminate those very inefficiencies.

In the case of blackjack, does eliminating the inefficiencies mean that the casinos went to the use of multiple decks?

I'm not an expert on blackjack, but it's my understanding that the casinos not only adopted specific game-related countermeasures of this sort, but they also became more aware of "card counters" and became more effective at expelling them from the casinos.

I know that classic arbitrage opportunities are long gone. Did such sitting-duck trades, however, exist when you first started?

Even then, those sorts of true arbitrage opportunities were few and far between. Every once in a while, we were able to engage in a small set of transactions in closely related instruments that, taken together, locked in a risk-free or nearly risk-free profit. Occasionally, we'd even find it possible to execute each component of a given arbitrage trade with a different department of the same major financial institution—something that would have been impossible if the institution had been using technology to effectively manage all of its positions on an integrated firmwide basis. But those sorts of opportunities were very rare even in those days, and now you basically don't see them at all.

Have the tremendous advances in computer technology, which greatly facilitate searching for market inefficiencies that provide a probabilistic edge, caused some previous inefficiencies to disappear and made new ones harder to find?

The game is largely over for most of the "easy" effects. Maybe someday, someone will discover a simple effect that has eluded all of us, but it's been our experience that the most obvious and mathematically straightforward ideas you might think of have largely disappeared as potential trading opportunities. What you are left with is a number of relatively small inefficiencies that are often fairly complex and which you're not likely to find by using a standard mathematical software package or the conventional analytical techniques you might learn in graduate school. Even if you were somehow able to find one of the remaining inefficiencies without going through an extremely expensive, long-term research effort of the sort we've conducted over the past eleven years, you'd probably find that one such inefficiency wouldn't be enough to cover your transaction costs.

As a result, the current barriers to entry in this field are very high. A firm like ours that has identified a couple dozen market inefficiencies in a given set of financial instruments may be able to make money even in the presence of transaction costs. In contrast, a new entrant into the field who has identified only one or two market inefficiencies would typically have a much harder time doing so.

What gives you that edge?

It's a subtle effect. A single inefficiency may not be sufficient to overcome transaction costs. When multiple inefficiencies happen to coincide, however, they may provide an opportunity to trade with a statistically expected profit that exceeds the associated transaction costs. Other things being equal, the more inefficiencies you can identify, the more trading opportunities you're likely to have.

How could the use of multiple strategies, none of which independently yields a profit, be profitable? As a simple illustration, imagine that there are two strategies, each of which has an expected gain of $100 and a transaction cost of $110. Neither of these strategies could be applied profitably on its own. Further assume that the subset of trades in which both strategies provide signals in the same direction has an average profit of $180 and the same $110 transaction cost. Trading the subset could be highly profitable, even though each individual strategy is ineffective by itself. Of course, for Shaw's company, which trades scores of strategies in many related markets, the effect of strategy interdependencies is tremendously more complex.

As the field matures, you need to be aware of more and more inefficiencies to identify trades, and it becomes increasingly harder for new entrants. When we started trading eleven years ago, you could have identified one or two inefficiencies and still beat transaction costs. That meant you could do a limited amount of research and begin trading profitably, which gave you a way to fund future research. Nowadays, things are a lot tougher. If we hadn't gotten started when we did, I think it would have been prohibitively expensive for us to get where we are today.

Do you use only price data in your model, or do you also employ fundamental data?

It's definitely not just price data. We look at balance sheets, income statements, volume information, and almost any other sort of data we can get our hands on in digital form. I can't say much about the sorts of variables we find most useful in practice, but I can say that we use an extraordinary amount of data, and spend a lot of money not just acquiring it but also putting it into a form in which it's useful to us.

Would it be fair to summarize the philosophy of your firm as follows? Markets can be predicted only to a very limited extent, and any single strategy cannot provide an attractive return-to-risk ratio. If you combine enough strategies, however, you can create a trading model that has a meaningful edge.

That's a really good description. The one thing that I would add is that we try to hedge as many systematic risk factors as possible.

I assume you mean that you balance all long positions with correlated short positions, thereby removing directional moves in the market as a risk factor.

Hedging against overall market moves within the various markets we trade is one important element of our approach to risk management, but there are also a number of other risk factors with respect to which we try to control our exposure whenever we're not specifically betting on them. For example, if you invest in IBM, you're placing an implicit bet not only on the direction of the stock market as a whole and on the performance of the computer industry relative to the overall stock market, but also on a number of other risk factors.

Such as?

Examples would include the overall level of activity within the economy, any unhedged exchange rate exposure attributable to IBM's export activities, the net effective interest rate exposure associated with the firm's assets, liabilities, and commercial activities, and a number of other mathematically derived risk factors that would be more difficult to describe in intuitively meaningful terms. Although it's neither possible nor cost-effective to hedge *all* forms of risk, we try to minimize our net exposure to those sources of risk that we aren't able to predict while maintaining our exposure to those variables for which we do have some predictive ability, at least on a statistical basis.

Some of the strategies you were using in your early years are now completely obsolete. Could you talk about one of these just to provide an illustration of the type of market inefficiency that at least at one time offered a trading opportunity.

In general, I try not to say much about historical inefficiencies that have disappeared from the markets, since even that type of information could help competitors decide how to more effectively allocate scarce research resources, allowing them a "free ride" on our own negative findings, which would give them an unfair competitive advantage. One example I can give you, though, is undervalued options [options trading at prices below the levels implied by theoretical models]. Nowadays, if you find an option that appears to be mispriced, there is usually a reason. Years ago, that wasn't necessarily the case.

When you find an apparent anomaly or pattern in the historical data, how do you know it represents something real as opposed to a chance occurrence?

The more variables you have, the greater the number of statistical artifacts that you're likely to find, and the more difficult it will generally be to tell whether a pattern you uncover actually has any predictive value. We take great care to avoid the methodological pitfalls associated with "overfitting the data."

Although we use a number of different mathematical techniques to establish the robustness and predictive value of our strategies, one of our most powerful tools is the straightforward application of the scientific method. Rather than blindly searching through the data for patterns—an approach whose methodological dangers are widely appreciated within, for example, the natural science and medical research communities—we typically start by formulating a hypothesis based on some sort of structural theory or qualitative understanding of the market, and then test that hypothesis to see whether it is supported by the data.

Unfortunately, the most common outcome is that the actual data fail to provide evidence that would allow us to reject the "null hypothesis" of market efficiency. Every once in a while, though, we do find a new market anomaly that passes all our tests, and which we wind up incorporating in an actual trading strategy.

I heard that your firm ran into major problems last year [1998], but when I look at your performance numbers, I see that your worst equity decline ever was only 11 percent—and even that loss was recovered in only a few months. I don't understand how there could have been much of a problem. What happened?

The performance results you're referring to are for our equity and equity-linked trading strategies, which have formed the core of our proprietary trading activities since our start over eleven years ago. For a few years, though, we also traded a fixed income strategy. That strategy was qualitatively different from the equity-related strategies we'd historically employed and exposed us to fundamentally different sorts of risks. Although we initially made a lot of money on our fixed income trading, we experienced significant losses during the global liquidity crisis in late 1998, as was the case for most fixed income arbitrage traders during that period. While our losses were much smaller, in both percentage and absolute dollar terms, than those suffered by, for example, Long Term Capital Management, they were significant enough that we're no longer engaged in this sort of trading at all.

LTCM—a hedge fund headed by renowned former Salomon bond trader John Meriwether and whose principals included economics Nobel laureates Robert Merton and Myron Scholes—was on the brink of extinction during the second half of 1998. After registering an average annual gain of 34 percent in its first three years and expanding its assets under management to near $5 billion, LTCM lost a staggering 44 percent (roughly $2 billion) in August 1998 alone. These losses were due to a variety of factors, but their magnitude was primarily attributable to excessive leverage: the firm used borrowing to leverage its holdings by an estimated factor of over 40 to 1. The combination of large losses and large debt would have resulted in LTCM's collapse. The firm, however, was saved by a Federal Reserve coordinated $3.5 billion bailout (financed by private financial institutions, not government money).

With all the ventures you have going, do you manage to take any time off?

I just took a week off—the first one in a long time.

So you don't take much vacation?

Not much. When I take a vacation, I find I need a few hours of work each day just to keep myself sane.

You have a reputation for recruiting brilliant Ph.D.s in math and sciences. Do you hire people just for their raw intellectual capability, even if there is no specific job slot to fill?

Compared with most organizations, we tend to hire more on the basis of raw ability and less on the basis of experience. If we run across someone truly gifted, we try to make them an offer, even if we don't have an immediate position in mind for that person. The most famous example is probably Jeff Bezos. One of my partners approached me and said, "I've just interviewed this terrific candidate named Jeff Bezos. We don't really have a slot for him, but I think he's going to make someone a lot of money someday, and I think you should at least spend some time with him." I met with Jeff and was really impressed by his intellect, creativity, and entrepreneurial instincts. I told my partner that he was right and that even though we didn't have a position for him, we should hire him anyway and figure something out.

Did Bezos leave your firm to start Amazon?

Yes. Jeff did a number of things during the course of his tenure at D. E. Shaw, but his last assignment was to work with me on the formulation of ideas for various technology-related new ventures. One of those ideas was to create what amounted to a universal electronic bookstore. When we discovered that there was an electronic catalog with millions of titles that could be ordered through Ingram's [a major book distributor], Jeff and I did a few back-of-the-envelope calculations and realized that it ought to be possible to start such a venture without a prohibitively large initial investment. Although I don't think either of us had any idea at the time how successful such a business could be, we both thought it had possibilities. One day, before things had progressed much further, Jeff asked to speak with me. We took a walk through Central Park, during which he told me that he'd "gotten the entrepreneurial bug" and asked how I'd feel about it if he decided he wanted to pursue this idea on his own.

What was your reaction?

I told him I'd be genuinely sorry to lose him, and made sure he knew how highly I thought of his work at D. E. Shaw, and how promising I thought his prospects were within the firm. But I also told him that, having made a similar decision myself at one point, I'd understand completely if he decided the time had come to strike out on his own and would not try to talk him out of it. I assured him that given the relatively short period of time we'd been talking about the electronic bookstore concept, I'd have no objections whatsoever if he decided that he wanted to pursue this idea on his own. I told him that we might or might not decide to compete with him at some point, and he said that seemed perfectly fair to him.

Jeff's departure was completely amicable, and when he finished the alpha version of the first Amazon system, he invited me and others at D. E. Shaw to test it. It wasn't until I used this alpha version to order my first book that I realized how powerful this concept could really be. Although we'd talked about the *idea* of an electronic bookstore while Jeff was still at D. E. Shaw, it's the things Jeff did since leaving that made Amazon what it is today.

★

Shaw's trading approach, which requires highly complex mathematical models, vast computer power, constant monitoring of worldwide markets by a staff of traders, and near instantaneous, extreme low-cost trade executions, is clearly out of the reach of the ordinary investor. One concept that came up in this interview, however, that could have applicability to the individual investor is the idea that market patterns ("inefficiencies" in Shaw's terminology) that are not profitable on their own might still provide the basis for a profitable strategy when combined with other patterns. Although Shaw disdains chart patterns and traditional technical indicators, an analogous idea would apply: It is theoretically possible that a combination

of patterns (or indicators) could yield a useful trading model, even if the individual elements are worthless when used alone.

This synergistic effect would apply to fundamental inputs as well. For example, a researcher might test ten different fundamental factors and find that none are worthwhile as price indicators. Does this imply that these fundamental inputs should be dismissed as useless? Absolutely not. Even though no single factor provides a meaningful predictor, it is entirely possible that some combination of these inputs could yield a useful price indicator.

Another important principle that came up in this interview concerns the appropriate methodology in testing trading ideas. A trader trying to develop a systematic approach, or any approach that incorporates computer patterns as signals, should caution against data mining—letting the computer cycle through the data, testing thousands or millions of input combinations in search of profitable patterns. Although the expense of computer time is usually no longer an issue, such computational profligacy has a more critical cost: it will tend to generate trading models (systems) that look great, but have no predictive power—a combination that could lead to large trading losses.

Why? Because patterns can be found even in random data. For example, if you flipped one million coins ten times apiece, on average, about 977 of those coins would land on heads all ten times. Obviously, it would be foolish to assume that these coins are more likely to land on heads in the future. But this type of naive reasoning is precisely what some system developers do when they test huge numbers of input combinations on price data and then trade the combination that is most profitable. If you test enough variations of any trading system, some of them will be profitable by chance—just as some coins will land on heads on every toss if you flip enough coins. Shaw avoids this problem of data mining by requiring that a theoretical hypothesis precede each computer test and by using rigorous statistical measures to evaluate the significance of the results.

★

Update on David Shaw

The D. E. Shaw group's equity and equity-linked strategies have continued to roar ahead in recent years, with performance actually improving despite a significant increase in assets managed in these strategies over this period. The strategies were up 58 percent in 2000, 23 percent in 2001, and an estimated 22 percent during the first nine months of 2002 (in net terms). As a result, the average annual compounded return of these strategies during their nearly fourteen-year history has now risen to over 24 percent, applying current fees. The lifetime Sharpe ratio (a return/risk measure) is now about 2.00, an extraordinarily high figure for such a long track record.

Your performance alone during the past 3½ years would have led to a tripling of assets under management. How much are you currently managing in your equity and equity-linked strategies? Has the increase in assets led to capacity problems?

We're currently managing around $4.3 billion, of which about $2.9 billion is in our equity and equity-linked strategies. At this point, the demand for our investment management services is sufficiently strong that we could easily raise more capital, but it's important to us to avoid accepting more money than we believe we can invest effectively. Although the capacity of these strategies has increased over the past few years as a result of new research results and certain market-related factors, the amount we're managing is still limited by capacity rather than the availability of capital.

Since you are often managing close to your estimated capacity in some strategies, what happens when your own positive performance causes assets under management to grow beyond this perceived capacity level?

We return profits to investors to an extent sufficient to bring our assets under management back to the desired level.

Have there been any significant changes to your methodology since we first spoke?

The basic methodology remains unchanged for the bulk of our strategies. We have, however, added several newly researched market effects to the couple of dozen we were already trading. We've also launched a new strategy focusing on the distressed securities markets.

Do the market effects or inefficiencies you trade have only limited life spans?

It depends. The market anomalies that are relatively easy to spot and exploit tend not to last. However, more subtle inefficiencies that require complex quantitative techniques to identify and extract tend to persist for a longer period of time. These are the types of inefficiencies we tend to focus on, rather than the much simpler effects that are not likely to last. Over the years, we've had to retire only a few effects out of the many that we trade.

Any thoughts about the corporate and accounting scandals we've seen recently?

I believe the regulatory and legislative scrutiny that the corporate world is experiencing right now is very healthy. A number of CEOs and CFOs were playing close to the edge—and in some cases, as we're now seeing, over the edge—in "managing" their earnings and executing dubious complex financial maneuvers to obscure the true health of their companies. This type of activity undermines the effective functioning of the global capital markets and should be of serious concern to a nation that has historically been a leader in accounting transparency. It's a very positive development that steps are being taken to ensure that investors and analysts have access to accurate, reliable information about the companies in which they invest.

STEVE COHEN

The Trading Room

"He's the best," said an industry contact, referring to Steve Cohen, when I asked him to recommend possible interview candidates. I would hear virtually the same assessment repeated several more times whenever Cohen's name was mentioned by industry acquaintances. When I looked at Cohen's numbers, I understood the reason for their ebullient praise. In the seven years he has managed money, Cohen has averaged a compounded annual return of 45 percent, with only three losing months in the entire period—the worst a tiny 2 percent decline.

These numbers, however, dramatically understate Cohen's trading talent. Cohen is so good that he is able to charge a 50 percent profit incentive fee, which means that his actual *trading* profits have averaged approximately 90 percent per year. Despite stratospheric fees—approximately two and a half times the hedge fund industry average—Cohen has not had a problem attracting investors. In fact, his flagship fund is closed to new investment.

Cohen's firm, S.A.C., which derives its name from his initials, is located in an office building whose architectural style can best be described as "Connecticut Corporate"—a low-rise, rectangular facade of glass squares. I expected to find Cohen sitting in a window-encased office with a glass and steel desk. Instead, the receptionist led me into a huge, windowless room with six long rows of desks, seating approximately sixty traders, each trader with an array of six to twelve computer screens. Despite its size, the room was so filled with people and equipment that it felt more cavelike than cavernous. The absence of windows created a bunkerlike atmosphere.

The traders were all dressed casually, with attire ranging from T-shirts and shorts, which was appropriate for the weather, to jeans or slacks and polar fleeces for those who found the air conditioning too cold. Cohen was seated near the middle of one row of desks, totally indistinguishable from any of the other traders in the room. (He was one of the polar fleece contingent.) Cohen has used his trading success to lure traders specializing in a whole range of market sectors. He has chosen to surround himself with traders, figuratively and literally.

When I arrived, Cohen was in the midst of a lengthy phone conversation—ironically, he was being interviewed by *The Wall Street Journal*. ("This is media day down here!" Cohen would later exclaim to a caller, referring to the dual interviews.) I squeezed a chair in alongside Cohen's slot within the room-length desk while I waited for him to get off the phone. Throughout his phone conversation, Cohen kept his eyes glued on the quote screens in front of him. At one point, he interrupted his conversation to call out an order. "Sell 20 [20,000] Pokémon." As an aside to the rest of the room, he said, "My kids love it, but what the hell." He reminded me of Jason Alexander from *Seinfeld*—a combination of a slight physical resemblance, speech patterns, and sense of humor.

The room was surprisingly quiet, considering the number of traders. I realized what was missing—ringing phones; the order clerks had open lines to the exchange floors. Every now and then there would be a flurry of activity and an accompanying wave of increased noise. Traders continually shouted out buy and sell orders, news items, and queries to others in the room. Sample: "Anyone know—Is Martha Stewart going to be a hot offering?" Every couple of minutes, Cohen called out a buy or sell order to be executed, in a tone so casual that you might have thought he was placing an order for a tuna fish on rye, instead of buying or selling 25,000 to 100,000 shares at a clip.

★

What is the stock you shorted that has a product that your kids love?

Nintendo. They do Pokémon. Do you know Pokémon?

Afraid not. [This interview preceded the media crescendo that led to a Pokémon *Time* magazine cover.]

It's a Japanese cartoon character that is very popular right now.

Why are you shorting it, if your kids like it?

Because I think it's a fad. It's a one-product company.

[Looking at the screen, Cohen comments] I think the market may go a little higher, but I'm actually turning very negative.

Why is that?

The big caps are moving higher, but the rally has no breadth. The market is moving up on light volume. Also, people will start to get more concerned about Y2K as we get closer to the end of the year.

A Fed announcement concerning interest rates is scheduled for the day I am visiting. As we approach within fifteen minutes of the announcement, Cohen begins entering a slew of buy and sell orders well removed from the prevailing market prices. "In case the market does something stupid," he explains. In other words, he is positioning himself to take the opposite side of any extreme reaction—price run-up or sell-off—in response to the Fed report.

Just before the announcement, the TV is turned on, just like in the movie *Trading Places*. (Although, for the record, the *Trading Places* sequence, which takes place on the commodity trading floor, is divorced from reality because the release of agricultural reports is deliberately delayed until after the close of the futures markets—but then again it's only a comedy.) As the clock ticks down to 2 P.M., the tension and anticipation build. Cohen claps his hands and laughs, shouting in eagerness, "Here we go!" A minute before the announcement, a spontaneous rhythmic clapping—the let's go [team name] beat one hears at sports events—ripples through the room.

The Fed announcement of a ¼ percent hike in interest rates is exactly in line with expectations, and the market response is muted. There is a small flurry of trading activity in the room, which quickly peters out. "Okay, that was exciting, let's go home," Cohen jokingly announces.

Cohen methodically types quote symbols into his keyboard at the rate of approximately one per second, bringing up companies that are not on one of his numerous quote screens. The market begins to rally, and Cohen considers buying but then decides to hold off. Ten minutes later the market reverses direction, more than erasing its prior gains.

How much of what you do is gut feel?

A lot, probably at least 50 percent.

I attempt to continue the interview, but it is virtually impossible with all the distractions and interruptions. Cohen is intently focused on his computer screens, frequently calling out trades, and also taking phone calls. The few questions and answers that I manage to record contain nothing that I wish to retain. The remainder of the interview, with the exception of the final section, is conducted in the more sedate environs of Cohen's office.

When did you first become aware that there was a stock market?

When I was about thirteen years old. My father used to bring home the *New York Post* every evening. I always checked the sports pages. I noticed that there were all these other pages filled with numbers. I was fascinated when I found out that these numbers were prices, which were changing every day.

I started hanging out at the local brokerage office, watching the stock quotes. When I was in high school, I took a summer job at a clothing store, located just down the block from a brokerage office, so that I could run in and watch the tape during my lunch hour. In those days, the tape was so slow that you could follow it. You could see volume coming into a stock and get the sense that it was going higher. You can't do that nowadays; the tape is far too fast. But everything I do today has its roots in those early tape-reading experiences.

Did your economics education at Wharton help at all in your career as a stock trader?

Not much. A few things they taught you were helpful.

Like what?

They taught you that 40 percent of a stock's price movement was due to the market, 30 percent to the sector, and only 30 percent to the stock itself, which is something that I believe is true. I don't know if the percentages are exactly correct, but conceptually the idea makes sense.

When you put on a trade and it goes against you, how do you decide when you're wrong?

If I am in the trade because of a catalyst, the first thing I check is whether the catalyst still applies. For example, about a month ago, I expected that IBM would report disappointing earnings, and I went short ahead of the report. I was bearish because a lot of computer and software companies were missing their numbers [reporting lower-than-expected earnings] due to Y2K issues. Customers were delaying the installation of new systems because with the year 2000 just around the corner, they figured that they might as well stick with their existing systems.

I went short the stock at $169. The earnings came out and they were just phenomenal—a complete blowout! I got out sharply higher in after-the-close trading, buying back my position at $187. The trade just didn't work. The next day the stock opened at $197. So thank God I covered that night in after-hours trading.

Has that been something you were always able to do—that is, turn on a dime when you think you're wrong?

You better be able to do that. This is not a perfect game. I compile statistics on my traders. My best trader makes money only 63 percent of the time. Most traders make money only in the 50 to 55 percent range. That means you're going to be wrong a lot. If that's the case, you better make sure your losses are as small as they can be, and that your winners are bigger.

Any trade stand out as being particularly emotional?

I held a 23 percent position in a private company that was bought by XYZ. [Cohen asked me not to use the actual name because of his contacts with the company.] As a result, I ended up with a stock position in XYZ, which I held for four or five years in my personal account without the stock doing much of anything.

XYZ had a subsidiary, which had an Internet Web site for financial commentary. They decided to take this subsidiary public. XYZ stock started to run up in front of the scheduled offering, rallying to $13, which was higher than it had been at any time I held it. I got out, and was happy to do so.

The public offering, which was originally scheduled for December, was delayed and the stock drifted down. A few weeks later, they announced a new offering date in January, and the stock skyrocketed as part of the Internet mania. In two weeks, XYZ went up from $10 to over $30.

I couldn't stand the idea that after holding the stock for all those years, I got out just before it exploded on the upside. But I was really pissed off because I knew the company, and there was no way the stock was remotely worth more than $30. The subsidiary was going public at $15. If it traded at $100, it would be worth only about $10 to the company. If it traded at $200, it would add only about $20 to the company's value. The rest of the company was worth maybe $5. So you had a stock, which under the most optimistic circumstances was worth only $15 to $25, trading at over $30.

I started shorting the hell out of the stock. I ended up selling 900,000 shares of stock and a couple of thousand calls. My average sales price was around $35, and the stock went as high as $45. On Friday, the day of the offering, XYZ plummeted. On Friday afternoon I covered the stock at $22, $21, and $20. I bought back the calls, which I had sold at $10 to $15, for $1.

This trade worked out phenomenally well. But when you go short, the risk is open-ended. Even here, you said your average price was around $35 and the stock did go as high as $45. What if it kept going higher? At what point would you throw in the towel? Or, if your assessment that the stock was tremendously overvalued remained unchanged, would you just hold it?

A basic principle in going short is that there has to be a catalyst. Here, the catalyst was the offering. The offering was on Friday, and I started going short on Tuesday, so that I would be fully positioned by that time. If the offering took place, and the stock didn't go down, then I probably would have covered. What had made me so angry was that I had sold out my original position.

So you got redemption.

I got redemption. That was cool.

What happens when you are short a stock that is moving against you, and there is no imminent catalyst? You sold it at $40, and it goes to $45, $50. When do you get out?

If a stock is moving against me, I'm probably buying in some every day.

Even if there's no change in the fundamentals?

Oh sure. I always tell my traders, "If you think you're wrong, or if the market is moving against you and you don't know why, take in half. You can always put it on again." If you do that twice, you've taken in three-quarters of your position. Then what's left is no longer a big deal. The thing is to start moving your feet. I find that too many traders just stand there and let the truck roll over them. A common mistake traders make in shorting is that they take on too big of a position relative to their portfolio. Then when the stock moves against them, the pain becomes too great to handle, and they end up panicking or freezing.

What other mistakes do people make?

They make trades without a good reason. They step in front of freight trains. They short stocks because they are up, as if that were a reason. They'll say, "I can't believe the stock is so high," and that's their total research. That makes no sense to me. My response is: "You have to do better than that." I have friends who get emotional about the market. They fight it. Why put yourself in that position?

But the XYZ trade that you told me about, wasn't that fighting the market?

The difference is that there was a catalyst. I knew the offering was scheduled for Friday. I knew what was going on. I also knew what I expected to happen. It was actually a well-planned trade, even though I was pissed off at having liquidated my stock position so much lower.

What else do people do wrong?

You have to know what you are, and not try to be what you're not. If you are a day trader, day trade. If you are an investor, then be an investor. It's like a comedian who gets up onstage and starts singing. What's he singing for? He's a comedian. Here's one I really don't understand: I know these guys who set up a hedge fund that was part trading and part small cap. Small caps are incredibly illiquid, and you have to hold them forever—it's the exact opposite of trading!

How do you interact with the traders who work for you?

I have different traders covering different sectors for a number of reasons. There are a lot of people in the room, and it would be cumbersome to have different traders trading the same names. Also, since we're trading over one billion dollars now, we want to cover as many situations as we can. This firm is very horizontal in nature, and I'm sort of orchestrating the whole thing. You could say I'm the hub and the traders are the spokes.

How do you handle a situation when a trader wants to put on a trade that you disagree with?

I don't want to tell my traders what to do. I don't have a corner on what's right. All I want to do is make sure they have the same facts that I do, and if they still want to do the trade, then they can. I encourage my guys to play. I have to. I'm running over one billion dollars. I can't do it all myself.

How do you pick your traders?

A lot of the traders who work here were referred to me. I have also trained people who have grown up within the system. I've had people who began as clerks and are now trading tens of millions of dollars, and doing it very well.

One thing I like to do is pair up traders. You need a sounding board. You need someone who will say, "Why are we in this position?" There is a check and balance, as opposed to being in your own world.

We also have teams where the trader is teamed up with an analyst of the same industry. I like that idea because it helps the trader learn the subtleties of the industry and understand what factors really move the stocks in that sector.

Are these trading teams informal or are they literally pooling their trading capital?

No, they're working together. Their livelihood depends on each other.

Have you seen improvements in the trading performance by using this team approach?

The results speak for themselves.

Was the team approach your idea?

It was an evolutionary process. Most traders want to trade everything. One minute they are trading Yahoo!, the next Exxon. They're traders!

My place operates very differently. I want my traders to be highly focused. I want them to know a lot about something, instead of a little about everything.

That means they can't diversify.

They can't, but the firm is diversified. As long as they can trade the short side as well as the long side, I don't think anyone in this room thinks being focused on a single sector is a negative.

Are you looking for any special skills when you hire potential traders?

I'm looking for people who are not afraid to take risks. One of the questions I ask is: "Tell me some of the riskiest things you've ever done in your life." I want guys who have the confidence to be out there; to be risk takers.

What would make you wary about a trader?

I'm concerned about traders who wait for someone else to tell them what to do. I know someone who could be a great trader. He has only one problem: He refuses to make his own decisions. He wants everyone else to tell him what to buy and sell. And then when he's wrong, he doesn't know when to get out. I've known him for a long time, and he's done this all along.

Do you give him advice?

Yeah! It doesn't matter. He still does it. He finds a new way to make it look like he's making his own decisions, but he really isn't. Ironically, if he just made his own decisions, he would do great. Obviously, on some level he's afraid. Maybe he is afraid of looking stupid.

You have had quite a run—years of mammoth returns and a sizeable amount of capital under management. Are you ever tempted to just cash in the chips and retire?

A lot of people get scared and think that since they made a lot of money they'd better protect it. That's a very limiting philosophy. I am just the opposite. I want to keep the firm growing. I have no interest in retiring. First, I have nothing else to do. I don't want to go play golf. You know the old saying: "Golf is great until you can play three times a week, and then it's no fun anymore." Second, I enjoy what I'm doing.

I've grown the company in a way that has kept my interest.

We've expanded from just traditional trading to a whole range of new strategies: market neutral, risk arbitrage, event driven, and so on. Also, my traders teach me about their sectors. I'm always learning, which keeps it exciting and new. I'm not doing the same thing that I was doing ten years ago. I have evolved and will continue to evolve.

Do you have a scenario about how the current long-running bull market will end ?

It's going to end badly; it always ends badly. Everybody in the world is talking stocks now. Everybody wants to be a trader. To me that is the sign of something ending, not something beginning. You can't have everybody on one side of the fence. The world doesn't work that way.

Any final words?

You can't control what the market does, but you can control your reaction to the market. I examine what I do all the time. That's what trading is all about.

These turn out not to be his final words for the interview. After my visit, I called Cohen with some follow-up questions. This phone portion of the interview follows.

How would you describe your methodology?

I combine lots of information coming at me from all directions with a good feel for how the markets are moving to make market bets.

What differentiates you from other traders?

I'm not a lone wolf. Many traders like to fight their own battles. I prefer to get a lot of support. The main reason I am as successful as I am is that I've built an incredible team.

Hypothetically, what would happen if you were trading in a room on your own?

I would still be very profitable, but I wouldn't do as well. There is no way I could cover the same breadth of the market.

What about the timing of your trades? Why do you put on a trade today versus yesterday or tomorrow, or for that matter, at a given moment, as opposed to an hour earlier or later?

It depends on the trade. I put on trades for lots of different reasons. Sometimes I trade off the tape—the individual stock price action; sometimes I trade off the sector; and sometimes I trade based on a catalyst.

When I was there last week, you were bullish on bonds. Since then, prices initially went a little higher but then sold off. Did you stay long?

No, I got out of the position. The basic idea is that you trade your theory and then let the market tell you whether you are right.

I have heard that you have a psychiatrist on staff to work with your traders.

Ari Kiev. He works here three days a week. [Kiev is interviewed in this book.]

How did this come about?

Ari's experience includes working with Olympic athletes. I saw some similarities: Traders also work in a highly competitive environment and are performance driven. I felt that the inability of some traders to achieve success was usually due to personal flaws rather than a consequence of bad ideas versus good ideas. All traders have something holding them back.

Has the counseling arrangement with Ari been helpful?

I've seen results. If you look around, baseball players have coaches, tennis players have coaches, and so on. Why shouldn't traders have coaches?

Of the tens of thousands of trades that you have done, do any stand out?

One time, I shorted a million shares of a stock and it dropped $10 the next day. That was pretty good.

What was the story there?

Without naming any names—or else the company will never speak to me again—there were a number of other stocks in the sector that were under pressure, but this stock was going up because it was being added to the S&P index. I figured that once the index fund buying was completed, the stock would sell off. The day after I went short, the company reported disappointing earnings, and the trade turned into a home run.

Any positions you ever lost sleep over?

Nah, I think I sleep pretty good. I don't lose sleep over any positions. Maybe a better question might be: What was the worst day I ever had?

Okay, what was the worst day you ever had?

One day I lost about $4 to $5 million.

What happened on that day?

I don't even remember. The reality is that if you trade long enough everything happens.

★

What is gut feel? It is just an expression for intelligence that we can't explain. I have seen gut feel firsthand in a number of traders—traders who can view the same information as everyone else and somehow see clearly which direction the market is likely to go. Watching Steve Cohen, you are left with the unmistakable impression that he has a real sense of where the market is headed. This sense, or gut feel, is nothing more that a distillation of the experiences and lessons drawn from tens of thousands of trades. It is the trader as a human computer.

So-called gut feel is a combination of experience and talent. It cannot be taught. Novice traders cannot expect to have gut feel, and experienced traders may also not possess it. Even many of the *Market Wizards* don't possess gut feel; in many cases, their trading success is due to a different talent—for example, a skill for market analysis or system building.

Although Steve Cohen's trading style cannot be emulated, his trading disciplines can. Insofar as Cohen's behavior demonstrates some of the key attributes of the successful trader, the accounts of his trading experiences contain important information even for the beginning trader. For example, Cohen provides an excellent model of the expert trader's approach to risk control.

As good as he is, Cohen makes mistakes too—sometimes big ones. Consider the trade in which he shorted IBM before an earnings report. He was dead wrong on his expectations, and the stock gapped up $18 against him in the first trades after the report's release. Since his reason for placing the trade had been violated, Cohen covered his position immediately. He didn't try to rationalize the situation; he didn't give the market a little more time. Although he took a sizable loss, had he waited just until the next morning, the stock would have gone another $10 against him. All traders make mistakes; the great traders, however, limit the damage.

For Cohen, cutting losses is almost a reflex action. Although developing such loss control skills usually takes many years of experience, Cohen offers one piece of related advice that should be as useful to the novice as to the professional: "If you think you're wrong, or if the market is moving against you and you don't know why, take in half. You can always put it on again."

Another important lesson provided by Cohen is that it is critical that your style of trading match your personality. There is no single right way to trade the markets. Know who you are. For example, don't try to be both an investor and a day trader. Choose an approach that is comfortable for you.

Cohen also advises that it is important to make sure you have a good reason for putting on a trade. Buying a stock because it is "too low" or selling it because it is "too high" is not a good reason. If that is the extent of your analysis, there is no reason why you should expect to win in the markets.

Being a great trader is a process. It's a race with no finish line. The markets are not static. No single style or approach can provide superior results over long periods of time. To continue to outperform, the great traders continue to learn and adapt. Cohen constantly tries to learn more about the markets—to expand his expertise to encompass additional stocks, sectors, and styles of trading. As Cohen explains, trading for him is an evolutionary process.

Update on Steve Cohen

Steve Cohen declined to do a follow-up interview. He has continued his phenomenal performance. If the massive bear market that began in April 2000 has made trading difficult, someone obviously forgot to tell Cohen.

Since the start of the bear market through August 2002, Cohen was up over 100 percent—and that's in net terms; his gross returns were presumably at least double that level! Even more remarkable, he has not had a single down month during the entire bear market to date. In fact, he has not had a negative return month in four years (since August 1998). Perhaps somewhere there is a trader with better return/risk numbers than Steve Cohen; it's just that I don't know who it is.

ARI KIEV, M.D.

The Mind of a Winner

Ari Kiev is not a Market Wizard; he is not even a trader. Why then should you pay attention to his advice? Because Steve Cohen, who is unquestionably one of the world's greatest traders (see interview in this book), thinks enough of Dr. Kiev to have made him a permanent fixture at his firm, S.A.C. Dr. Kiev began working with traders at S.A.C. in 1992, conducting weekly seminars. This role steadily expanded over the years, and he now spends three full days each week at S.A.C, working with traders both individually and within groups. He also consults with a small number of professional traders at other firms.

Dr. Kiev graduated from Harvard and received his medical degree at Cornell. After a residency at Johns Hopkins Hospital and the Maudsley Hospital in London and serving as a research associate at Columbia, he returned to Cornell Medical College to head their social psychiatry department, focusing on suicide prevention research. In 1970, he founded the Social Psychiatry Research Institute, which participated in major trials of the antidepressant drugs, such as Prozac, Paxil, Zoloft, and Celexa, among others.

Dr. Kiev was the first psychiatrist appointed to the U.S. Olympic Sports Medicine Committee and worked with Olympic athletes during 1977–82. It was his work in helping Olympic athletes enhance their performance that years later attracted Steve Cohen's attention, because Cohen believed that there were strong parallels between top athletes and top traders.

Dr. Kiev has authored fourteen books, including *Trading to Win: The Psychology of Mastering the Markets*, and *Trading in the Zone*, based on his experience working with professional traders; the best-selling *A Strategy for Daily Living* and a popular anthropology text, *Magic, Faith, and Healing: Studies in Primitive Psychiatry Today*.

I interviewed Dr. Kiev at his Manhattan office. (No, I didn't ask him to lie down on the couch.)

★

You began your career working with suicidal and depressed patients and then ended up working with Olympic athletes and traders. That's quite a transition. It doesn't sound like there would be much of a connection.

One of the therapies for depressed and suicidal patients is to help them become more sell-reliant and assertive. These same skills are applicable to athletes and traders as well.

How did you get involved in working with Olympic athletes?

My kids went to a health club that was run by the head of the U.S. Olympic Sports Medicine Committee, and I met some Olympic athletes there. As a result of that association, I became the first psychiatrist on the committee.

What sports did the athletes you worked with participate in?

Bobsledding—my son was on the U.S. world team in 1981—basketball, archery, fencing, kayaking, sculling, and a number of others.

That's quite a range of sports. Are there common denominators among the sports or are different approaches required for different types of athletes?

There are some common denominators, but different sports require different mental frameworks. For example, in bobsledding, you need to start off with a maximum amount of exertion as you run and push the sled. But as soon as you get into the sled, you have to slow down your adrenaline so that you are calm and centered while steering the sled down the course. A similar transition is required in the biathlon, where the athletes race on cross-country skis, with their heart rate exceeding 120 beats per minute, and then have to stop and focus on shooting a target, with their heartbeat ideally slowing down to 40 beats per minute. These types of athletes can condition themselves by practicing abrupt mental shifts between exertion and relaxation.

In a sport like archery, however, the critical element is for the athletes to be able to empty their minds. For example, I worked with an archer who had won the gold medal in the previous Olympics, and that achievement was interfering with his ability to have his mind totally empty and centered on the target. He needed to develop the skill of letting go of the thought of his previous gold medal win so that he could be relaxed and completely focused on the target.

How do you accomplish that?

By relaxation and imagery. There are many techniques, but the essential idea is that you want to notice a thought and then let it go. For example, you might picture the thought in a bubble and then visualize it fading off and disappearing.

Are there some winning traits that are common across all sports?

In any sport, it's very difficult to win a gold medal unless you *decide* you're going to win it. Making the Olympic team and winning a gold medal may be a ten-year quest. If you're going to make it, then you have to start today to do those things that are compatible with what someone who is performing at that level is doing. Most people don't believe it is possible and settle for not succeeding, or at least not succeeding at the level they have chosen. You have to be willing to put yourself on the line and go for it, even with the thought that you will feel humiliated if you don't make it after you have promised that you would.

Promised yourself or promised the world?

Promised the world—that makes it much more powerful. Promising the result commits you to doing it and leaves you no alternative but to do it if you are going to live by your word. Letting others know that you have set a goal and are committed to achieving it makes it more likely you will achieve that goal, whether it is in the realm of athletics, trading, or something else.

One procedure I introduced at S.A.C. seven years ago was to go around the room and have each trader promise his results. In the early years, I got a lot of resistance from just about everyone except Steve Cohen, who was always very willing to promise an extraordinary result. It took a long time for people to accept this process, but now it is amazing how much it has become part of the company culture.

Almost everyone is willing to commit to making more than he or she did in the previous year, often promising to double the amount. It's not a matter of making positive affirmations; the key is promising to do something, and then on a daily basis doing what you need to do to realize that result.

Steve Cohen set a target for this year that was off the charts. He had to plan a strategy consistent with that target. He starts working at four in the afternoon on Sunday and works until ten that night. "I don't want to do that," he says, "but I have to in order to play at this level. I don't want to come into the office at seven-thirty every morning. I don't want to go through all these charts every night. But it's what I have to do if I'm going to be true to my goal."

Are you implying that simply committing to a higher target makes it possible?

Believing that an outcome is possible makes it achievable. The classic example is Roger Bannister's penetration of the four-minute mile mark. Before he ran his sub-four-minute mile in 1954, this feat was considered an impossible barrier that was beyond human physical capabilities. After he ran his so-called magic mile, many other runners suddenly began breaking this once seemingly impossible barrier.

As the barriers are being broken down by Steve, other traders at his firm are discovering that they can make a lot more than they once thought possible. One trader who was a clerk five years ago is on target to make $70 million this year.

What are the implications of setting a target and then not reaching it? Certainly not everyone who sets a higher target makes it.

The objective of setting a target is not necessarily to reach it, but rather to establish a standard against which to measure your performance. If you are not reaching your target, it forces you to focus on what you are doing wrong or what you may not be doing that you should. The target holds you to a higher standard of performance.

Why do some athletes or traders excel, whereas others with equal skill manage only moderate success?

Sometimes when people reach their target and nothing happens, they stop paying attention to whatever the commitment was to get there. This explains why some people begin to lose after they succeed. They can't sustain the effort. When someone achieves his goal, the question is often, "What now?" My answer, which is based on comparing athletes who have won gold medals with those who haven't, is to set up another target that will provide a challenge. The gold medal winners are always stretching for a goal that is uncertain.

Failing to redefine the goal can limit success. For example, one ski jumper prepared for the Olympic trials for years by visualizing himself doing perfect jumps over and over. He came to the trials, made the perfect jump, and achieved his goal of making the Olympic team. The problem was that the qualifying jumps ended up being his best performance because he hadn't visualized or mentally prepared himself for going beyond the trials.

Some traders have trouble maintaining the discipline that made them successful once they get ahead by a certain amount. One trader I worked with did well at the beginning of each month, but whenever he got ahead by $300,000, he would revert to bad habits. When I pressed him to explain the reasons for the deterioration in his performance during the latter part of each month, he said, "I begin trading each month from the perspective that I am flat. Therefore, I am very selective about my trades and use strict risk control. Once there is money in the till, I get lax. I become overconfident. I stop having respect for the market."

What else impedes skilled athletes and traders from excelling?

There are people who hold the world record but have never won a gold medal. One athlete held the world record in his event and participated in four Olympics, but never won the gold medal. It turns out that the time he set the world record, he had a beesting that distracted him from thoughts like: "I'm not winning. I have to win."

Is there an applicable lesson to trading?

Yes, being preoccupied with not losing interferes with winning. Trading not to lose is not a good strategy. You need to trade to win.

How did you get involved working with traders?

Steve Cohen had heard of my work with Olympic athletes and thought it would be relevant to traders. I've been working with his firm for seven years. When I started, they were a $25 million hedge fund; they have now grown to $1.5 billion. I know that you interviewed Steve Cohen. I'm curious, what was your impression of him?

I was struck by his casualness in trading. He was throwing out 100,000-share orders with the same level of emotion that he might use ordering a sandwich for lunch. He also seemed to maintain a constant sense of humor while trading. Another thing I noticed about Steve that I've also seen in a number of other great traders is that he can look at the same one hundred facts everyone else sees—some of which are bullish and some of which are bearish—and somehow pick out the one or two elements that are most relevant to the market at that moment in time.

You saw that? I think part of it is preparation and part of it is experience. The trades he's doing are not new trades. He has a vast repertoire of trades and is able to access them. Great traders like Steve are also able to notice when the sweet spot is visible and to pile in. According to S.A.C.'s risk manager's statistics, 5 percent of his trades account for virtually all of his profits. He is also willing to cut his position when he is wrong.

Do you work with just professional traders, or do you also work with ordinary people who want to become successful traders?

Just professional traders. I see myself as a trading coach—helping someone who is a trader improve, not teaching someone who is not a trader to be a trader. My job is to diagnose how a trader might be trapped by his own emotional response to the market and then help tweak his approach to correct the problem.

For example.

One trader came to me and said, "When I'm winning, I keep winning—I can do no wrong; when I'm losing, I keep losing—I can't do anything right." The solution was to create the same state of mind when he was losing as when he was winning.

How do you do that?

By getting him to re-create the same mind-set that he has on a winning streak. When he is on a winning streak, he is fearless, intuitive, and makes the right choices. When he is on a losing streak, he needs to visualize, remember, and feel those same positive traits so that when he comes into the office, he has the same attitude toward his trading as when he is in the middle of a winning streak. You repeatedly hear traders say that when they are in a hot streak, they can do no wrong. I'm suggesting that people can re-create that hot streak in their mind.

Is that what you did with athletes as well—get them to imagine doing their particular event perfectly?

I once worked with an ice skater who couldn't do a triple jump. Every time he attempted the third turn, he would fall. I asked him if he could begin to do it in his mind. At first, when he attempted doing it in his mind, he would also fall. I had him keep practicing the jump in his mind until he felt comfortable doing it mentally. In order to be able to do it physically on the ice, he had to first have a mental image of his doing the jump successfully. Not long after he became comfortable doing the jump in his mind, he was able to do it on the ice.

Another athlete I worked with was a bobsled driver who had crashed at Zigzag in Lake Placid, which is a ninety-degree turn. Subsequently, every time he made that turn, he overcompensated. I had him visualize the perfect run. The actual bobsled run takes about a minute, and you can run through the entire course in your mind in about ten seconds. He practiced coming down the perfect route in his mind hundreds of times. This mental imaging allowed him to overcome his anxiety, and he was ultimately able to make the turn without overcompensating.

I don't want to make this sound simple or magical. I don't mean to suggest that all that is involved is learning some set of visualization techniques. What I do is better described as a dialogue process to find out what is impeding a person's performance.

Do people know the answer to that question?

They frequently do. I worked with one trader who whenever he decided it was time to liquidate his position would hold on to a small part of it, just in case the market continued to move in his direction. On balance, these remnant positions were costing him money. He had to learn to get rid of his entire position when he decided it was time to liquidate, which at first was anxiety producing.

I'm not trying to badger people. I'm just trying to get them to do what is in their best self-interest. Human beings want to feel comfortable. My job is to be a bit of a gadfly so that I can get them to make the necessary changes.

Any other examples of personal flaws that prevented a trader from reaching his full potential?

One trader who runs a large hedge fund is never willing to buy a stock at the market; he is always trying to bid it lower. As a result, he misses a lot of trades.

How did this flaw come to light?

I asked him, "How did things go today?"

"Not so good. I just missed getting into a big trade in XYZ. I tried to buy it, but I couldn't get into the position because the price was too high. I put in a bid, but the market was already up one dollar, and I didn't want to pay up for it."

I'm trying to get him into a different mental perspective. He has been successful for a number of years. He wins on the vast majority of his trades. Why is he being such a penny-pincher?

Why do you think he is?

I think that's his personality. It's the way he was brought up. He nickels-and-dimes everything.

And it's getting in his way?

It's getting in his way of greater success. All I'm trying to do is hear where a trader is at and then help him see what is holding him back.

What is another example of a behavioral pattern that was holding a trader back?

One trader selected his stocks fundamentally and then scaled into the position as the stock declined. Even though he had chosen to enter his positions by averaging down, when a stock got back to even, he was so relieved that he would often get out.

Didn't he realize that his entry approach would always lead to an initial loss?

He knew it intellectually, but psychologically he was still experiencing it as a loss. Therefore, when a stock got back to even, he was just glad to get out. The first step was to get him to perceive what he was doing. Now he can stay in much longer. Consciousness is one of the most critical tools I use. In this case, the trader needed to be confronted because he was fooling himself.

Did he change what he was doing?

Yes, he now catches himself when he is tempted to get out of a stock when it goes back to even. Not only does he catch it, but I can identify this same tendency in other traders.

Has his trading improved as a result?

Dramatically. Last year he made $28 million. At the start of this year, I asked him, "What is your goal for this year?"

"Fifty [million]," he answered.

"Fifty?" I asked.

"Well . . ."

I hear that "well" and I say, "Let's amplify that *well*. How much is in the well?"

"I probably could make more."

"How much more?" I asked

"I don't want to say," he replied.

"Come on, say it."

"I don't want to say it, or else you'll make me do it."

"I'm not going to make you do it. But how much do you think you could make?"

"I think I can make a hundred," he whispered.

"Well, then say it."

"Okay, I'm going to make a hundred."

I tell him, "We're going to get the guys who work with you in here.

We call them in and he says, "I was just talking to Ari and we're going to make one hundred million this year."

Three weeks ago he came in and told me that he had reached a hundred million for the year. The key was getting him to recognize his own hesitation when he said that fifty million was his target. If the conversation had ended there, he would not have made a hundred million. There had to be an exchange for me to sense where he was really at. One hundred million wasn't my number; it was my number for him. If there's anything unique in what I do, it's hearing that bit of uncertainty that reflects where a trader is holding back.

You've written an entire book about the psychology of trading. What if I asked you for your advice on how to win at trading, but required you to say it in twenty-five words or less.

Define a target, a strategy consistent with the target, a set of disciplines to follow, and risk management guidelines. Then trade, track, and evaluate your performance.

★

Dr. Kiev's advice regarding goal achievement in general and trading success in particular can be summarized as follows:

- Believing makes it possible.
- To achieve a goal, you not only have to believe it is possible, but you also have to commit to achieving it.
- A commitment that promises the goal to others is more powerful than a commitment made to oneself.
- Extraordinary performers—Olympic gold medal winners, supertraders—continually redefine their goals so they are a stretch. Maintaining exceptional performance requires leaving the comfort zone.
- After setting a goal, the trader or athlete needs to define a strategy that is consistent with the target.
- Traders, athletes, and other goal-oriented individuals need to monitor their performance to make sure they are on track with their target and to diagnose what is holding them back if they are not.

★

Update on Ari Kiev, MD

Since the original interview Dr. Kiev has continued his focus on working with traders and has written two more books on the subject: Trading in the Zone *and* Psychology of Risk.

What changes have you seen in the traders you work with during the massive bear market that has emerged and prevailed since our last interview?

Confidence levels are much lower. I've been dealing more and more with traders who call me because they feel burned out and don't have the stomach for the markets anymore, or they perceive their market analysis and methodology are no longer working. They want to know what they should do.

What do you tell them?

I advise them to take time off to replenish their energy, and then start back up small. I've worked with them to lower their expectations so that they could regain some sense of mastery. If expectations remain too high, there is likely to be too much frustration. I also caution them against the temptation to make large bets to try to get it all back.

Can you give me a specific example of a trader you work with who has been having significant difficulty in the current market environment?

I recently met with a trader with a long side bias who is running $35 million and is down over $3 million for the year. He had greatly reduced his position size, trying to scratch his way back to respectability. He was in great distress. As he has done poorly, he has become reluctant to come out of his office and interact with other people in the group. He has some of the classic signs of mild depression. He is caught in a self-perpetuating cycle where his poor performance has caused him to lose confidence and withdraw, which in turn impedes his performance.

What advice did you give him?

The problem is that he was defining himself in terms of his results. I told him to become more engaged by contributing ideas and interacting with other people in the firm.

How has your work with traders changed during the bear market?

I have not changed my basic strategy. I still focus on encouraging traders to go for the gold, committing to targets that are a stretch, and then developing strategies consistent with these targets: cutting losses quickly, and sizing positions upward when they have high conviction, an edge, and a sufficient profit cushion.

This approach has continued to work well for a broad spectrum of markets and strategies: foreign exchange traders, macro traders, convertible bond arbitrageurs, and even *quant* traders using black box systems. Among equity traders, it has worked for those traders with an ability to go short and the conviction to ride out short squeezes because of their understanding of the fundamental vulnerability of their short positions. Some equity traders, however, have had difficulty adapting to the powerful bear market of recent years. For these traders, it's been less a matter of going for the gold, and more a matter of staying in the game. Although I prefer to emphasize performance enhancement—that is, helping traders make more money on the assumption they could make more—for some traders, it has been more appropriate to focus on preservation of capital and risk management.

Specifically, how have you worked with the traders who have had difficulty?

It has often been a matter of getting these traders to face their tendency toward denial and rationalization. For example, for some traders this has meant learning to cut their losses, even if the fundamentals were sound. For others it has meant helping them overcome their visceral discomfort in going short. I have also advised traders to take larger risks only after they have built up a profit cushion. This works both ways, though. For some more cautious souls who were reluctant to use all the capital allocated to them, I've encouraged them to trade larger when they had a profit cushion and their Sharpe ratios warranted it.

Any other changes in emphasis?

I find myself dealing a lot more with management issues such as maintaining firm morale, team building, and communication skills with support staff. For example, a hedge fund manager recently told me, "I instructed my trader to go short 100,000 shares, but he only sold 40,000." I asked him why he simply didn't tell the trader to sell another 60,000. "Well," he said, "I didn't want to undermine his confidence." The bull market allowed managers to run their teams in a much more easygoing manner, and a lot of them never learned the skill of getting their staff to understand when they say X, they mean X, not Y. In this market, you can't afford to make those types of mistakes.

Presumably, some of the managers you work with did well in the bull market, not because of innate skill, but because the market was a one-way street. How do you differentiate between a trader

who may be having temporary trouble and one who may never have had any special talent to begin with?

As a starting point, you look at performance. If the manager is consistently losing money, then maybe he should be doing something else. Also, you have to look at the degree of work and sophistication of the approach, or the lack of it. I recently had lunch with a manager who had been successful in raising a large sum of money to start a new hedge fund. I was amazed by how elementary his approach was. He wanted his analysts to give him a list of stocks near the low end of their range so he could buy them and stocks near the high end of their range so he could sell them. He didn't have more of a subtle distinction than that. I was shocked. I advised him to bring in some first-rate analysts to strengthen the investment process.

In our original interview, you stressed the importance of traders committing to higher targets. Surely, in this bear market, many traders must be falling far short of their targets or even losing money. What do you tell them to do?

A trader may have said that $10 million was his target, and he is only up $2 million, and the year is more than half over. In that instance, maybe $5 million is a better target. There is no shame in reducing the target. It's better to reach a lower target than feel frustrated in trying to reach a higher target.

So, now you find yourself often counseling traders to revise their target down, whereas previously you were advising them to revise their target up.

Exactly.

What about the trader who is not just falling short of his target, but is actually losing a significant amount of money? Say his target was $10 million, the year is more than half over, and he is down $3 million.

The problem is that the guy who is down $3 million is thinking too much about the $3 million. You shouldn't think about making the loss back—that's too burdensome. You have to start where you are. OK, you're down, but what can you do this week, this month, and for the rest of the year? You have to try to regain a sense of control.

WIZARD LESSONS

1. There Is No Single True Path

There is no single true path for succeeding in the markets. The methods employed by great traders are extraordinarily diverse. Some are pure fundamentalists; others use only technical analysis; and still others combine the two methodologies. Some traders consider two days to be long term, while others consider two months to be short term. Some are highly quantitative, while other rely primarily on qualitative market decisions.

2. The Universal Trait

Although the traders interviewed differed dramatically in terms of their methods, backgrounds, and personalities, there were numerous traits common to many of them. One trait that was shared by *all* the traders is discipline.

Successful trading is essentially a two-stage process:

1. Develop an effective trading strategy and an accompanying trading plan that addresses all contingencies.
2. Follow the plan without exception. (By definition, any valid reason for an exception—for example, correcting an oversight—would become part of the plan.) No matter how sound the trading strategy, its success will depend on this execution phase, which requires absolute discipline.

3. You Have to Trade Your Personality

Cohen emphasizes that it is critical to trade a style that matches your personality. There is no single right way to trade the markets; you have to know who you are. For example, don't try to be both an investor and a day trader. Choose an approach that is comfortable for you. Minervini offers similar advice: "Concentrate on mastering one style that suits your personality, which is a lifetime process."

Successful traders invariably gravitate to an approach that fits their personality. For example, Cook is happy to take a small profit on a trade, but hates to take even a small loss. Given this predisposition, the methodologies he has developed, which accept a low return/risk ratio on each trade in exchange for a high probability of winning, are right for him. These same methods, however, could be a mismatch for others. Trading is not a one-size-fits-all proposition; each trader must tailor an individual approach.

4. Failure and Perseverance

Although some of the traders in this book were successful from the start, the early market experiences of others were marked by complete failure. Mark Cook not only lost his entire trading stake several times, but on one of these occasions ended up several hundred thousand dollars in debt and a hair away from personal bankruptcy. Stuart Walton wiped out once with money borrowed from his father and several years later came close to losing not only all his trading capital, but also the money he borrowed on a home equity loan. Mark Minervini lost not only all his own money in the markets, but some borrowed money as well.

Despite their horrendous beginnings, these traders ultimately went on to spectacular success. How were they able to achieve such a complete metamorphosis? Of course, part of the answer is that they had the inner strength to not be defeated by defeat. But tenacity without flexibility is no virtue. Had they continued to do what they had been doing before, they would have experienced the same results. The key is that they completely changed what they were doing.

5. Great Traders Are Marked by Their Flexibility

Even great traders sometimes have completely wrongheaded ideas when they start. They ultimately succeed, however, because they have the flexibility to change their approach. La Rochefoucauld said, "One of the greatest tragedies of life is the murder of a beautiful theory by a gang of brutal facts." Great traders are able to face such "tragedies" and choose reality over their preconceptions.

Walton, for example, started out by selling powerhouse stocks and buying bargain stocks. When his empirical observations of what actually worked in the market contradicted this original inclination, he was flexible enough to completely reverse his approach. As another example, as a novice trader, Minervini favored buying low-priced stocks that were making new lows, an approach that was almost precisely the opposite of the methodology he ended up using.

Markets are dynamic. Approaches that work in one period may cease to work in another. Success in the markets requires the ability to adapt to changing conditions and altered realities. Some examples:

- Walton adjusts his strategy to fit his perception of the prevailing market environment. As a result, he might be a buyer of momentum stocks in one year and a buyer of value stocks in another. "My philosophy," he says, "is to float like a jellyfish, and let the market push me where it wants to go."
- Even though Lescarbeau has developed systems whose performance almost defy belief, he continues his research to develop their replacements so that he is prepared when market conditions change.
- Fletcher's primary current strategy evolved in several stages from a much simpler earlier strategy. As competitors increase in the current approaches he is utilizing, Fletcher is busy developing new strategies.
- Cohen says, "I'm always learning, which keeps it exciting and new. I'm not doing the same thing that I was doing ten years ago. I have evolved, and will continue to evolve."

6. It Requires Time to Become a Successful Trader

Experience is a minimum requirement for success in trading, just as it is in any other profession, and experience can be acquired only in real time. As Cook says, "You can't expect to become a doctor or an attorney overnight, and trading is no different."

7. Keep a Record of Your Market Observations

Although the process of gaining experience can't be rushed, it can be made much more efficient by writing down market observations instead of depending on memory. Keeping a daily diary in which he recorded the recurrent patterns he noticed in the market was instrumental to Cook's transition from failure to great success. All of the many trading strategies he uses grew out of these notes. Masters jots down observations on the backs of his business cards. A compilation of these notes provided the basis for his trading model.

8. Develop a Trading Philosophy

Develop a specific trading philosophy—an integration of market concepts and trading methods—that is based on your market experience and is consistent with your personality (item 3). Developing a trading philosophy is a dynamic process—as you gather more experience and knowledge, the existing philosophy should be revised accordingly.

9. What Is Your Edge?

Unless you can answer this question clearly and decisively, you are not ready to trade. Every trader in this book has a specific edge. To offer a few examples:

- Masters has developed a catalyst-based model that identifies high probability trades.
- Cook has identified price patterns that correctly predict the short-term direction of the market approximately 85 percent of the time.
- Cohen combines the information flow provided by the select group of traders and analysts he has assembled with his innate timing skills as a trader.
- A tremendous investment in research and very low transaction costs have made it possible for Shaw's firm to identify and profit from small market inefficiencies.
- By combining carefully structured financing deals with hedging techniques, Fletcher implements transactions that have a high probability of being profitable in virtually any scenario.
- Watson's extensive communication-based research allows him to identify overlooked stocks that are likely to advance sharply well before those opportunities become well recognized on Wall Street.

10. The Confidence Chicken-and-Egg Question

One of the most strikingly evident traits among all the *market wizards* is their high level of confidence. This leads to the question: Are they confident because they have done so well, or is their success a consequence of their confidence? Of course, it would hardly be surprising that anyone who has done as extraordinarily well as the traders in this book would be confident. But the more interviews I do with *market wizard* types, the more convinced I become that confidence is an inherent trait shared by these traders, as much a contributing factor to their success as a consequence of it. To cite only a few of the many possible examples:

- When Watson was asked what gave him the confidence to pursue a career in money management when he had no prior success picking stocks, he replied, "Once I decide I am going to do something, I become determined to succeed, regardless of the obstacles. If I didn't have that attitude, I never would have made it."
- Masters, who launched his fund when he was an unemployed stockbroker with virtually no track record, responded to a similar question, "I realized that if somebody could make money trading, so could I. Also, the fact that I had competed successfully at the highest levels of swimming gave me confidence that I could excel in this business as well."
- Lescarbeau's confidence seemed to border on the irrational. When asked why he didn't delay a split with his partner, who was the money manager of the team, until he had developed his own approach, Lescarbeau replied, "I knew I would come up with something. There was absolutely no doubt in my mind. I had never failed to succeed at anything that I put my mind to, and this was no different."

An honest self-appraisal in respect to confidence may be one of the best predictors of a trader's prospects for success in the markets. At the very least, those who consider career changes to become traders or risking a sizable portion of their assets in the market should ask themselves whether they have absolute confidence in their ultimate success. Any hesitation in the answer should be viewed as a cautionary flag.

11. Hard Work

The irony is that so many people are drawn to the markets because it seems like an easy way to make a lot of money, yet those who excel tend to be extraordinarily hard workers—almost to a fault. Consider just some of the examples in this book:

- As if running a huge trading company were not enough, Shaw has also founded a number of successful technology companies, provided venture capital funding and support to two computational chemistry software firms, and chaired a presidential advisory committee. Even when he is on a rare vacation, he acknowledges, "I need a few hours of work each day just to keep myself sane."
- Lescarbeau continues to spend long hours doing computer research even though his systems, which require very little time to run, are performing spectacularly well. He continues to work as if these systems were about to become ineffective tomorrow. He never misses a market day, to the point of hobbling across his house in pain on the day of his knee surgery so that he could check on the markets.
- Minervini works six-day workweeks, fourteen-hour trading days, and claims not to have missed a market day in ten years, even when he had pneumonia.
- Cook continues to do regular farm work in addition to spending fifty to sixty hours a week at trading. Moreover, for years after the disastrous trade that brought him to the brink of bankruptcy, Cook worked the equivalent of two full-time jobs.
- Bender not only spends a full day trading in the U.S. markets, but then is up half the night trading the Japanese stock market.

12. Obsessiveness

There is often a fine line between hard work and obsession, a line that is frequently crossed by the *market wizards*. Certainly some of the examples just cited contain elements of obsession. It may well be that a tendency toward obsessiveness in respect to the markets, and often other endeavors as well, is simply a trait associated with success.

13. The *Market Wizards* Tend to Be Innovators, Not Followers

To list a few examples:

- When Fletcher started his first job, he was given a desk and told to "figure it out." He never stopped. Fletcher has made a career of thinking up and implementing innovative market strategies.
- Bender not only developed his own style of trading options but cre-

ated an approach that sought to profit by betting against conventional option models.

- Shaw's entire life has been defined by innovation: the software company he launched as a graduate student; his pioneering work in designing the architecture of supercomputers; the various companies he founded; and his central role in developing the unique complex mathematical trading model used by D. E. Shaw.
- By compiling detailed daily diaries of his market observations for over a decade, Cook was able to develop a slew of original, high-reliability trading strategies.
- Minervini uncovered his own menagerie of chart patterns rather than using the patterns popularized in market books.
- By jotting down all his market observations, Masters was able to design his own catalyst-based trading model.
- Although he was secretive about the details, based on their incredible performance alone, it is quite clear that Lescarbeau's systems are unique.

14. To Be a Winner You Have to Be Willing to Take a Loss

In Watson's words, "You can't be afraid to take a loss. The people who are successful in this business are the people who are willing to lose money."

15. Risk Control

Minervini believes that one of the common mistakes made by novices is that they "spend too much time trying to discover great entry strategies and not enough time on money management." "Containing your losses," he says, "is 90 percent of the battle, regardless of the strategy." Cohen explains the importance of limiting losses as follows: "Most traders make money only in the 50 to 55 percent range. My best trader makes money only 63 percent of the time. That means you're going to be wrong a lot. If that's the case, you better make sure your losses are as small as they can be."

Risk control methods used by the traders interviewed included the following:

- **Stop-loss points.** Both Minervini and Cook predetermine where they will get out of a trade that goes against them. This approach allows them to limit the potential loss on any position to a well-defined risk level (barring a huge overnight price move). Both Minervini and Cook indicated that the stop point for any trade depends on the expected gain—that is, trades with greater profit potential will use wider stops (accept more risk).

- **Reducing the position.** Cook has a sheet taped to his computer reading: GET SMALLER. "The first thing I do when I'm losing," he says, "is to stop the bleeding." Cohen expresses the virtual identical sentiment: "If you think you're wrong, or if the market is moving against you and you don't know why, take in half. You can always put it on again. If you do that twice, you've taken in three-quarters of your position. Then what's left is no longer a big deal."
- **Selecting low-risk positions.** Some traders rely on very restrictive stock selection conditions to control risk as an alternative to stop-loss liquidation or position reduction (detailed in item 17).
- **Limiting the initial position size.** Cohen cautions, "A common mistake traders make . . . is that they take on too big of a position relative to their portfolio. Then when the stock moves against them, the pain becomes too great to handle, and they end up panicking or freezing." On a similar note, Fletcher quotes his mentor, Elliot Wolk, "Never make a bet you can't afford to lose."
- **Diversification.** The more diversified the holdings, the lower the risk. Diversification by itself, however, is not a sufficient risk-control measure, because of the significant correlation of most stocks to the broader market and hence to each other. Also, as discussed in item 52, too much diversification can have significant drawbacks.
- **Short selling.** Although the common perception is that short selling is risky, it can actually be an effective tool for reducing portfolio risk (see item 58).
- **Hedged strategies.** Some traders (Fletcher, Shaw, and Bender) use methodologies in which positions are hedged from the onset. For these traders, risk control is a matter of restricting leverage, since even a low-risk strategy can become a high-risk trade if the leverage is excessive. (See, for example, the discussion of LTCM in the Shaw interview.)

16. You Can't Be Afraid of Risk

Risk control should not be confused with fear of risk. A willingness to accept risk is probably an essential personality trait for a trader. As Watson states, "You have be willing to accept a certain level of risk, or else you will never pull the trigger." When asked what he looks for when he hires new traders, Cohen replies, "I'm looking for people who are not afraid to take risks."

17. Limiting the Downside by Focusing on Undervalued Stocks

A number of the traders interviewed restrict their stock selection to the universe of undervalued securities. Watson focuses on the stocks with relatively low price/earnings ratios (8 to 12). Okumus buys stocks that have declined 60 percent or more off their highs and are trading at price/earnings ratios under 12. He also prefers to buy stocks with prices as close as possible to book value.

One reason all these traders focus on buying stocks that meet their definition of value is that by doing so they limit the downside. Another advantage of buying stocks that are trading at depressed levels is that the stocks in this group that do turn around will often have tremendous upside potential.

18. Value Alone Is Not Enough

It should be stressed that although a number of traders considered undervaluation a necessary condition for purchasing a stock, none of them viewed it as a sufficient condition. There always had to be other compelling reasons for the trade because a stock could be low priced and stay that way for years. Even if you don't lose much in buying a value stock that just sits there, it could represent a serious investment blunder by tying up capital that can be used much more effectively elsewhere.

19. The Importance of Catalysts

A stock can represent great value and still stagnate for years, tying up valuable capital. Therefore, an essential question that needs to be asked is: What is going to make the stock go up?

Watson's stock selection process contains two essential steps. First, the identification of stocks that fulfill his value criteria, which is the easy part of the process that merely defines the universe of stocks in which he prospects for buy candidates. Second, the search for catalysts (recent or impending) that will identify which of these value stocks have a compelling reason to move higher over the near term. To discover these catalysts, he conducts extensive communication with companies, as well as their competitors, distributors, and consumers. By definition, every trade requires a catalyst.

Masters has developed an entire trading model based primarily on catalysts. Through years of research and observation, he has been able to find scores of patterns in how stocks respond to catalysts. Although most of these patterns may provide only a small edge by themselves, when grouped together, they help identify high-probability trades.

20. Most Traders Focus on When to Get in and Forget About When to Get Out

When to get out of a position is as important as when to get in. Any market strategy that ignores trade liquidation is by definition incomplete. A liquidation strategy can include one or more of the following elements:

- **Stop-loss points.** Detailed in item 15.
- **Profit objective.** A number of traders interviewed (e.g., Okumus, Cook) will liquidate a stock (or index) if the market reaches their predetermined profit target.
- **Time stop.** A stock (or index) is liquidated if it fails to reach a target within a specified time frame. Both Masters and Cook cited time stops as a helpful trading strategy.
- **Violation of trade premise.** A trade is immediately liquidated if the reason for its implementation is contradicted. For example, when IBM, which Cohen shorted in anticipation of poor earnings, reported better-than-expected earnings, Cohen immediately covered his position. Although he still took a large loss on the trade, the loss would have been significantly greater if he had hesitated.
- Counter-to-anticipated market behavior (see item 21).
- Portfolio considerations (see item 22).

Some of these elements may make sense for all traders (e.g., exiting on counter-to-anticipated market behavior); others are very dependent on a trader's style. For example, the use of stops to limit losses is essential to Minervini, who uses a timing-based methodology, but is contradictory to the approach used by Okumus and Watson, who tend to buy undervalued stocks after very sharp declines. (The latter traders, however, would still use stop-loss strategies for short positions, which are subject to open-ended losses.) As another example, profit objectives, which are an integral part of some traders' methodologies, could be detrimental to other traders and investors by limiting profit potential.

21. If Market Behavior Doesn't Conform to Expectations, Get Out

A number of traders mentioned that if the market fails to respond to an event (e.g., earnings report) as expected, they will view it as evidence that they are wrong and liquidate their position. When I interviewed Cohen, he was bullish on the bond market, which at the time was in a long-term decline. He gave me a number of reasons why he believed the bond market would witness a substantial rebound in the ensuing months, and he implemented a long position as I sat next to him. The next few days, the bond market did indeed witness a bounce, but the rally soon faltered, with bond prices sliding to new lows. When I spoke to Cohen on a follow-up phone interview a week after my visit to his firm, I asked him whether he was still long the bond market, which he had been so bullish on several weeks earlier. "No," Cohen replied, "you trade your theory and then let the market tell you whether you are right."

22. The Question of When to Liquidate Depends Not Only on the Stock but Also on Whether a Better Investment Can Be Identified

Investable funds are finite. Continuing to hold one stock position precludes using those funds to purchase another stock. Therefore, it may often make sense to liquidate an investment that still looks sound if an even better investment opportunity exists. Watson, for example, employs what he calls a pig-at-the-trough philosophy. He is constantly upgrading his portfolio—replacing stocks that he still expects will go higher with other stocks that appear to have an even better return/risk outlook. Thus, the key question an investor needs to ask regarding a current holding is not "Will the stock move higher?" but rather "Is this stock still a better investment than any other equity I can hold with the same capital?"

23. The Virtue of Patience

Whatever criteria you use to select a stock and determine an entry level, you need to have the patience to wait for those conditions to be met. For example, Okumus will patiently wait for a stock to decline to his "bargain" price level, even if it means missing more than 80 percent of the stocks he wants to buy. In mid-1999, Okumus was only 13 percent invested because, as he stated at the time, "There are no bargains around. I'm not risking the money I'm investing until I find stocks that are very cheap."

24. The Importance of Setting Goals

Dr. Kiev, who has worked with both Olympic athletes and professional traders, is a strong advocate of the power of setting goals. He contends that believing that an outcome is possible makes it achievable. Believing in a goal, however, is not sufficient. To achieve a goal, Kiev says, you need to not only believe in it but also commit to it. Promising results to others, he maintains, is particularly effective.

Dr. Kiev stresses that exceptional performance requires setting goals that are outside a trader's comfort zone. Thus, the trader seeking to excel needs to continually redefine goals so that they are always a stretch. Traders also need to monitor their performance to make sure they are on track toward reaching their goals and to diagnose what is holding them back if they are not.

25. This Time Is Never Different

Every time there is a market mania, the refrain is heard, "This time is different," followed by some explanation of why the particular bull market will continue, despite already stratospheric prices. When gold soared to near $1,000 an ounce in 1980, the explanation was that gold was "different from every other commodity." Supposedly, the ordinary laws of supply and demand did not apply to gold because of its special role as a store of value in an increasingly inflationary world. (Remember double-digit inflation?) When the Japanese stock market soared in the 1980s, with price/earnings ratios often five to ten times as high as corresponding levels for U.S. companies, the bulls were ready with a reassuring explanation: The Japanese stock market is different because companies hold large blocks of each other's shares, and they rarely sell these holdings.

As this book was being written, there was an explosive rally in technology stocks, particularly Internet issues. Stocks with no earnings, or even a glimmer of the prospect of earnings, were being bid up to incredible levels. Once again, there was no shortage of pundits to explain why this time was different; why earnings were no longer important (at least for these companies). Warnings about the aspects of mania in the current market were mentioned by a number of the traders interviewed. By the time this manuscript was submitted, many of the Internet stocks had already witnessed enormous percentage declines. The message, however, remains relevant because there will always be some market or sector that rekindles the cry, "This time is different." Just remember: It never is.

26. Fundamentals Are Not Bullish or Bearish in a Vacuum; They Are Bullish or Bearish Only *Relative* to Price

A great company could be a terrible investment if its price rise has already more than discounted the bullish fundamentals. Conversely, a company that has been experiencing problems and is the subject of negative news could be a great investment if its price decline has more than discounted the bearish information. As Galante expressed when asked for her advice to investors, "A good company could be a bad stock and vice versa."

27. Successful Investing and Trading Has Nothing to Do with Forecasting

Lescarbeau, for example, emphasized that he never made any predictions and scoffed at those who made claim to such abilities. When asked why he laughed when the subject of market forecasting came up, he replied: "I'm laughing about the people who do make predictions about the stock market. They don't know. Nobody knows."

28. Never Assume a Market Fact Based on What You Read or What Others Say; Verify Everything Yourself

When Cook first inquired about the interpretation of the *tick* (the number of New York Stock Exchange stocks whose last trade was an uptick minus the number whose last trade was a downtick), he was told by an experienced broker that if the *tick* was very high, it was a buy signal. By doing his own research and recording his own observations, he discovered that the truth was exactly the opposite.

Bender began his option trading career by questioning the very core premises underlying the option pricing models used throughout the industry. Convinced that the conventional wisdom was wrong, he developed a methodology that was actually based on betting against the implications of the option pricing models in wide use.

29. Never, Ever Listen to Other Opinions

To succeed in the markets, it is essential to make your own decisions. Numerous traders cited listening to others as their worst blunder. Walton and Minervini lost their entire investment stake because of this misjudgment. Talking about this experience, Minervini said, "My mistake had been surrendering the decision-making responsibility to someone else." Watson got off cheap, learning this lesson at the bargain basement price of a blown grade on a class project. Cohen talks about someone he knows that has the skill to be a great trader, but will never be one because "he refuses to make his own decisions."

30. Beware of Ego

Walton warns, "The odd thing about this industry is that no matter how successful you become, if you let your ego get involved, one bad phone call can put you out of business."

31. The Need for Self-Awareness

Each trader must be aware of personal weaknesses that may impede trading success and make the appropriate adjustments. For example, Walton ultimately realized his weakness was listening to other people's opinions. His awareness of this personal flaw compelled him to make sure that he worked alone, even when the level of assets under management would seem to dictate the need for a staff. In addition, to safely vent his tip-following, gambling urges, he set aside a small amount of capital—too small to do any damage—to be used for such trades.

Dr. Kiev describes his work with traders as "a dialogue process to find out what [personal flaws are] impeding a person's performance." Some examples of these personal flaws he helped traders identify included:

- a trader whose bargain-hunting predisposition caused him to miss many good trades because he was always trying to get a slightly better entry price;
- a trader whose scale-down entry approach was in conflict with his experiencing these trades as a loss, even though they were entered in accordance with his plan;
- a trader who, to his detriment, always kept a partial position after he made the decision to get out because of his anxiety that the stock would go higher after he liquidated.

Awareness alone is not enough; a trader must also be willing to make the necessary changes. Cook, who also works with traders, has seen people with good trading skills fail because they wouldn't deal with their personal weaknesses. One example he offered was a client who was addicted to the excitement of trading on expiration Fridays. Although the trader did well across all other market sessions, these far more numerous small gains were more than swamped by his large losses on the four-per-year expiration Fridays. Despite being made aware of his weakness, the trader refused to change and ultimately wiped out.

32. Don't Get Emotionally Involved

Ironically, although many people are drawn to the markets for excitement, the *market wizards* frequently cite keeping emotion out of trading as essential advice to investors. Watson says, "You have to invest without emotions. If you let emotions get involved, you will make bad decisions."

33. View Personal Problems as a Major Cautionary Flag to Your Trading

Health problems or emotional stress can sometimes decimate a trader's performance. For example, all of Cook's losing periods (after he became a consistent winning trader) coincided with times of personal difficulties (e.g., a painful injury, his father's heart attack). It is a sign of Walton's maturity as a trader that he decided to take a trading hiatus when an impending divorce coincided with a rare losing period. The morale is: Be extremely vigilant to signs of deteriorating trading performance if you are experiencing health problems or other personal difficulties. During such times, it is probably a good idea to cut trading size and to be prepared to stop trading altogether at the first sign of trouble.

34. Analyze Your Past Trades for Possible Insights

Analyzing your past trades might reveal patterns that could be used to improve future performance. For example, in analyzing his past trades, Minervini found that his returns would have been substantially higher if he had capped his losses to a fixed maximum level. This discovery prompted a change in his trading rules that dramatically improved his performance.

35. Don't Worry About Looking Stupid

Never let your market decisions be restricted or influenced by concern over what others might think. As a perfect example of the danger of worrying about other people's opinions, early in his career, Minervini held on to many losing positions long after he decided they should be liquidated because of concern about being teased by his broker.

36. The Danger of Leverage

Ironically, even though Mark Cook won on most of his trades in his initial market endeavor, he wiped out because of excessive leverage. If you are too heavily leveraged, all it takes is one mistake to knock you out of the game.

37. The Importance of Position Size

Superior performance requires not only picking the right stock, but also having the conviction to implement major potential trades in meaningful size. Dr. Kiev, who sees Cohen's trading statistics, said that nearly 100 percent of Cohen's very substantial gains come from 5 percent of his trades. Cohen himself estimates that perhaps only about 55 percent of his trades are winners. Implicit in these statements is that when Cohen bets big, he is usually right. Indeed, his uncanny skill in determining which trades warrant stepping on the accelerator is an essential element in his success.

As another example, even though Lescarbeau is a systematic trader, he will occasionally increase the leverage on trades that he perceives have a particularly high likelihood of winning. Interestingly, he has never lost money on one of these trades.

The point is that all trades are *not* the same. Trades that are perceived to have particularly favorable potential relative to risk or a particularly high probability of success should be implemented in a larger size than other trades. Of course, what constitutes "larger size" is relative to each individual, but the concept is as applicable to the trader whose average position size is one hundred shares as the fund manager whose average position size is one million shares.

38. Complexity Is Not a Necessary Ingredient for Success

Some of the patterns and indicators that Cook uses to signal trades are actually quite simple, but it is his skill in their application that accounts for his success.

39. View Trading as a Vocation, Not a Hobby

As both Cook and Minervini said, "Hobbies cost money." Walton offered similar advice, "Either go at it full force or don't go at it at all. Don't dabble."

40. Trading, Like Any Other Business Endeavor, Requires a Sound Business Plan

Cook advises that every trader should develop a business plan that answers all the following essential questions:

- What markets will be traded?
- What is the capitalization?
- How will orders be entered?
- What type of drawdown will cause trading cessation and reevaluation?
- What are the profit goals?
- What procedure will be used for analyzing trades?
- How will trading procedures change if personal problems arise?

- How will the working environment be set up?
- What rewards will the trader take for successful trading?
- What will the trader do to continue to improve market skills?

41. Define High-Probability Trades

Although the methodologies of the traders interviewed differ greatly, in their own style, they have all found ways of identifying high-probability trades.

42. Find Low-Risk Opportunities

Many of the traders interviewed have developed methods that focus on identifying low-risk trades. The merit of a low-risk trade is that it combines two essential elements: patience (because only a small portion of ideas will qualify) and risk control (inherent in the definition).

43. Be Sure You Have a Good Reason for Any Trade You Make

As Cohen explains, buying a stock because it is "too low" or selling it because it is "too high" is not a good reason. Watson paraphrases Peter Lynch's principle: "If you can't summarize the reasons why you own a stock in four sentences, you probably shouldn't own it."

44. Use Common Sense in Investing

Taking a cue from his role model, Peter Lynch, Watson is a strong proponent of commonsense research. As he illustrated through numerous examples, frequently, the most important research one can do is simply trying a company's product or visiting its mall outlets in the case of retailers.

45. Buy Stocks That Are Difficult to Buy

Walton says, "One of the things I like to see when I'm trying to buy stocks is that they become very difficult to buy. I put an order in to buy Dell at 42, and I got a fill back at 45. I love that." Minervini says, "Stocks that are ready to blast off are usually very difficult to buy without pushing the market higher." He says that one of the mistakes "less skilled traders" make is "wait[ing] to buy these stocks on a pullback, which never comes."

46. Don't Let a Prior Lower-Priced Liquidation Keep You from Purchasing a Stock That You Would Have Bought Otherwise

Walton considers his willingness to buy back good stocks, even when they are trading higher than where he got out, as one of the changes that helped him succeed as a trader. Minervini stresses the need for having a plan to get back into a trade if you're stopped out. "Otherwise," he says, "you'll often find yourself . . . watching the position go up 50 percent or 100 percent while you're on the sidelines."

47. Holding on to a Losing Stock Can Be a Mistake, *Even If It Bounces Back,* If the Money Could Have Been Utilized More Effectively Elsewhere

When a stock is down a lot from where it was purchased, it is very easy for the investor to rationalize, "How can I get out now? I can't lose much more anyway." Even if this is true, this type of thinking can keep money tied up in stocks that are going nowhere, causing the trader to miss other opportunities. Talking about why he dumped some stocks after their prices had already declined as much as 70 percent from where he got in, Walton said: "By cleaning out my portfolio and reinvesting in solid stocks, I made back much more money than I would have if I had kept [these] stocks and waited for a dead cat bounce."

48. You Don't Have to Make All-or-Nothing Trading Decisions

As an illustration of this advice offered by Minervini, if you can't decide whether to take profits on a position, there's nothing wrong with taking profits on part of it.

49. Pay Attention to How a Stock Responds to News

Walton looks for stocks that move higher on good news but don't give much ground on negative news. If a stock responds poorly to negative news, then in Walton's words, "[it] hasn't been blessed [by the market]."

50. Insider Buying Is an Important Confirming Condition

The willingness of management or the company to buy its own stock may not be a sufficient condition to buy a stock, but it does provide strong confirmation that the stock is a good investment. A number of traders cited insider buying as a critical element in their stock selection process (e.g., Okumus and Watson).

Okumus stresses that insider buying statistics need to be viewed in relative terms. "I compare the amount of stock someone buys with his net worth and salary. For example, if the amount he buys is more than his annual salary, I consider that significant." Okumus also points out the necessity of making sure that insider buying actually represents the purchase of new shares, not the exercise of options.

51. Hope Is a Four-Letter Word

Cook advises that if you ever find yourself saying, "I hope this position comes back," get out or reduce your size.

52. The Argument *Against* Diversification

Diversification is often extolled as a virtue because it is an instrumental tool in reducing risk. This argument is valid insofar as it generally unwise to risk all your assets on one or two equities, as opposed to spreading the investment across a broader number of diversified stocks. Beyond a certain minimum level, however, diversification may sometimes have negative consequences. Okumus, for example, explains why he limits his portfolio to approximately ten holdings as follows: "Simple logic: My top ten ideas will always perform better than my top hundred."

The foregoing is not intended as an argument against diversification. Indeed, some minimal diversification is almost always desirable. The point is that although some diversification is beneficial, more diversification may sometimes be detrimental. Each trader needs to consider the appropriate level of diversification as an individual decision.

53. Caution Against Data Mining

If enough data is tested, patterns will arise simply by chance—even in random data. Data mining—letting the computer cycle through data, testing thousands or millions of input combinations in search of profitable patterns—will tend to generate trading models (systems) that look great, but have no predictive power. Such hindsight analysis can entice the researcher to trade a worthless system. Shaw avoids this trap by first developing a hypothesis of market behavior to be tested rather than blindly searching the data for patterns.

54. Synergy and Marginal Indicators

Shaw mentioned that although the individual market inefficiencies his firm has identified cannot be traded profitably on their own, they can be combined to identify profit opportunities. The general implication is that it is possible for technical or fundamental indicators that are marginal on their own to provide the basis for a much more reliable indicator when combined.

55. Past Superior Performance Is Relevant Only If the Same Conditions Are Expected to Prevail

It is important to understand why an investment (stock or fund) outperformed in the past. For example, in the late 1990s a number of the better performing funds owed their superior results to a strategy of buying the most highly capitalized stocks. As a result, the high-cap stocks were bid up to extremely high price/earnings ratios relative to the rest of the market. A new investor expecting these funds to continue to outperform in the future would, in effect, be making an investment bet that was dependent on high-cap stocks becoming even more overpriced relative to the rest of the market.

As columnist George J. Church once wrote, "Every generation has its characteristic folly, but the basic cause is the same: people persist in believing that what has happened in the recent past will go on happening into the indefinite future, even while the ground is shifting under their feet."

56. Popularity Can Destroy a Sound Approach

A classic example of this principle was provided by the 1980s experience with *portfolio insurance* (the systematic sale of stock index futures as the value of a stock portfolio declines in order to reduce risk exposure). In the early years of its implementation, portfolio insurance provided a reasonable strategy for investors to limit losses in the event of market declines. As the strategy became more popular, however, it set the stage for its own destruction. By the time of the October 1987 crash, portfolio insurance was in wide usage, which contributed to the domino effect of price declines triggering portfolio insurance selling, which pushed prices still lower, causing more portfolio selling, and so on. It can even be argued that the mere knowledge of the existence of large portfolio insurance sell orders below the market was one of the reasons for the enormous magnitude of the October 19, 1987, decline.

57. Like a Coin, the Market Has Two Sides—But the Coin Is Unfair

Just as you can bet heads or tails on a coin, you can go long or short a stock. Unlike a normal coin, however, the odds for each side are not equal: The long-term uptrend in stock prices results in a strong negative bias in short selling trades. As Lescarbeau says, "Shorting stocks is dumb because the odds are stacked against you. The stock market has been rising by over 10 percent a year for many decades. Why would you want to go against that trend?" (Actually, there is a good reason why, which we will get to shortly.)

Another disadvantage to the short side is that the upside is capped. Whereas a well-chosen buy could result in hundreds or even thousands of percent profit on the trade, the most perfect short position is limited to a profit of 100 percent (if the stock goes to zero). Conversely, whereas a long position can't lose more than 100 percent (assuming no use of margin), the loss on a short position is theoretically unlimited.

Finally, with the exception of index products, the system is stacked against short selling. The short seller has to borrow the stock to sell it, an action that introduces the risk of the borrowed stock being called in at a future date, forcing the trader to cover (buy in) the position. Frequently, deliberate attempts to force shorts to cover their positions (short squeezes) can cause overvalued, and even worthless, stocks to rally sharply before collapsing. Thus, the short seller faces the real risk of being right on the trade and still losing money because of an artificially forced liquidation. Another obstacle faced by shorts is that positions can be implemented only on an uptick (when the stock trades up from its last sale price)—a rule that can cause a trade to be executed at a much worse price than the prevailing market price when the order was entered.

58. The Why of Short Selling

With all the disadvantages of short selling, it would appear reasonable to conclude that it is foolhardy ever to go short. Reasonable, but wrong. As proof, consider this amazing fact: fourteen of the fifteen traders interviewed in this book incorporate short selling! (The only exception is Lescarbeau.) Obviously, there must be some very compelling reason for short selling.

The key to understanding the raison d'être for short selling is to view these trades within the context of the total portfolio rather than as standalone transactions. With all their inherent disadvantages, short positions have one powerful attribute: they are inversely correlated to the rest of the portfolio (they will tend to make money when long holdings are losing and vice versa). This property makes short selling one of the most useful tools for reducing risk.

To understand how short selling can reduce risk, we will compare two hypothetical portfolios. Portfolio A holds only long positions and makes 20 percent for the year. Portfolio B makes all the same trades as Portfolio A, but also adds a smaller component of short trades. To keep the example simple, assume the short positions in Portfolio B exactly break even for the year. Based on the stated assumptions, Portfolio B will also make 20 percent for the year. There is, however, one critical difference: the magnitude of equity declines will tend to be smaller in Portfolio B. Why? Because the short positions in the portfolio will tend to do best when the rest of the portfolio is declining.

In our example, we assumed short positions broke even. If a trader can make a net profit on short positions, then short selling offers the opportunity to both reduce risk and increase return. Actually, short selling offers the opportunity to increase returns without increasing risk, *even if the short positions themselves only break even.** How? By trading long positions with greater leverage (using margin if the trader is fully invested)—a step that can be taken without increasing risk because the short positions are a hedge against the rest of the portfolio.

It should now be clear why so many of the traders interviewed supplement their long positions with short trades: It allows them to increase their return/risk levels (lower risk, or higher return, or some combination of the two).

* To be precise, this statement would be true even for small *net losses* in the short component of the portfolio, but an adequate explanation is beyond the scope of this book.

If short selling can help reduce portfolio risk, why is it so often considered to be exactly the opposite: a high-risk endeavor? Two reasons. First, short trades are often naively viewed as independent transactions rather than in the context of the total portfolio. Second, the open-ended loss exposure of short positions can indeed lead to enormous risk. Fortunately, however, this risk can be controlled, which brings us to our next point.

59. The One Indispensable Rule for Short Selling

Although short selling will tend to reduce portfolio risk, any individual short position is subject to losses far beyond the original capital commitment. A few examples:

- A $10,000 short position in Amazon in June 1998 would have lost $120,000 in seven months.
- A $10,000 short position in Ebay in October 1998 would have lost $230,000 in seven months.
- A $10,000 short position in Yahoo! in January 1997 would have lost $680,000 in two years.

As these examples make clear, it takes only one bad mistake to wipe out an account on the short side. Because of the theoretically unlimited risk in short positions, the one essential rule for short selling is: Define a specific plan for limiting losses and adhere rigorously to it.

The following are some of the risk-control methods for short positions mentioned by the interviewed traders:

- A short position is liquidated when it reaches a predetermined maximum loss point, *even if the trader's bearish analysis is completely unchanged*. As Watson says, "I will cover even if I am convinced that the company will ultimately go bankrupt . . . I'm not going to let [a 1 percent short in the portfolio] turn into a 5 percent loss."
- A short position is limited to a specific maximum percentage of the portfolio. Therefore, as the price of a short position rises, the size of the position would have to be reduced to keep its percentage share of the portfolio from increasing.
- Short positions are treated as short-term trades, often tied to a specific catalyst, such as an earnings report. Win or lose, the trade is liquidated within weeks or even days.

60. Identifying Short-Selling Candidates (or Stocks to Avoid for Long-Only Traders)

Galante, whose total focus is on short selling, looks for the following red flags in finding potential shorts:

- high receivables (large outstanding billings for goods and services);
- change in accountants;
- high turnover in chief financial officers;
- a company blaming short sellers for their stock's decline;
- a company completely changing their core business to take advantage of a prevailing hot trend.

The stocks flagged must meet three additional conditions to qualify for an actual short sale:

- very high P/E ratio;
- a catalyst that will make the stock vulnerable over the near term;
- an uptrend that has stalled or reversed.

Watson's ideal short-selling candidate is a high-priced, one-product company. He looks for companies whose future sales will be vulnerable because their single or primary product does not live up to promotional claims or because there is no barrier to entry for competitors.

61. Use Options to Express Specific Price Expectations

Prevailing option prices will reflect the assumption that price movements are random. If you have specific expectations about the relative probabilities of a stock's future price movements, then it will frequently be possible to define option trades that offer a higher profit potential (at an equivalent risk level) than buying the stock.

62. Sell Out-of-the-Money Puts in Stocks You Want to Buy

This is a technique used by Okumus that could be very useful to many investors, but is probably utilized by very few. The idea is for an investor to sell puts at a strike price at which he would want to buy the stock anyway. This strategy will assure making some profit if the stock fails to decline to the intended buying point and will reduce the cost for the stock by the option premium received if it does reach the intended purchase price.

For example, let's say XYZ Corporation is trading at $24 and you want to buy the stock at $20. Typically, to achieve this investment goal, you would place a buy order for the stock at a price limit of $20. The alternative Okumus suggests is selling $20 puts in the stock. In this way, if the stock fails to decline to your buy price, you will at least make some money from the sale of the $20 puts, which by definition will expire worthless. If, on the other hand, the stock declines to under $20, put buyers will exercise their option and you will end up long the stock at $20, which is the price that you wanted to buy it at anyway. Moreover, in this latter event, your purchase price will be reduced by the premium collected from the sale of the options.

63. Wall Street Research Reports Will Tend to Be Biased

A number of traders mentioned the tendency for Wall Street research reports to be biased. Watson cites the bias due to investment banking relationships—analysts will typically feel implicit pressure to issue buy ratings on companies that are clients of the firm, even if they don't particularly like the stock.

64. The Universality of Success

This chapter was intended to summarize the elements of successful trading and investing. I believe, however, that the same traits that lead to success in trading are also instrumental to success in any field. Virtually all the items listed, with the exception of those that are exclusively market-specific, would be pertinent as a blueprint for success in any endeavor.

APPENDIX

Options—Understanding the Basics

There are two basic types of options: calls and puts. The purchase of a *call option* provides the buyer with the right—but not the obligation—to purchase the underlying stock (or other financial instrument) at a specified price, called the *strike price* or *exercise price*, at any time up to and including the expiration date. A *put option* provides the buyer with the right—but not the obligation—to sell the underlying stock at the strike price at any time prior to expiration. (Note, therefore, that buying a put is a *bearish* trade, whereas selling a put is a *bullish* trade.) The price of an option is called *premium*. As an example of an option, an IBM April 130 call gives the purchaser the right to buy 100 shares of IBM at $130 per share at any time during the life of the option.

The buyer of a call seeks to profit from an anticipated price rise by locking in a specified purchase price. The call buyer's maximum possible loss will be equal to the dollar amount of the premium paid for the option. This maximum loss would occur on an option held until expiration if the strike price were above the prevailing market price. For example, if IBM were trading at $125 when the 130 option expired, the option would expire worthless. If at expiration the price of the underlying market was above the strike price, the option would have some value and would hence be exercised. However, if the differenct between the market price and the strike price was less than the premium paid for the option, the net result of the trade would still be a loss. In order for a call buyer to realize a net profit, the difference between the market price and

Adapted from Jack D. Schwager, *A Complete Guide to the Futures Market* (New York: John Wiley, 1984). Reprinted by permission of John Wiley & Sons, Inc.

the strike price would have to exceed the premium paid when the call was purchased (after adjusting for commission cost). The higher the market price, the greater the resulting profit.

The buyer of a put seeks to profit from an anticipated price decline by locking in a sales price. Like the call buyer, his maximum possible loss is limited to the dollar amount of the premium paid for the option. In the case of a put held until expiration, the trade would show a net profit if the strike price exceeded the market price by an amount greater than the premium of the put at purchase (after adjusting for commission cost).

Whereas the buyer of a call or put has limited risk and unlimited potential gain, the reverse is true for the seller. The option seller (often called the *writer*) receives the dollar value of the premium in return for undertaking the obligation to assume an opposite position *at the strike price* if an option is exercised. For example, if a call is exercised, the seller must assume a short position in the underlying market at the strike price (because, by exercising the call, the buyer assumes a long position at that price).

The seller of a call seeks to profit from an anticipated sideways to modestly declining market. In such a situation, the premium earned by selling a call provides the most attractive trading opportunity. However, if the trader expected a large price decline, he would be usually better off going short the underlying market or buying a put—trades with open-ended profit potential. In a similar fashion, the seller of a put seeks to profit from an anticipated sideways to modestly rising market.

Some novices have trouble understanding why a trader would not always prefer the buy side of the option (call or put, depending on market opinion), since such a trade has unlimited potential and limited risk. Such confusion reflects the failure to take probability into account. Although the option seller's theoretical risk is unlimited, the price levels that have the greatest probability of occurrence, (i.e., prices in the vicinity of the market price when the option trade occurs) would result in a net gain to the option seller. Roughly speaking, the option buyer accepts a large probability of a small loss in return for a small probability of a large gain, whereas the option seller accepts a small probability of a large loss in exchange for a large probability of a small gain. In an efficient market, neither the consistent option buyer nor the consistent option seller should have any significant advantage over the long run.

The option premium consists of two components: intrinsic value plus time value. The *intrinsic value* of a call option is the amount by which the current market price is above the strike price. (The intrinsic value of a put option is the amount by which the current market price is below the strike price.) In effect, the intrinsic value is that part of the premium that could be realized if the option were exercised at the current market price. The intrinsic value serves as a floor price for an option. Why? Because if the premium were less than the intrinsic value, a trader could buy and exercise the option and immediately offset the resulting market position, thereby realizing a net gain (assuming that the trader covers at least transaction costs).

Options that have intrinsic value (i.e., calls with strike prices below the market price and puts with strike prices above the market price) are said to be *in the money*. Options that have no intrinsic value are called *out of the money* options. Options with a strike price closest to the market price are called *at the money* options.

An out of the money option, which by definition has an intrinsic value equal to zero, will still have some value because of the possibility that the market price will move beyond the strike price prior to the expiration date. An in the money option will have a value greater than the intrinsic value because a position in the option will be preferred to a position in the underlying market. Why? Because both the option and the market position will gain equally in the event of a favorable price movement, but the option's maximum loss is limited. The portion of the premium that exceeds the intrinsic value is called the time value.

The three most important factors that influence an option's time value are the following:

1. *Relationship between the strike price and market price.* Deeply out of the money options will have little time value, since it is unlikely that the market price will move to the strike price—or beyond—prior to expiration. Deeply in the money options have little time value because these options offer positions very similar to the underlying market—both will gain and lose equivalent amounts for all but an extremely adverse price move. In other words, for a deeply in the money option, risk being limited is not worth very much because the strike price is so far from the prevailing market place.

2. *Time remaining until expiration.* The more time remaining until expiration, the greater the value of the option. This is true because a longer life span increases the probability of the intrinsic value increasing by any specified amount prior to expiration.
3. *Volatility.* Time value will vary directly with the estimated *volatility* (a measure of the degree of price variability) of the underlying market for the remaining life span of the option. This relationship results because greater volatility raises the probability of the intrinsic value increasing by any specified amount prior to expiration. In other words, the greater the volatility, the greater the probable price range of the market.

Although volatility is an extremely important factor in the determination of option premium values, it should be stressed that the future volatility of a market is never precisely known until after the fact. (In contrast, the time remaining until expiration and the relationship between the current market price and the strike price can be exactly specified at any juncture.) Thus, volatility must always be estimated on the basis of *historical volatility* data. The future volatility estimate implied by market prices (i.e., option premiums), which may be higher or lower than the historical volatility, is called the *implied volatility.*

INDEX